Marx, Nietzsche, and Modernity

MARX, NIETZSCHE, and MODERNITY

NANCY S. LOVE

New York   Columbia University Press   *1986*

Library of Congress Cataloging-in-Publication Data

Love, Nancy Sue, 1954–
Marx, Nietzsche, and modernity.

Bibliography: p.
Includes index.
1. Marx, Karl, 1818–1883.   2. Nietzsche, Friedrich
Wilhelm, 1844–1900.   3. Civilization, Modern—19th
century.   I. Title.
B3305.M74L67   1986   193   86-6118
ISBN 0-231-06238-9

Columbia University Press
New York   Guildford, Surrey
Copyright © 1986 Columbia University Press
All rights reserved

Printed in the United States of America

This book is Smyth-sewn.

To Jim

CONTENTS

PREFACE

This study is a comparison of Karl Marx's and Friedrich Nietzsche's critiques of modern society. I provide an intellectual justification for such a comparison in Chapter 1. Here I explain my interpretive strategy.

I do not review the already vast and rapidly expanding secondary literature on Marx and Nietzsche, except where my argument differs from prominent positions. Instead, I focus upon Marx and Nietzsche themselves. I quote extensively from their work; especially with so subtle a stylist as Nietzsche, the reader is better served by the original, even in translation, than a paraphrase.

I organize my comparison around issues. That is, instead of providing separate sections on Marx and Nietzsche linked by shared introductions and conclusions, I discuss their views on common topics virtually simultaneously. This expository procedure has advantages and disadvantages. It allows me to demonstrate striking similarities and differences between them; it also forces me to limit discussion of the internal arguments of each philosopher. For a book on Marx *and* Nietzsche, the advantages outweigh the disadvantages. Still, I want to warn the reader that an extensive interpretation of each philosophy only gradually emerges, and to promise that it does emerge as the sum of these many parts.

This organization also de-emphasizes Marx's and Nietzsche's philosophical development, but that is not a disadvantage. Internal divisions in their work are often overemphasized. Both later revise some of their early ideas, but these are evolutionary transformations. By stressing the continuity between dispersed remarks, I provide a more complex, complete picture of their views than sequential analysis of separate texts yields. Although I include early works, I respect their intellectual growth by focusing upon mature writings. My interpretation of Marx centers around *The German Ideology* and *Capital.* With Nietzsche, I concentrate upon *Beyond Good and Evil, The Genealogy of Morals,* and *The Will to Power.* The material from Nietzsche's unpublished notebooks collected in *The Will to Power* poses particular problems for interpreters of his philosophy. We cannot know how, if at all, he might have used it. Yet the sudden end of his intellectual life while he was accumulating notes for future projects creates a *prima facie* case for considering it. However, because of its uncertain status, I use it primarily to corroborate and clarify positions expressed in his published works.

My use of gender-specific language also requires explanation. I find such language offensive, but also recognize that occasionally it is appropriate. This is, in my opinion, such an occasion. The relationship between Marxism and feminism is promising and troubling. Nietzsche was arguably a misogynist. To discuss their philosophies in sexually neutral terms might conceal, rather than reveal, sexual biases. I could analyze their many arguments, deciding which apply to women as well as to men. But that is another book, one others have already written. Readers cannot do better than Alison Jaggar's discussion of Marxism in *Feminist Politics and Human Nature* (Totowa, N.J.: Rowman and Allenheld, 1984) and Ofelia Schutte's analysis of Nietzsche's views on women in *Beyond Nihilism.* Although these authors may have intended otherwise, they have convinced me that Marx's and Nietzsche's ambiguous relationships to feminism warrant retaining gender-specific language.

I do not expect that readers sympathetic to Marx or Nietzsche will be pleased with my interpretation of their philosophies, though supporters of each may like what I say about the other. I criticize Marx and Nietzsche, but not by judging their philosophies myself; I do not presume to possess sufficient standards for such judgments. Instead, I show through a Marxian critique of Nietzsche and Nietzschean critique of Marx that neither attains his aim, neither overcomes the oppression of modern society. Nor do attempts to combine their critiques obviate their limitations; rather, they incorporate them. This is then a negative work, but not a pessimistic one. It is written with the conviction that a successful critique proposes a new project.

I want to thank many institutions and individuals for their assistance. Fellowships from the Charlotte W. Newcombe and Josephine De Kármán foundations allowed me to begin this project. The Swarthmore College Faculty Research Fund defrayed costs for preparing an early version of the manuscript. The political science department at Pennsylvania State University has provided intellectual and logistical support for subsequent drafts.

My deepest thanks go to Allen W. Wood of the Sage School of Philosophy at Cornell University. He supported this project in its infancy; it has grown largely because of his continual support and perceptive criticisms. I also want to thank Charles Beitz, Susan Buck-Morss, Joseph Flay, Isaac Kramnick, and Larry Spence, who read the entire manuscript and offered helpful suggestions. Parts of it have also been read by James Curtis, Thomas Dumm, and Mark Warren; they have shaped it perhaps more than they realize. My thanks as well to Kate Wittenberg of Columbia University Press for her enthusiasm and assistance on this project. Only one of her contributions was assigning a reader, Tracy Strong, whose astute comments helped me to revise and refine my argument. Equally essential was Melanie Romig, who typed several drafts with great care and patience. Finally, I owe Jim Curtis another thanks since we share far more than the profession of political theory. I have joked over the last few years about writing what unfortunately remains an unusual acknowledgment—from a wife to her husband. I am serious when I thank him for his constant support, especially for his failure to understand my crises of confidence.

Together these individuals are responsible for much of what is good here, but any mistakes are my own.

ACKNOWLEDGMENTS

I wish to acknowledge permission to quote from the following:

Karl Marx, *Early Writings*, Quinton Hoare, ed.; Gregor Benton and Rodney Livingstone, trs. Copyright © 1975 New Left Review. Reprinted by permission of Random House, Inc.

Marx, Nietzsche, and Modernity

CHAPTER ONE

THE PROBLEM OF MODERNITY

The only connection which still links them with the productive forces and with their own existence—labour—has lost all semblance of self-activity and only sustains their life by stunting it...material life appears as the end, and what produces this material life, labour (which is now the only possible but, as we see, negative form of self-activity), as the means. (Marx and Engels, *The German Ideology*. p. 92)

This is my *basic objection* to all philosophic-moralistic cosmologies and theodicies, to all *wherefores* and *highest values* in philosophy and theology hitherto. One kind of means has been misunderstood as an end; conversely, life and the enhancement of its power has been debased as a means. (Nietzsche, *The Will to Power*, aphorism #707)

For nearly two centuries social and political theorists have been ambivalent about modern society. Three interdependent historical developments shaped that society: the Enlightenment, with its faith in reason and science; the French Revolution, with its defense of free, equal individuals; and the industrial revolution, with its expansion of production beyond all previous expectations. None of these developments—the ascendancy of scientific reason over religion, of contractual over status relations, and of modern industry over feudal production—is an unambiguous improvement. Each raises disturbing questions. Does the expansion of man's ability to understand and to control the natural world through science destroy cultural beliefs necessary for individual and social life? Does the victory of individual freedom over feudal relations lead to the subordination of individuals to a mass culture or a bureaucratic iron cage? And, does the triumph of human productivity in the industrial revolution necessitate the exploitation of laboring class? Underlying these questions is a more basic one: Has modern man created a world where his creative capacities frustrate rather than fulfill him? If so, he should explore the limitations of modern society and even question its premises.

This book is a comparison of Karl Marx and Friedrich Nietzsche, two of the earliest and greatest critics of modern society. I have three interrelated purposes in undertaking this comparison. The first concerns our continuing ambivalence about modern society. By comparing Marx's critique of capitalism and Nietzsche's critique of asceticism, I will illuminate the problems of modern man, potentially better than either critique does alone. Recognizing this potential, numerous twentieth-century social and political theorists have attempted a more ambitious and less promising task: I compare Marx and Nietzsche; they combine them. The second purpose of my comparison is to show where Marx's and Nietzsche's critiques converge and diverge, suggesting and subverting such combinations. Marx and Nietzsche have different perspectives on modern society, each of which reveals the other's limitations, but they are contradictory, not complementary. My third purpose is most appropriately seen as a corollary of this comparison of Marx and Nietzsche. Contrary to interpretations of Nietzsche's philosophy as apolitical, my goal is to establish his status as a political philosopher, one whose analysis of modern society rivals Marx's in its richness. The remainder of this introduction provides a preliminary sense of how I plan to pursue each facet of this threefold project.

Although differences between Marx's and Nietzsche's critiques of modern society ultimately render them contradictory, numerous similarities still provide a basis for comparing them to learn about the limitations of modern society. Each identifies conditions in modern society which frustrate man's creative capacities: Marx criticizes his alienation under capitalist economics; Nietzsche attacks ascetic psychology, which sickens him.

For Marx, the capitalist mode of production alienates men,

who are first and foremost producing animals, from their products, their productive activity, and their fellow men.[1] Commodity production for exchange is the alienated form which men's alienated productive activity assumes under capitalism. The labor power expended by men to produce a product takes the quantitative form of the exchange value of the commodity produced, and this exchange value is thought to inhere in the commodity itself. The origin of value in men's productive activity is consequently obscured. Further, productivity itself is separated from its basis in men's activity and is attributed to capital: capital produces surplus value and purchases labor power and means of production. Finally, the social character of men's labor is obscured by the individual, in this case, capitalist, appropriation of commodities. The social character of labor only manifests itself as a "social," i.e., exchange, relationship between commodities. In sum, "a definite social relation between men" assumes "the fantastic form of a relation between things."[2]

Marx describes these fetishes of capitalist commodity production by analogy with the religious world: as God is man's alienated essence perceived as an autonomous being, so commodities are the alienated products of man's social production under capitalism. However, while the religious fetish does not really possess the power men attribute to it, the commodity fetish does: capitalist commodity production controls men's productive activity, instead of being controlled by them. The bourgeoisie control and exploit the workers' products and productive activity, and exchange—the vicissitudes of the world market—controls bourgeoisie and proletariat alike. Marx argues that commodity fetishes express the absurdity, not of men's productive activity per se, but of the historical capitalist mode of production, in which the laborer's life activity assumes an alienated commodity form as capital.[3]

According to Nietzsche, it is ascetic ideals which sicken modern man. Nietzsche argues that men need horizons, unconditional beliefs which give life meaning, in order to be healthy.

This is a universal law: a living thing can only be healthy, strong, and productive within a certain horizon; if it is incapable of drawing one round itself, or too selfish to lose its own view in another's, it will come to an untimely end. Cheerfulness, a good conscience, belief in the future, the joyful deed—all depend, in the individual as well as the nation, on there being a line that divides the visible and clear from the vague and shadowy.[4]

Throughout history men have created such meaning(s); all past philosophies have been the unconscious creations of men's wills to power projected upon reality and believed as truth(s).[5]

Thus far, however, these creations have been ascetic ideals. They have denied life as will to power in the name of Forms, of God, of Being, in the name of Truth. In other words, historically the will to power has assumed a life-denying form as the will to truth. The life-denying will to truth reaches its nadir in science and atheism, the products of Enlightenment reason and the culmination of a philosophical tradition which began in Socratic Greece. Science "kills" God (read: truth), leaving men atheists, and science cannot provide a counterideal.

> Unconditional honest atheism . . . is . . . *not* the antithesis of that ideal [the will to truth], as it appears to be; it is rather only one of the latest phases of its evolution, one of its terminal forms and inner consequences—it is the awe-inspiring *catastrophe* of two thousand years of training in truthfulness that finally forbids itself the *lie involved in belief in God.*[6]

Atheism—the result of man's domination of nature by reason and science—is a catastrophe because it does not provide men with the meaning they need. They remain without truth, with a structure of understanding which forces them to continue searching for it, even though that structure of understanding also tells them that it is not to be found. The outcome is paralysis and weariness as men see flux everywhere and accumulate masses of meaningless data. In modern society, the will to truth results in the inability of man, the esteeming animal, to esteem.[7]

Capitalism and nihilism not only involve man's pursuit of goals—commodities and truths—in such a way that he cannot fulfill himself. Each also is a social condition man has created which now confronts him as a power beyond his control. To show man that the conditions which frustrate his creative powers are his own creations, Marx and Nietzsche question the premises of modern society. Marx asks of that society why labor—men's productive activity—assumes an alienated form as commodity exchange. Nietzsche asks why the will to power—men's value-creating power—assumes a life-denying form in ascetic ideals.

In order to answer these analogous questions, both examine societies historically. That is, both ask another series of related questions: What are the historical origins of societies? More specifically, how did the society of the Enlightenment, liberal democracy, and capitalism arise? What do its origins reveal about its scope? Its limits? Even its contradictions? How Marx and Nietzsche respond to these questions, the way they analyze the origins of societies, requires considerable explanation. These introductory comments are intended only to clarify my basis for comparing their critiques of modern society.

Marx and Nietzsche understand origins as beginnings in the sense of historical reasons for something of consequence. As nineteenth-century heirs of Feuerbach, they reject theories which find origins in an absolute essence behind/beyond the existential world or in a *Weltgeist* which manifests itself in a particular form in a particular historical setting. Both argue that men create the meaning of history from within history. While Marx's primary concern lies with men as producing animals[8] and Nietzsche's lies with men as value-creating animals,[9] neither acknowledges any ultimate antithesis between history and nature.

Since societies originate in history, they reflect particular socioeconomic and/or sociopsychological contexts. Marx's and Nietzsche's searches for origins are attempts to discover why men create particular societies in particular historical circumstances. For each, this means that the study of the historical origins of societies becomes a critical enterprise. By relating a society to its historical context, they reveal the factors which contribute to its formation and its scope or limits. That is, by portraying the "givens" of a society as historical products, Marx and Nietzsche expose the previously unquestioned and unquestionable to question. Through the pursuit of origins, their descriptions of societies become critiques of those societies.[10]

However, although Marx and Nietzsche question social "givens" by revealing their historical origins in man's expanding powers, they question from different perspectives because they understand his powers differently. Marx exposes social structures as products of man's developing productive powers, and Nietzsche explores their origins in man's developing will to power. Marx's focus is upon socioeconomic conditions, and Nietzsche's concern is sociopsychological ones.

In describing his genealogical questioning of social "givens," Nietzsche says,

> We need a *critique* of moral values, *the value of these values themselves must first be called into question*—and for that there is needed a knowledge of the conditions and circumstances in which they grew, under which they evolved and changed ... a knowledge of a kind that has never yet existed or even been desired. One has taken the *value* of these "values" as given, as factual, as beyond all question.[11]

Nietzsche explains truths, indeed truth itself, as values shaped by the psychology of their progenitors, as expressions of the basic order of their creators' drives. He regards all great philosophies as personal confessions, as involuntary and unconscious memoirs of their authors. He says,

> Indeed, if one would explain how the abstrusest metaphysical claims of a philosopher really came about, it is always well (and wise) to ask first: at what morality does all this (does he) aim? Accordingly, I do not believe that a "drive to knowledge" is the father of philosophy; but rather that another drive has, here as elsewhere, employed understanding (and misunderstanding) as a mere instrument. But anyone who considers the basic drives of man ... will find that all of them have done philosophy at some time—and that every single one of them would like only too well to represent just *itself* as the ultimate purpose of existence and the legitimate *master* of all the other drives. For every drive wants to be master—and it attempts to philosophize in *that spirit*.[12]

Regarding modern society, he questions the "given" expression of the will to power in ascetic ideals, specifically in the will to truth. He suggests that men

> consider on this question both the earliest and most recent philosophers: they are all oblivious of how much the will to truth itself first requires justification; here there is a lacuna in every philosophy—how did this come about? Because the ascetic ideal has hitherto *dominated* all philosophy, because truth was posited as being, as God, as the highest court of appeal—because truth was not *permitted* to be a problem at all. Is this "permitted" understood? From the moment faith in the God of the ascetic ideal is denied, a *new problem arises*: that of the *value* of truth.
>
> The will to truth requires a critique—let us thus define our own task—the value of truth must for once be experimentally *called into question*.[13]

Marx analogously depicts his historical materialist questioning of socioeconomic "givens." He criticizes political economists for their attempts to "present production ... as encased in eternal natural laws independent of history, at which opportunity *bourgeois* relations are then quietly smuggled in as the inviolable natural laws on which society in the abstract is founded."[14] But Marx's focus differs from Nietzsche's. Marx explains how social "givens" originate in man's productive powers. In a well-known passage which I later examine at length, he argues that

> in the social production of their existence, men inevitably enter into definite relations, which are independent of their will, namely, relations of production appropriate to a given stage in the development of their material forces of production. The totality of these relations of production constitutes the economic structure of society, the real foundation on which arises a legal and political superstructure and to which correspond definite forms of social consciousness. The mode of production of material life conditions the general process of social, political and intellectual life.[15]

For Marx, political economists' "inviolable natural laws" are the laws of a specific, historical mode of production, that is, capitalist production. Political economy in Marx's case, like philosophy in Nietzsche's, has

> never once asked the question why labour is represented by the value of its product and labour time by the magnitude of that value. These formulae, which bear it stamped upon them in unmistakable letters that they belong to a state of society, in which the process of production has the mastery over man, instead of being controlled by him, such formulae appear to the bourgeois intellect to be as much a self-evident necessity imposed by Nature as productive labour itself.[16]

By pursuing the origins of modern society, Marx discovers its dominant economic interests and Nietzsche reveals its dominant psychological ones. In each case, they show how these interests are implicated in the creation and perpetuation of social structures which once were functional for man's creative powers but now frustrate them. That is, each exposes a contradiction at the core of modern society. Both also suggest how this contradiction will be overcome.

This glance at Marx's and Nietzsche's critiques of modern society suggests how a comparison of them speaks to my initial purpose, to illuminate potential problems in modern society. However, the issue of Nietzsche's political philosophy has been implicit in the discussion so far. That too now requires some explicit introductory remarks.

The political relevance of Marx's analysis of man's alienation under capitalist economics and its superstructural forms, among them, the state, is generally acknowledged, but controversy continues regarding Nietzsche's relationship to political philosophy. That relationship has a complex and varied history which contains three general approaches.

The first approach links Nietzsche to the Nazis. These interpretations vary in their subtlety. Standard texts often try to show a historical connection.[17] This is unsatisfactory, however, because (as those texts often acknowledge) that connection is so indirect, largely depending upon Elizabeth Förster-Nietzsche, and because Nietzsche's politics are not overtly Nazi. After all, he did condemn both German nationalism and anti-Semitism. More subtle interpreters refrain from direct comparisons of Nietzsche and Nazism, and try instead to show how Nietzsche's philosophy may indirectly, even unintentionally, produce such politics.[18] The argument here proceeds roughly as follows. Nietzsche is seen as a superb diagnostician of a crisis in Western values, whose treatment intensifies, rather than resolves, that crisis. His philosophical alternative to nihilism, advocacy of the individual's creative will, produces a politics without moral limits. Although Nietzsche does not defend fascism, this leaves him without a philosophical basis for attacking it. Problems also arise here, however, because the political implications of nihilism are indeterminate. Fascism is certainly one possible outcome of Nietzsche's philosophy, but even power politics does not necessitate it. Ample evidence exists that numerous political movements have found Nietzsche's philosophy to be fertile ground.[19] The crucial component is the social and moral context in which politically inclined creative individuals arise.

A second strain of interpretations severs the link between Nietzsche and Nazism by denying his political importance altogether. This approach characterizes much of the contemporary philosophical literature. For example, Danto discusses Nietzsche's psychology of power, but argues that that psychology is philosophical, not social and political; Heidegger discusses willing as mastery, but does not specify the object of that mastery; Kaufmann acknowledges Nietzsche's conception of life as commanding and obeying, but maintains that greatness reveals itself in self-mastery, not political power; and Schacht discusses Nietzsche's notion of creativity as "ordering transformation," but neglects exploitation, domination, and legislation.[20] Obvious problems also exist with this approach: Nietzsche not only talks about politics, he also seems to think that his philosophy has implications for politics broadly construed.

Nietzsche's concern with the sociopsychological origins of domination can only be misconstrued and/or misrepresented as apolitical if one adopts a narrow, legal-rational view of politics as a means and neglects the political implications of the choice of communal ends. This view of sociopolitical relations as a means typifies modern society, according to Marx and Nietzsche, and both regard it as one of many modern problems. Marx criticizes the capitalist mode of production because it makes men's social interactions, their species-life, merely a means to their individual existence: "Life itself appears only as a *means of life*."[21] Nietzsche criticizes the decline of peoples and the rise of the last man, the man who is unable to create goals. He says of modern society: "Alas, the time is coming when man will no longer give birth to a star. Alas, the time of the most despicable man is coming, he that is no longer able to despise himself. Behold, I show you the *last man*. What is love? What is creation? What is longing? What is a star? Thus asks the last man, and he blinks."[22]

However, if one adopts Marx's and Nietzsche's view that politics involves the choice of communal ends, that those ends are imposed and defended by potentially violent political means, and that political legitimacy can only be understood in terms of dominant powers, not conformity to principles of morality or justice, then Nietzsche's political relevance becomes clear. By denying the possibility of truth, Nietzsche makes such principles the objects of social and political analysis.

He generally portrays truths as part of the realm of practical wisdom, of the customary morality created by a people to sustain their form of communal life. For example, in the *Genealogy of Morals*, he traces the historical origins of the moral world of modern men to the psychological conditions surrounding their social existence.[23] That he understands the creation of social values, indeed society itself, in terms of political domination is also clear. He explicitly says, "All unity is unity only as organization and cooperation—just as a human community is a unity— as opposed to an atomistic anarchy, as a pattern of domination that *signifies* a unity, but *is* not a unity."[24] Domination as the creation and imposition of communal ends is an explicitly political concern. Although Nietzsche's political pronouncements are often offensive, this does not justify portraying his analysis of the complex psychological origins of social values, especially of the ascetic ideals of modern man, as apolitical.

This brings us to a third, more recent approach to Nietzsche as a political philosopher. Recognizing the relevance of Nietzsche's genealogy in our postmetaphysical age, many political philosophers have tried to combine his philosophy with different, presumably better, politics.[25] Their task is to sever Nietzsche's philosophy from his political assumptions and to use it to further other ones. This approach also poses problems, however. Methodologically, it is difficult to defend adopting a philosophical position independent of its assumptions. If one could do so, presumably one would no longer have the same philosophy; any resemblance would be purely formal. But can one even do so? Are assumptions so arbitrary? This approach has been justified in Nietzsche's case by the suggestion that his politics flow from his philosophy only because of several arbitrary (or at least time-bound) assumptions. Those political assumptions can hence be severed from his philosophy (the politics of which is presumably indeterminate), leaving that philosophy intact and amenable to other uses. Yet although nihilism is politically indeterminate, Nietzsche's philosophy is not necessarily so. That is, might his philosophy not also flow from his politics? Or, to avoid a crude reductionism, might there not be some subtle symbiosis between the two?

My purpose here is not to argue that nihilism necessitates Nazism; it does not. Nor is it to argue that Nietzsche's philosophy does so. As we will see, that philosophy does have fascistic, or at least aristocratic, elements, and it also possesses seemingly socialist and anarchist strains. Still, it is not indeterminate. Solipsism is, I will argue, its most consistent consequence. Instead, my purpose is to illustrate problems Nietzsche's philosophy poses for attempts to link it with the quasi-Marxist politics many contemporary "Nietzscheans," perhaps quite rightly, desire. With this, I turn to my remaining purpose, to illustrate where Marx's and Nietzsche's critiques of modern society converge and diverge, suggesting and ultimately subverting attempts to combine them.

Given the similarities I have already suggested, it is not surprising that brief references to parallels between Marx's and Nietzsche's critiques of modern society abound. Paul Tillich maintains that they, like other "philosophers of Existence," "share a common opposition to a common foe, and have a common aim, though they try to attain it in very different ways." He characterizes their common foe as man's self-estrangement under the rational systems of Western industrial society and their common aim as the creation of a new meaning for life after the "two great traditions, the Christian and the humanistic, have lost their comprehensive character and their convincing power."[26] Arthur Mitzmann argues that the logic of rationalization permits a comparison not only of Marx and Weber, but also of Nietzsche with both: "All three men saw it [rationalization] leading to an unparalleled reification of institutions and values and a corresponding destruction of essential aspects of human personality: grace, dignity, personal creativity, spontaneity, ultimate meaningfulness."[27] Karl Löwith also argues that, although Nietzsche never concerned himself directly with Marx, "a comparison of the two is nonetheless justified, because Nietzsche is the only man after Marx and Kierkegaard, who made the decline of the bourgeois-Christian world the theme of such a fundamental analysis."[28] Recognizing that Marx's and Nietzsche's critiques differ substantively, Tracy Strong argues that structurally they respond similarly to bourgeois civilization: Marx begins with production and Nietzsche with ideology, but commodity fetishes parallel idols as human creations beyond human control.[29] Continuing this structural emphasis, Hans Barth compares their analyses of truth and ideology, exploring how each differently "functionalized ideas."[30] Mark Warren also suggests parallels in their materialist orientations, i.e., their agreement that our concrete, sensuous existence is the practical foundation of values.[31]

Explicitly or implicitly acknowledging these parallels, many twentieth-century social theorists concerned with man's domination by capitalism and asceticism have tried to combine their critiques. Early in the century, Max Weber admitted his debt to Marx and Nietzsche, a debt particularly evident in his analysis of the relationship between capitalism and Protestantism. He claimed that "one can measure the honesty of a contemporary scholar, and above all, of a contemporary philosopher, in his posture toward Nietzsche and Marx. Whoever does not admit that he could not perform the most important parts of his own work without the work that those two have done swindles himself and others. Our intellectual world has to a great extent been shaped by Marx and Nietzsche."[32] Franz Mehring also referred to Nietzsche as a "moment of passage to socialism," one especially attractive for the disillusioned bourgeoisie.[33] Georges Sorel, their contemporary, tried to combine Marxist economic and Nietzschean psychological weapons—general strikes and heroic myths—in the war against modern society as well.[34]

More recently, French structuralists, poststructuralists, and existentialists have assimilated aspects of Nietzsche's philosophy. Michel Foucault associates his disciplinary approach to power with Nietzsche's notion of politics as relations of force. The role of power is "perpetually to re-inscribe this relation [of force] through a form of unspoken warfare; to re-inscribe it in social institutions, in economic inequalities, in language, in the bodies themselves of each and every one of us."[35] Foucault retains the notion of power as repression here (although he also assigns power positive roles), but he moves away from conceptions of a sovereign power. He augments liberal versions of the social contract and Marxist analyses of economic functions with tools for analyzing the "multiple forms of subjugation that have a place and function within the social organism."[36] Jacques Derrida portrays Nietzsche as a patron of deconstruction, one who teaches the elusiveness of truth and whose own works deconstruct.[37] Derrida is circumspect regarding any affinity between deconstruction and Marxism. But he responded to a direct question about their relationship by saying: "If one wished to schematize—but truly this is only a schema—what I have attempted can *also* be inscribed under the rubric of the 'critique of idealism.'"[38] This also raises the issue of Nietzsche's compatibility with Marx, if both are to remain even ambiguously associated with deconstruction. Additional Nietzschean strains appear in Albert Camus', Maurice Merleau-Ponty's, and Jean-Paul Sartre's complex and changing relations with Marxism, especially in their confrontations with Stalinism as the legacy of scientific materialism in a nihilistic world.[39]

Perhaps the strongest contemporary Nietzschean influence is found among the first generation of critical theorists, specifically in the works of Theodor Adorno, Max Horkheimer, and Herbert Marcuse.[40] To transcend Marx's complicity in the dialectic of enlightenment, Adorno and Horkheimer turn to Nietzsche. Although they criticize his ahistorical identification of reason per se with domination, they praise him as a historian of modern society, one who mercilessly exposed the bourgeois *ratio*. Nietzsche influenced their interrelated epistemological and sociological critiques of that *ratio*. Adorno's rejection of identity and Hork-heimer's critique of instrumental reason are deeply rooted in Nietzsche's analysis of psychological exchange relations as the foundation of society. Their joint attack upon the culture industry, which sublimates repressed needs in modern society, also springs directly from Nietzsche's *Genealogy of Morals*.

Marcuse's attack upon the Western ontological tradition reflects Nietzsche's influence as well. He argues that Nietzsche exposed the fallacies of Western philosophy and morality, i.e., the transformation of facts into essences and of history into meta-physical conditions. He also defends Nietzsche's notion of eternal recurrence as a new erotic attitude toward being. Finally, al-though he argues that the self owes society its very existence, Marcuse, like Adorno and Horkheimer, pursues a Nietzschean reassertion of individuality against an administered world.

This discussion provisionally suggests that attempts to com-bine Marx's and Nietzsche's critiques of modern society are prompted not only by similarities between them, but also by the sense that each critique is incomplete. Some preliminary remarks on Marx's and Nietzsche's standards for evaluating modern society clarify how their different perspectives are limited in scope, and how each exposes the other's limitations.

As my description of similarities between Marx's and Nietzsche's approaches to history revealed, neither regards his pursuit of social origins as relativistic. That is, neither concludes from his socioeconomic or sociopsychological analysis that different values are right at different times and/or in different places. Each criticizes modern society from a perspective which indicates that he thinks something is objectively wrong with it. Yet, in the absence of absolute principles of morality or justice, how can either claim that capitalism or asceticism frustrates life? Their standards of evaluation seem to require some initial explor-ation.

Marx stresses the scientific, non-utopian character of histori-cal materialism and argues that communist society is not an ideal posited from some abstract conception of morality or justice, but the inevitable product of real historical forces. Justice and morality, according to Marx, are elements of the superstructure of particular societies and are by definition ideological. This suggests that Marx does not condemn capitalism on the basis of a conscious principle of morality or standard of justice. Instead, he tries to illustrate adequate reasons for condemning it through his description of its genesis, operation, and prognosis. Those reasons include his analyses of expropriation (the so-called "primitive accumulation"), disguised and unnecessary exploitation (the extraction of surplus value), and ensuing economic inefficiency and instability (crises of overproduction and underconsumption). If true, these are seemingly good reasons for condemning an economic system.[41]

Yet the absence of principles of morality and standards of justice in Marx's critique of capitalism may still reveal a significant gap in historical materialism. Marx describes how capitalism may be overthrown and even why it should be overthrown, but his analysis of its historical limitations may not adequately explain why men would—or, more important, would not—overthrow it. Many of the social and political theorists who turn to Nietzsche, while remaining sympathetic to Marx, argue that the explanation of why men would not overthrow capitalism must include (and may even hinge upon) superstructural phenomena. They focus upon such ideological components of social control as the culture industry, discourses, or grammar, and argue that, although these social structures may change in relation to productive forces, they may also follow their own logic.

The complex implications of their diverse arguments for historical materialism are beyond the boundaries of this introduction. But they do raise several questions relevant to our present context. Can social phenomena be adequately understood in terms of economic production, or must one also consider social psychology, which may play an independent role in history? That is, is historical materialism incomplete? Does it need to be supplemented by an examination of psychological dimensions of domination? Further, if our Enlightenment tradition is characterized, as Nietzsche argues, by asceticism, what does this suggest about the limitations of Marx's own critique of modern society? Does Marx fail to account for an ascetic psychology which may preclude social revolution? More important, does scientific socialism itself idealize this ascetic psychology in its image of rational, social, productive man?

Marx's critique of capitalism, whatever its possible limitations, does rest upon empirical evidence, whereas Nietzsche's critique of asceticism has a less coherent base. Nietzsche exposes all previous truths, indeed, the will to truth itself, as the unconscious creations of man's will to power. But if truth is dead, what is the status of the will to power? Is the will to power the truth about life? If it is the truth about life, is it not consequently false? If it is not the truth about life, if it is merely Nietzsche's view of reality, how can Nietzsche condemn ascetic ideals as denials of life as will to power? Nietzsche seems to argue simultaneously that there are no truths—that the will to power is his "truth"—and that the will to power is the truth about life. Nietzsche may ultimately be an ethical naturalist. Like Marx, he may argue that life has built-in, though different, values, i.e., that strength, exploitation, and overcoming are good, while weakness, pity, and decline (all of which are expressed in ascetic ideals) are bad. But if Nietzsche is an ethical naturalist, then something, however enigmatically it is expressed, is true and his philosophy is incoherent.

Nonetheless, the enhancement of life as will to power is the standard by which Nietzsche criticizes modern society. As Nietzsche's insights may reveal the sociopsychological limitations of historical materialism, so a Marxian critique of the will to power may reveal the socioeconomic limitations of Nietzsche's genealogy. Does Nietzsche, who understands men and societies in terms of the values which they esteem, ignore the material reality which shapes their consciousness? That is, is Nietzsche's genealogy also incomplete? Does it need to be supplemented by an examination of economic dimensions of power? If domination is economic as well as psychological, might ascetic ideals persist because they are powerful instruments by which the ruling economic class manipulates those beneath them? More important, does Nietzsche's own conception of life as will to power itself idealize his exploitative capitalist economic context?

These questions suggest that combinations of Marx's and Nietzsche's critiques of modern society may be appropriately construed as attempts to synthesize them in a genuine dialectical sense. That is, they are attempts to transcend the limitations of each critique by embracing aspects of the other. My comparison of their critiques does show, through a Nietzschean critique of Marx and a Marxian critique of Nietzsche, that neither fully escapes his "given" social structures. Marx questions capitalist economics, but not ascetic psychology; Nietzsche questions ascetic psychology, but not capitalist economics. However, that comparison also illustrates how each mistakes the "given" oppression which the other attacks for man's emancipation: Nietzsche criticizes ascetic psychology *from* a capitalist economic perspective; Marx criticizes capitalist economics *from* an ascetic psychological one. This suggests that Marx's and Nietzsche's different perspectives on modern society illuminate but do not obviate the other's limitations; their critiques are contradictory, not complementary.[42] That is, if the political implications of Nietzsche's philosophy are clearly and completely confronted, it cannot be combined with Marxism. The two positions negate one another, and this is not a dialectical negation. The result of attempts to combine them is schizophrenia, not synthesis.

Although my analysis suggests that syntheses of Marx and Nietzsche are caught in the contradictions between them, it is not my purpose here to criticize any specific attempt. I largely confine my commentary to Marx's and Nietzsche's critiques of modern society. Still, I do try to demonstrate the contradictions between them convincingly enough to shift the burden of proof, to suggest that those who would synthesize their critiques should show how they avoid or resolve the contradictions I explore. I also try to indicate where one might begin to look for those contradictions in attempts at synthesis. I ask that those who would combine Marx and Nietzsche assume this burden because, although I too find elements of socialism and Dionysianism attractive, I fear that attempts to combine them, at least in their Marxian and Nietzschean forms, take us toward a dead end.

My comparison of Marx and Nietzsche proceeds in the following fashion. I begin with similarities in their critiques of modern society which make comparison possible and which encourage attempts to synthesize them. In chapter 2, I examine how Marx and Nietzsche, through their critiques of German idealism and also of their own youthful alternatives to it, arrive at a view of man as a being who creates himself historically. I compare their analyses of how man projects his powers over nature and how he forms social relations which facilitate the expansion of those powers. In chapter 3, I turn to related similarities in their dialectical explanations of the development (rise, functioning, and fall) of societies. I discuss their analyses of how man's developing powers functionally order social organisms, and functionally determine social change through contradictions. I show how, for Marx, capitalist economics and, for Nietzsche, ascetic psychology are social structures which once were, but no longer are, functional for man's historical development. For this reason, each maintains that modern society must and will be overcome.

Then, in chapters 4 through 6, I increasingly emphasize how their historical dialectics differ, how each criticizes modern society from a different perspective. In chapter 4, I compare their critiques of modern ideology, Christian and scientific metaphysics, focusing upon the differences between Marxian science and Nietzschean skepticism. In chapter 5, I consider why Marx from a socialist perspective and Nietzsche from an individualist one criticize liberal-democratic freedom. In chapter 6, I explore their analyses of capitalist production and their contrasting alternatives—Marxian production and Nietzschean play—to it.

In each chapter, I examine why each thinks that these social structures frustrate man's creative capacities, how each illuminates the limitations of the other's critique, and why their critiques are contradictory, not complementary. That is, I show how neither escapes what the other regards as the locus of man's oppression. Marx's critique of capitalist society in the name of science, society, and production is an expression of ascetic psychology. By attacking ascetic ideals, in the name of skepticism, individuality, and play, Nietzsche expresses capitalist economics. In my conclusion, I suggest that, because of the contradictions between their critiques of modern society, syntheses of Marx and Nietzsche escape neither the economics nor the psychology of modern society. However, although Marx's, Nietzsche's, and their mutual heirs' failure to escape our self-created iron cage may express the demise of the tradition of political theory, this should not be regarded as the demise of reason. Perhaps it is once again "essential to educate the educator himself."[43]

CHAPTER TWO

NATURAL, HISTORICAL MAN

As individuals express their life, so they are. What they are, therefore, coincides with their production, both with *what* they produce and with *how* they produce. (Marx and Engels, *The German Ideology*, p. 42)

Man projects his drive to truth, his "goal" in a certain sense, outside himself as a world that has being. . . . His needs as creator invent the world upon which he works, anticipate it; this anticipation (this "belief" in truth) is his support. (Nietzsche, *The Will to Power*, aphorism #552)

Nietzsche was not born until 1844, the year Marx wrote the *Economic and Philosophical Manuscripts,* and Marx died in 1883, the year Nietzsche published part one of *Zarathustra.* Still, their historical experiences serve more to unite than to divide them. Their critiques of modern society revolve around common nineteenth-century concerns, the death of God and the birth of science, the French Revolution and the Paris Commune, industrialization and mechanization, to mention only a few. As they criticize modern society drawing upon these same developments, so they also develop the basis for their critiques reacting against the same philosophical tradition: German idealism.

In this chapter, I focus upon Marx's and Nietzsche's views of man, explaining substantive similarities between them as, in part, products of their responses to German idealist philosophy. First, I discuss their overlapping intellectual origins and their similar critiques of Kant and Hegel. Second, I examine parallels in the development of their mature views of man, stressing their major intellectual changes, i.e., Marx's evolution from anthropological to historical materialist conceptions of man and Nietzsche's movement from romantic to Dionysian pessimism. I argue that both develop mature views of man as a natural, historical being to solve strikingly similar problems with their youthful origins. Third, I compare their mature views of man, examining similarities between Marx's production and Nietzsche's will to power as forms of man's life activity, and setting the stage for my exploration of why both think modern society frustrates it.

Overlapping Intellectual Origins

Marx and Romanticism; Nietzsche and Left Hegelianism

Marx and Nietzsche have long been regarded as members of different schools, Marx as the heir of Hegel and the Left Hegelians, and Nietzsche as the heir of the German romantics, especially Schopenhauer and Wagner. These are the predominant lines in their respective intellectual genealogies. However, as occasional references to Marx as a romantic[1] and to Nietzsche as a Left Hegelian[2] indicate, their intellectual origins overlap in ways which are frequently ignored. These overlapping origins help to explain some of the similarities in their views of man.

Disagreements abound regarding what constitutes romanticism and hence when and to what extent Nietzsche was a romantic.[3] Still, Nietzsche shared these romantic themes: aesthetic idealism; subjectivism; images of the isolated, creative genius; attacks on cultural philistinism and the fragmentation of modern life. These themes also appear in the poetry of the young Marx, whose models were many of the same figures who influenced Nietzsche, e.g., Heine, Goethe, Schiller, who attended Schlegel's romantic lectures at the University of Bonn, and who initially rejected Hegel as "too realistic."

Marx soon abandoned his aesthetic idealism and sought a resolution of the romantic opposition between is and ought. This development began with his decision to study law at the University of Berlin and reached a critical point when he grew dissatisfied with the gap between is and ought in his metaphysics of law, written under Kant's and Fichte's influence. He turned to Hegel, whom he then considered to have bridged this gap by seeking the

Idea in the real, with new interest.[4] His movement to and subsequently beyond Hegel (who only bridged the gap in thought, not practice) to historical materialism has been seen as a realistic solution to Hegel's romantic problem, that is, to how man as a dynamic being realizes himself in the world.[5]

In addition to aesthetic idealism, Marx's work retains permutations of other romantic themes: cultural philistinism and fragmentation of modern life become socioeconomic, not aesthetic, problems; subjectivism becomes a dialectic of subject and object; and the creative genius becomes social man, who creates an existence corresponding to his essence. In fact, Marx may have drawn his image of man in the *Economic and Philosophical Manuscripts* as much from romantic as from Left Hegelian sources.[6]

Unlike Marx, Nietzsche was initially influenced by Schopenhauer's atheistic aesthetics. He regarded this as the background of his own enmity toward Hegel's philosophical theism.[7] Still, Nietzsche also has indirect ties to Hegel and the Left Hegelians, and through them to Marx. These connections may account for some of the Left Hegelian themes, e.g., transformative method, religious and cultural criticism, and emphasis on sensuous man, which Marx and Nietzsche share.

Some of Nietzsche's connections with the Left Hegelians are more direct and more extensive than others. Among the least direct, but still significant, in his connection to Max Stirner. Nietzsche does not mention Stirner in his writings, but Overbeck claims that Nietzsche knew Stirner's work. Certainly, there are parallels in their critiques of Christian humanitarianism and the liberal state (themes in Stirner's philosophy which also influenced Marx) and in the overman concept.[8] Nietzsche may have avoided explicit references to Stirner because, despite other areas of agreement, Stirner's *petit bourgeois* individualism repelled him and he did not want readers to confuse his aristocratic individualism with it.[9]

In contrast to his silence on Stirner, Nietzsche refers repeatedly in his letters and occasionally in his published works to Bruno Bauer, whom he praises as an attentive reader and a supporter of his attack on David Strauss as a cultural philistine.[10] Löwith argues that Nietzsche's *AntiChrist* parallels Bauer's analysis in *Das entdeckte Christentum*, which, in turn, developed out of Hegel's philosophy of religion.[11] Bauer's work also inspired Marx's study of religion and his use of religious images as paradigms of social and economic contradictions.[12]

Possibly most interesting, because of his extensive influence upon Marx's philosophy, is Nietzsche's indirect connection to Feuerbach through Wagner. Descriptions of Nietzsche as the heir of Schopenhauer and Wagner often ignore the tensions between these progenitors of his philosophy.[13] Although Schopenhauer influenced Nietzsche's notion of life as will to power, Nietzsche rejected his pessimistic metaphysics as early as *The Birth of Tragedy* and wrote with revolutionary fervor derived from the Feuerbachian Wagner of the 1830s and 1840s. Wagner then "regarded Feuerbach as the ideal exponent of the radical release of the individual from the thraldom of accepted notions, founded on the belief in authority."[14] Wagner especially praised Feuerbach's critique of Hegel because it established the value of art over philosophy and of sensuality over "spirit." In addition, after reading Feuerbach's *Philosophy of the Future*, Wagner wrote his *Art of the Future* and dedicated it to Feuerbach. Nietzsche similarly elevates art over philosophy, praises Feuerbach's "healthy sensuality," and writes a Left Hegelian cultural critique, *The Future of Our Educational Institutions*.

Nietzsche's rejection of Wagner when Wagner abandoned Feuerbach and wholeheartedly embraced Schopenhauer confirms the importance of this link. Wagner initially criticized the same aspects of Schopenhauer's philosophy as Nietzsche, saying,

> Here [Schopenhauer's philosophy] the annihilation of the will and complete abnegation are represented as the sole true and final deliverance from those bonds of individual limitation in estimating and facing the world.... For those who hoped to find some philosophical justification for political and social agitation on behalf of so-called "individual freedom" there was certainly no support to be found here, where all that was demanded was absolute renunciation of all such methods of satisfying the claims of personality.[15]

Later, Wagner turned away from his hopes for humanity and found "under the influence of Schopenhauer a profound realization of the intense tragedy of life and the emptiness of its phenomena."[16] Nietzsche says of this change:

> One should recall how enthusiastically Wagner at one time followed in the footsteps of the philosopher Feuerbach: Feuerbach's cry of "healthy sensuality"—that sounded in the thirties and fourties, to Wagner as to many other Germans (they called themselves the *"young* Germans"), like a cry of redemption. Did he at last come to *learn otherwise*? For at least it seems that he finally had the will to *teach otherwise*. And not only from the stage with the trumpets of *Parsifal*; in the murky writings of his last years ... there are a hundred passages that betray a secret wish and will, a despairing, unsure, unacknowledged will to preach nothing other than reversion, conversion, denial, Christianity, medievalism, and to say to his disciples "it is no good! seek salvation elsewhere!"[17]

Elsewhere, Nietzsche describes Schopenhauer's philosophy as a reef upon which Wagner was shipwrecked.[18]

Given these connections between Marx's Left Hegelianism and Nietzsche's romanticism, it should not be surprising that their critiques of German idealism, from which they developed their mature philosophies, contain similar themes.

Critics of German Idealism

As Left Hegelians and romantics, Marx and Nietzsche developed their views of man partially in opposition to German idealist philosophy. Both attacked two main (and numerous minor) aspects of that philosophical tradition: the notion of spirit, essence, or being beyond or manifest in the natural world; and the notion that men are to be understood in terms of their consciousness and that history is the product of consciousness. Both of these criticisms appear in their remarks concerning Kant and Hegel.

The young Marx and the young Nietzsche were both to

varying extents Kantians. In his 1837 letter to his father, Marx describes himself as "setting out from idealism—which . . . I had compared to and nourished with that of Kant and Fichte."[19] In his 1886 "Self-Criticism," Nietzsche says of *The Birth of Tragedy*, where he obscured his opposition to moralistic distinctions between phenomena and noumena with Kant's and Schopenhauer's metaphysical language:

> How I regret now that in those days I still lacked the courage (or immodesty?) to permit myself in every way an individual language of my own for such individual views and hazards— and that instead I tried laboriously to express by means of Schopenhauerian and Kantian formulas strange and new valuations which were basically at odds with Kant's and Schopenhauer's spirit and taste![20]

Both Marx and Nietzsche soon rejected Kant's metaphysics outright. After "setting out from idealism," Marx "hit upon seeking the Idea in the real itself. If formerly the gods had dwelt above the world, they had now become its center."[21] As I mentioned earlier, Marx turned to Hegel to mediate the Kantian gap between phenomena and noumena. He describes *Cleanthes*, his next work after his metaphysics of law, as a "philosophic-dialectical discussion of the godhead manifested as a concept per se, as religion, as nature, and as history. My last sentence was the beginning of the Hegelian system."[22] After *Cleanthes*, he "was more and more chained to the current world philosophy from which [he] had thought to escape."[23]

Nietzsche also attacks Kant's juxtaposition of phenomena and noumena: "Any distinction between a 'true' and an 'apparent' world—whether in the Christian manner or in the manner of Kant (in the end an underhanded Christian)—is only a suggestion of decadence, a symptom of the *decline of life*."[24] Although he admires Kant's skepticism about our ability to know the thing-in-itself—Kant correctly perceives the limits of reason[25]—he argues that that skepticism mistakenly leads back to God: the distinction between a phenomenal world of appearances and a noumenal realm inaccessible to reason makes room for faith.[26] For Nietzsche, there is only this world; no true world exists behind or beyond it. Further, precisely because no other reality exists, this world is no longer an apparent world. It is *the* world. We know this world as actors within it and our actions are always a part of it. Nietzsche does not mean by this that we create the world in the act of perceiving it, however. This radical Kantian notion of the phenomenal realm still presumes that knowledge of the world is something a knower has. That is, it presumes a transcendent, timeless subject—a Kantian knower though not Kantian noumena. For Nietzsche, there is neither a subject before knowledge who could have it, nor knowledge of oneself to be had. Men are ever-changing parts of an ever-changing whole, and they can only know their manifold relations within it.[27]

Nietzsche agrees with Marx that Hegel tries to overcome the Kantian separation of noumena and phenomena by demonstrating the Idea in the real; both characterize Hegel as a pantheist. But whereas Marx temporarily thought that Hegel's demonstration succeeded, Nietzsche consistently criticized it. According to Nietzsche, Kant and Hegel differ only on whether or not the Idea is demonstrable historically. Neither questions the existence of the Idea itself.

> God is unknowable for *us* and not demonstrable by us (the hidden meaning of the epistemological movement);
>
> God is demonstrable but as something in process of becoming, and we are part of it, as witness our impulse toward the ideal (the hidden meaning of the historical movement).
>
> Observe: criticism is never directed at the ideal itself, but only at the problem, where the opposition to it originates: why it has not yet been achieved or why it is not demonstrable in small things and in great.[28]

Nietzsche argues that Hegel, like Kant, is a Platonist, i.e., Hegel continues to posit a true world of abstract universal concepts opposed to our apparent world, even though he argues in Aristotelian fashion that the true world manifests itself in our apparent world. "The Hegelian way out, following Plato, a piece of romanticism and reaction, at the same time a symptom of the historical sense, of a new *strength*: the 'spirit' itself is the 'self-revealing and self-realizing ideal.'"[29] By positing spirit as reality, Hegel, like Kant, places "that which comes at the end—unfortunately! for it ought not to come at all!—namely, the 'highest concepts,' which means the most general, the emptiest concepts, the last smoke of evaporating reality, in the beginning, *as* the beginning."[30] In contrast to Hegel's "metaphysical pantheism," Nietzsche posits naturalistic values by affirming this world as the only world.

Through Feuerbach's influence Marx soon arrived at a similar critique of Hegel. In his "Preliminary Theses" and *Philosophy of the Future*, Feuerbach argues that Hegel mystifies reality by inverting subject and predicate. In other words, by understanding history as the self-actualization of spirit (subject) in the real (predicate), Hegel understands man, the real subject of history, as merely the predicate of spirit. Conversely, Feuerbach argues that man and this world are subject and that spirit is man in self-alienation, i.e., man's predicate.

In his *Critique of Hegel's Doctrine of the State* and in the *Economic and Philosophical Manuscripts*, Marx uses Feuerbach's transformative method to attack Hegel's "metaphysical pantheism."

> This process [Hegel's dialectic] must have a bearer, a subject; but the subject comes into being only as the result; this result, the subject knowing itself as absolute self-consciousness, is therefore *God, absolute spirit, the self-knowing and self-manifesting idea.* Real man and real nature become mere predicates, symbols of this hidden, unreal man and this unreal nature. Subject and predicate therefore stand in a relation of absolute inversion to one another.[31]

Like Nietzsche, Marx now argues that Hegel is a Platonist, i.e., that he mistakenly posits the most abstract—spirit—as the real.

> If we abstract thus from every subject all the alleged accidents, animate or inanimate, men or things, we are right in saying that in the final abstraction, the only substance left is the logical categories. Thus the metaphysicians who, in making these abstractions, think they are making analyses, and who, the more they detach themselves from things, imagine themselves to be getting all the nearer to the point of penetrating to their core.[32]

Marx, then, who initially sought Hegel's philosophy to mediate the Kantian dichotomy between real and Idea, subsequently rejects Hegel's pantheism because it too fails adequately to understand the real. By positing history as the self-actualization of spirit, Hegel mystifies concrete reality and denies man's role as the subject of history. Like Nietzsche, Marx would establish the reality of this world and of natural man in opposition to Kant's noumena and Hegel's "metaphysical pantheism."

Closely related to the above, Marx and Nietzsche also attack the apologetic character of Hegel's philosophy. They argue that Hegel's view of history as moments in the life of the Idea rationalizes the status quo and induces passivity and/or false optimism. Marx attacks Hegel's *Philosophy of Right* as an apologetic work: "As Hegel's task is not to discover the truth of empirical existence but to discover the empirical existence of the truth, it is very easy to fasten on what lies nearest to hand and prove that it is an *actual* moment of the Idea."[33] Nietzsche similarly (and more humorously) criticizes Hegel:

History understood in this Hegelian way has been contemptuously called God's sojourn upon earth—though the God was first created by history. [Note Nietzsche's use of transformative method; he too would stand things on their feet again.] He, at any rate, became transparent and intelligible inside Hegelian skulls, and has risen through all the dialectically possible steps in his being up to the manifestation of the self; so that for Hegel the highest and final stage of the world-process came together in his own Berlin existence.... he has implanted in a generation leavened throughout by him the worship of the "power of history" that turns practically every moment into a sheer gaping at success, into an idolatry of the actual.... If each success has come by a "rational necessity," and every event shows the victory of logic or the "Idea," then—down on your knees quickly, and let every step in the ladder of success have its reverence![34]

Both admit that the Hegelian dialectic does have a revolutionary side, i.e., the conception of history as struggle and development. Although Nietzsche is disturbed because Hegel's teaching made Darwinism possible, he still praises him for introducing the notion of becoming into philosophy: "Let us take . . . the astonishing stroke of *Hegel,* who struck right through all our logical habits and bad habits when he dared to teach that species concepts develop *out of each other.*" He explains this insight as characteristically German: "We Germans are Hegelians even if there never had been any Hegel, insofar as we . . . instinctively attribute a deeper meaning and greater value to becoming and development than to what 'is'; we hardly believe in the justification of the concept of 'being'."[35] Marx similarly praises Hegel, saying: "The importance of Hegel's *Phenomenology* and its final result—the dialectic of negativity as the moving and producing principle—lies in the fact that Hegel conceives the self-creation of man as a process . . . that he therefore grasps the nature of *labour* and conceives objective man—true, because real man—as the result of his *own labour.*"[36]

Yet Hegel obscures the revolutionary aspects of his dialectic not only because he rationalizes existence as a manifestation of an external reality, but also because he understands that reality and man in terms of self-consciousness. With this, I turn to Marx's and Nietzsche's second major criticism of German idealist philosophy. Both attack Hegel's history of the Idea as abstract, formal history, and instead posit histories of real, concrete, active men.

According to Marx, Hegel, because he mistakenly understands the real as spirit, also mistakenly equates man with his self-consciousness. Although Hegel identifies labor as man's process of self-creation in history, he recognizes only abstract, mental labor.[37] Further, because Hegel regards man as self-consciousness and his labor as abstract, mental labor, he regards estrangement too as merely the estrangement of self-consciousness. He inverts the real relationship and fails to recognize that estrangement of self-consciousness is merely the expression of real estrangement.

> For Hegel *human nature, man,* is equivalent to *self-consciousness.* All estrangement of human nature is therefore *nothing* but *estrangement of self-consciousness.* Hegel regards the estrangement of self-consciousness not as the *expression,* reflected in knowledge and in thought, of the *real*

estrangement of human nature. On the contrary, *actual* estrangement, estrangement which appears real, is in its innermost hidden nature—which philosophy first brings to light—nothing more than the *appearance* of the estrangement of real human nature, of *self-consciousness.*[38]

In contrast, Marx describes man as a "natural, corporeal, sensuous, objective being," who has *"real,* natural *objects* for the objects of its being" and whose "self-alienation [takes] the form of the establishment of a *real* objective world, but as something *external* to it, a world which does not belong to its being and which overpowers it."[39] Man's consciousness is not pure consciousness, but rather develops out of his particular material and social relations.

Nietzsche also criticizes attempts to understand man in terms of his consciousness:

The awakened and knowing say: body am I entirely, and nothing else; and soul is only a word for something about the body.

The body is a great reason, a plurality with one sense, a war and a peace, a herd and a shepherd. An instrument of your body is also your little reason, my brother, which you call "spirit"—a little instrument and toy of your great reason....

Behind your thoughts and feelings, my brother, there stands a mighty ruler, an unknown sage—whose name is self. In your body he dwells; he is your body.[40]

Nietzsche agrees with Marx that pure consciousness does not exist and that consciousness is only a small part of man. For both, sensuous, corporeal man is the self. In Nietzsche's case, the body is the seat of the will to power, man's self-actualizing power.

Nietzsche and Marx also agree that man's alienation as a real being or self in modern society cannot be overcome merely by a change in consciousness, be it the development of Hegel's absolute spirit or Feuerbach's species-consciousness. Marx argues that theory must merge with practice and criticizes Hegel and his Left Hegelian progeny on this point in the "Theses on Feuerbach": "The philosophers have only *interpreted* the world, in various ways; the point is to *change* it."[41] Nietzsche, although he might at first glance be regarded as vulnerable to Marx's criticism because he primarily criticizes philosophical, religious, and cultural interpretations, concurs:

> *Theory and Practice.*—Fateful distinction, as if there were an actual *drive for knowledge* that, without regard to questions of usefulness and harm, went blindly for the truth; and then, separate from this, the whole world of *practical* interest—
>
> I tried to show, on the other hand, what instincts have been active behind all these *pure* theoreticians—how they have all, under the spell of their instincts, gone fatalistically for something that was "truth" *for them*—for them and only for them. The conflict between different systems, including that between epistemological scruples, is a conflict between quite definite instincts (forms of vitality, decline, classes, races, etc.).
>
> The so-called drive for knowledge can be traced back to a drive to appropriate and conquer.
>
> Morality is such a curious science because it is in the highest degree *practical*.[42]

There is a subtle difference between these two arguments, however. Marx argues that theory *should not* be separated from practice, and Nietzsche argues that theory *cannot* be separated from practice. The two arguments blur because, if pressed, Marx would probably speak of "pure theory" as incorrect "practice." They separate because Nietzsche understands theory itself as practice. Whereas Marx assumes in the Eleventh Thesis that interpretations might not (and should) change the world, Nietzsche argues that thinking and doing cannot be separated, and that a revolution in theory is a revolution in action.

Perhaps this partially explains Nietzsche's attraction for diverse twentieth-century marxists concerned with superstructural phenomena, ranging from Adorno's critique of identity to Foucault's analysis of discourses to Derrida's defense of deconstruction. It may also explain why marxists who, from necessity, conviction, or both, want to understand their theorizing as a form of practice find Nietzsche congenial.[43] Still, it must be remembered that Nietzsche, unlike such marxists and the Left Hegelians with whom both are often compared, understands theory as practice because he understands thinking as a form of willing. As with the proletarian revolution, it is not enough, in fact it may be impossible, simply to think correctly about the overman and the eternal recurrence. (Witness Zarathustra's inability to think the eternal recurrence, because he is not yet willing to will it.) One must will them: one must project them upon reality and live as if they are true.

There are, then, similarities not only in Marx's and Nietzsche's intellectual origins, but also in their critiques of German idealist philosophy. Both reject Kant's noumenal realm and Hegel's "metaphysical pantheism" in the name of this world and natural man. Both also deny that man can be understood solely in terms of his consciousness. And both question Hegel's rationalization of the status quo and call for a revolutionary linkage of theory and practice. But both do recognize revolutionary aspects hidden in Hegel's philosophy, e.g., his notions of man's self-creation and of historical development. These common reactions to German idealism foreshadow similarities in the development of Marx's and Nietzsche's mature views of man, to which I now turn. In fact, one might say of Marx and Nietzsche what Nietzsche, in a different context, said of Hegel and Schopenhauer: in their fight against German idealism, they were of one mind—"these two hostile brother geniuses in philosophy who strove apart toward opposite poles of the German spirit and in the process wronged each other as only brothers wrong each other."[44]

Parallel Development

Marx and Nietzsche developed their mature views of man in opposition not only to German idealism, but also to their own youthful Left Hegelian and romantic alternatives to it. Although permutations of Left Hegelian and romantic themes still appear in their mature work, both become critics of similar aspects of those philosophies for similar reasons. The mature Marx criticizes Feuerbach's Left Hegelianism and the mature Nietzsche criticizes Wagner's romanticism because both respond passively to life as suffering, resigning themselves to it. That is, Feuerbach and Wagner only counsel escape from life through ideal states of consciousness. Neither examines how men create the historical conditions, the economics or the psychology, in which alienation and asceticism flourish, and neither suggests how men might create new and better conditions. For these reasons, Marx moves beyond Feuerbach to a historical materialist understanding of man's alienation as the product of particular socioeconomic conditions, and Nietzsche moves beyond Wagner to a gene-alogical understanding of man's asceticism as the product of particular sociopsychological conditions. Each also argues that men can overcome alienation or ascetic ideals historically. By similar routes, each arrives at a mature view of man as a natural and historical being. I discuss Marx's and Nietzsche's develop-ment in some detail, focusing upon the major problems each tried to answer in his mature view of man.

Marx: From "Man" to "Real, Historical Man"

The central question regarding Marx's view of man is whe-ther, really when, he had one. Marx clearly had a Feuerbachian anthropological theory of man in the *Economic and Philosophical Manuscripts*, but does he abandon this early Feuerbachian anthropology when he begins to insist that "as individuals express their life, so they are"?[45] If Marx does abandon a Feuerbachian anthropology, does he thereby abandon a theory of man alto-gether? What does it mean to speak, as Marx does, of man's essence once one has declared that men create themselves historically? Or, what is the realtionship between Marx's theory of man in the *Economic and Philosophical Manuscripts* and his analysis of the "economic laws of motion in modern society" in *Capital*?

Marx scholars generally answer these questions in two diametrically opposed ways. First, many argue that Marx's views on man constitute a unified whole, i.e., that it does not make sense to speak of an early anthropological versus a late historical materialist Marx.[46] Second, in contrast to these humanistic interpretations which describe Marx's work as a unified whole, others, most prominent among them Louis Althusser, argue that Marx's early and late views of man differ qualitatively.[47] These conflicting interpretations introduce confusion about what changes and what remains constant in Marx's view of man. Further, neither interpretation adequately characterizes his development: the former overemphasizes continuity and ignores fundamental differences; the latter overemphasizes discontinuity and ignores fundamental similarities. In contrast to both, I argue that Marx continued to reformulate the same basic question— Why is man's life activity, his labor, alienated in capitalist society?—throughout his work, but that he only gradually developed the historical materialist means to answer this question. Since Althusser argues that Marx changes when he develops historical materialism, but characterizes this change as the introduction of a new basic question, I develop my interpretation in opposition to his.

In order to understand Althusser's argument, a brief outline of his philosophy of science is necessary. Althusser argues that an author's thought is unified by a particular problematic, that is, by an *"objective internal reference system of its particular* themes, a system of *questions* commanding the *answers* given."[48] This system of questions is more important than the objects of the author's thought: "It is not the material reflected on that characterizes and qualifies a reflection, but . . . the *modality of the reflection*, the actual relation the reflection has with its objects, that is the *basic problematic* that is the starting point for the reflection of the objects of the thought."[49] Science progresses not by changes in the objects of thought, but by the discovery of new problematics, e.g., "The many authors who talked of social classes or even of the class struggle before Marx have never . . . been taken for Marxists simply because they dealt with objects which were eventually destined to attract Marx's attention."[50] Following Gaston Bachelard, Althusser calls such changes in problematics "epistemological breaks."

Althusser argues that Marx underwent an "epistemological break" roughly between the *Economic and Philosophical Manuscripts* and *The German Ideology.* According to Althusser, the young Marx was "no more than an *avant-garde* Feuerbachian applying *an ethical problematic to the understanding of human history*."[51] As a Feuerbachian, Marx extended anthropology to new objects, e.g., politics and economics, "inverted" Hegel, i.e., maintained that economics shapes philosophy, not the converse, and "extracted" Hegel's dialectic from its mystical shell, i.e., practiced concrete-material as opposed to abstract-speculative criticism.[52] However, this extension, inversion, and extraction is merely a different application, due to Feuerbach's transformative criticism, of the same problematic—Hegel's idealist dialectic—to a different structure. Hence, according to Althusser's understanding of scientific development, the young Marx is still the slave of German idealism and is not yet a Marxist.[53]

Althusser says that Marx began to develop his mature historical materialist, i.e., Marxist, problematic in *The German Ideology*. Althusser states that the mature Marx abandoned anthropological views of man and alienation as key concepts; neither retained any explanatory power with regard to historical development.[54] Indeed, Marx criticized both—and philosophical humanism per se—as ideological formulations.[55] Althusser maintains that Marx abandoned "Man" and alienation as key concepts because he no longer understood history as a dialectic of negativity of a simple, unstructured whole, i.e., as the Feuerbachian inversion of Hegel's autogenesis of spirit into the autogenesis of man.[56] According to Althusser, beginning with *The German Ideology*, Marx substituted a new historical materialist problematic for his previous Feuerbachian anthropology. He "replaced the old couple individual/human essence in the theory of history by new concepts (forces of production, relations of production, etc.)," and he "replaced the old postulates (empiricism/idealism of the subject, empiricism/idealism of the essence) which were the basis not only for idealism but also for pre-Marxist materialism, by a historico-dialectical materialism of *praxis*."[57] Althusser regards Marx's "epistemological break" as critical for Marxism: "This rupture with every *philosophical* anthropology or humanism is no secondary detail; it is Marx's scientific discovery."[58]

Against Althusser, I argue that 1) Marx never fully accepted Feuerbach's anthropology, obviating the need for a "break" with it; 2) he began to seek historical explanations for alienated labor prior to *The German Ideology*, belying arguments that historical materialism constitutes a qualitative change; 3) he developed historical materialism in order to provide such explanations, in order to answer persistent questions.

Althusser correctly identifies Marx's use of Feuerbach's

transformative method to invert Hegel's dialectic. Yet Marx's continued use of this method not only in his *Critique of Hegel's Doctrine of the State* (1843) and in the *Manuscripts* (1844), but also in *Capital* (1867), casts doubt upon Althusser's argument regarding an "epistemological break."[59] More important, Marx indicated his major criticisms of Feuerbach—that Feuerbach overemphasizes nature, de-emphasizes man's historical activity, and regards species-consciousness as human fulfillment—prior to his supposed "epistemological break." In a letter to Ruge on March 13, 1843, Marx says, "I approve of Feuerbach's aphorisms except for one point: he directs himself too much to nature and too little to politics. But it is politics which happens to be the only link through which contemporary philosophy can become true."[60] In addition, Marx commences the "Contribution to the Critique of Hegel's *Philosophy of Right*" (1843–1844) by calling for social criticism because the criticism of religion (Feuerbach's Left Hegelian work) is complete and concludes it by calling for proletarian revolution, not species-consciousness.[61] Later, in the "Theses on Feuerbach" (1845) and *The German Ideology* (1845–46), when Marx develops historical materialism, discusses man's essence as an ensemble of social relations, not a natural condition, and exhorts philosophers to stop interpreting and to begin changing the world, he does not say anything qualitatively new about Feuerbach, but merely expands upon his previous criticisms.[62] Evidence, then, exists to show that Marx was similarly critical of Feuerbach's anthropology both before and after what Althusser regards as his "epistemological break."

In addition, Marx begins to develop his alternative to Feuerbach's anthropology in the *Economic and Philosophical Manuscripts* themselves. Having used Feuerbach's transformative method to invert Hegel's abstract spirit into concrete man, he then adopts Hegel's notion of man's self-creation through labor as an active materialist alternative to Feuerbach's passive materialism. He describes this new synthesis of Hegel and Feuerbach somewhat paradoxically as a historical anthropology: "Nature as it comes into being in human history—in the act of creation of human society—is the *true* nature of man; hence nature as it comes into being through industry, though in *estranged* form, is true *anthropological* nature."[63]

Althusser, who ignores the historical aspects of Marx's

analysis in the *Manuscripts*, cannot explain Hegel's role in the development of historical materialism. In fact, Althusser argues that the Marx who turns to Hegel's self-creative man in part IV of the *Manuscripts* is furthest from the mature Marx.[64] With this, Althusser contradicts Marx's own statements regarding his debt to Hegel.[65] In the first "Thesis on Feuerbach," Marx credits idealism with developing the active component materialism requires.[66] The conception of man's self-creation as a historical process is the "rational kernel" of Hegel's dialectic which Marx later says he has extracted from its "mystical shell," from Hegel's pantheistic metaphysics.[67] Engels also argues that Hegel's dialectic has a revolutionary, i.e., active, side which helped Marx to transform Feuerbach's natural materialism into historical materialism.[68]

As he begins to develop his conception of historical man in the *Manuscripts*, Marx also criticizes both Hegel and Feuerbach (acknowledging a similarity in their "problematics" which Althusser would later emphasize) for regarding alienation as the essence of human development.[69] In contrast to both, Marx tries to show that man's objectification is a process of alienation only under particular historical conditions.[70] In the *Manuscripts*, in order to answer his initial question—"What is the meaning, in the development of mankind, of this reduction of the greater part of mankind to abstract labour?"—he already examines capital, profit, labor, commodities, classes, etc. They are the historical conditions he associates with alienation in capitalist society.[71]

He fails to answer his question, however, because he reverts back to Hegelian and Feuerbachian language, ascribing explanatory power to man's species-essence and to alienation itself, referring to human history as a process predetermined by a mysterious species-essence which alienates itself and thereby causes alienation. Although he understands man historically and examines the historical conditions surrounding alienated labor, he does not yet possess the means to explain man's historical development or the historical causes of alienation. Marx later attests both to the presence of his basic question and the inadequacy of his early attempts to answer it in a passage which explicitly contradicts Althusser's interpretation of a change in problematic:

This path [to the materialistic outlook] was already indicated in the *Deutsch-Französische Jahrbücher*—in the *Einleitung zur Kritik der Hegelschen Rechtsphilosophie* and *Zur Judenfrage*. But since at that time this was done in philosophical phraseology, the traditionally occurring philosophical expressions such as "human essence," "genus," etc., gave the German theoreticians the desired excuse for misunderstanding the real trend of thought and believing that here again it was a question merely of giving a new turn to their worn-out theoretical garments.[72]

Marx begins to develop the historical materialist means to explain man's historical development and the historical causes of alienation in *The Poverty of Philosophy* and *The German Ideology*. When he develops these means, he does not abandon his concern with man's labor for an analysis of historical structures, as Althusser argues. He retains his understanding of labor as man's life activity, referring in *The German Ideology* and in *Capital* to production as that which distinguishes man from animals,[73] and in the *Grundrisse* to labor as man's life expression and to production as the determinant moment of human activity.[74] He reformulates his basic question in historical materialist terms by asking, "Why is labor represented by the value of its products?" but his concern with alienation also persists. Passages referring to the four types of alienation discussed in the *Manuscripts* appear in *Capital* and the *Grundrisse*, as do more general references to labor—man's process of self-realization—as a process of de-realization in capitalist society.[75]

However, Marx no longer ascribes explanatory power to man's species-essence alienating itself. Once he develops the premises of historical materialism, Marx understands man's labor in terms of material and social relations of production which correspond to expanding productive forces; alienation now describes labor under particular relations of production. In other words, Marx retains his concern with why man's labor—his life activity—is alienated in capitalist society, but turns to historical materialist analyses of social structures to explain why. His continued concern with man's alienated life activity prompts his historical materialist analysis of the "economic laws of motion" of modern society. Contrary to Althusser's analysis, Marx is not first a humanist of the subject (Man) and then a scientist of the object (social structures). Instead, he becomes a scientist of the object precisely because he remains a humanist of the subject.

Nietzsche: From Romantic to Dionysian Pessimism

Nietzsche's problems with romantic alternatives to German idealism are strikingly similar to those Marx experienced with Left Hegelianism. Paralleling Marx, who criticizes Feuerbach because of his passivity, emphasis upon nature, and idealization of species-consciousness, Nietzsche criticizes Wagner because of his resignation, ahistoricity, and asceticism. As Marx ultimately moves beyond Feuerbach, so Nietzsche ultimately moves beyond Wagner.

Unlike Marx, however, Nietzsche conveniently clarifies his development, describing four distinct phases: early Schopenhauerian student years (1864–69); Wagnerian period (1869–1876); positivistic criticism of all past ideals (1876–1882); mature doctrines of the will to power, overman, and eternal recurrence.[76]

As I discussed earlier, scholars who conflate Nietzsche's Schopenhauerian and Wagnerian years may obscure his early doubts about Schopenhauer's romantic pessimism and hence also his later criticisms of Wagner. As early as *The Birth of Tragedy* and *Richard Wagner in Bayreuth*, Nietzsche (despite his Schopenhauerian language) sees Wagner as a Dionysian pessimist, not a Schopenhauerian romantic one. Wagner's artistic creations affirm life as suffering instead of negating it through aesthetic or ascetic withdrawal. Later, Nietzsche describes Wagner's turn from Feuerbach to Schopenhauer as a shipwreck:

> For a long time, Wagner's ship followed *this* [the overturning of old deities who denied life] course gaily. No doubt, this was where Wagner sought his highest goal.— What happened? A misfortune. The ship struck a reef; Wagner was stuck. The reef was Schopenhauer's philosophy; Wagner was stranded on a *contrary* world view. What had he transposed into music? Optimism. Wagner was ashamed.

... Finally, a way out dawned on him: the reef on which he was shipwrecked—what if he interpreted it as the *goal*, as the secret intent, as the true significance of his voyage?[77]

Nietzsche also says that his shipwreck "gave to the artist of decadence—himself." Wagner had such tendencies all along. With this Nietzsche begins to define the romantic as a type, a type which he admits he had failed to recognize in Wagner, explaining his early overestimation of him.

With Schopenhauer and Wagner as examples, Nietzsche argues that romantics are weak-willed, too weak to affirm life. Schopenhauer understands life itself as will, by which he means ceaseless striving after ceaseless desires. Because desire is insatiable, happiness is only a momentary cessation of pain, and life is best characterized as suffering. According to Schopenhauer, art and asceticism are escapes from life as will and suffering. The artist escapes through aesthetic contemplation and creation which transcend will as desire; the ascetic escapes through a morality which, by denying will as desire, ultimately denies life itself.

Nietzsche regards ascetic and aesthetic ideals as metaphysical creations which condemn life as will to power and/or counsel resignation to it. According to Nietzsche, Wagner's romanticism is then not an alternative to idealism but merely another form of it.

With this extraordinary rise in the value of music that appeared to follow from Schopenhauerian philosophy, the value of *the musician* himself all at once went up in an unheard-of manner, too: from now on he became an oracle, a priest, indeed more than a priest, a kind of mouthpiece of the "in itself" of things, a telephone from the beyond— henceforth he uttered not only music, this ventriloquist of God—he uttered metaphysics: no wonder he one day finally uttered *ascetic ideals*.[78]

Instead of condemning life by creating ahistorical conceptions of being, Dionysian pessimists, who have a superabundant will, affirm life as suffering and becoming. Nietzsche characterizes the contrast:

> I was the first to see the real opposition: the degenerating instinct that turns against life with subterranean vengefulness (Christianity, the philosophy of Schopenhauer, in a certain sense already the philosophy of Plato, and all of idealism as typical forms) versus a formula for the highest affirmation, born of fullness, of overfullness, a Yes-saying without reservation, even to suffering, even to guilt, even to everything that is questionable and strange in existence.[79]

He describes the distinctively Dionysian as: "The affirmation of passing away *and destroying,* . . . saying Yes to opposition and war; *becoming,* along with a radical repudiation of the very concept of *being.*"[80]

In his third period, Nietzsche moves beyond Wagnerian-as-Schopenhauerian romanticism and rejects all metaphysical ideals. He depicts this—akin to Marx's and Engel's break with German idealism and Left Hegelianism, which "settled accounts with their philosophical consciences"—as a break with himself and all the decadence of his age which he embodied.[81] For as Marx relied on German idealist and Left Hegelian concepts in his early work, Nietzsche had adopted romantic strains. In *The Birth of Tragedy*, although his position is Dionysian, not romantic, and he does not advocate an ascetic metaphysics, he does argue that the world is only justified as an aesthetic phenomenon. In addition, though he does not posit Schopenhauerian ahistorical conceptions of being, he does explain history as the development of an "idea." His understanding of history as becoming is still tinged with Hegel's pantheistic metaphysics. This, I think, is the main reason why he later criticizes his *Birth of Tragedy* as offensively Hegelian. Still, I will return to the parody of dialectics (one reminiscent of Marx's caricature of thesis, antithesis, and synthesis in *The Poverty of Philosophy*) which is also evident here. He says,

> One might sooner believe that the essay was fifty years older. It is indifferent toward politics . . . it smells offensively Hegelian, and the cadaverous perfume of Schopenhauer sticks only to a few formulas. An "idea"—the antithesis of the Dionysian and the Appollinian—translated into the realm of metaphysics; history itself as the development of this "idea"; in tragedy this antithesis is sublimated into a unity.[82]

Once Nietzsche rejects his past ideals, he rejects all such metaphysical antitheses and declares all of life to be will to power. As Marx's notion of man's self-creation through labor overcomes the idealist antithesis between man's history and his nature, so Nietzsche's notion of life as the creative will to power overcomes that between becoming and being. Nietzsche exposes past conceptions of being as creations of the will to power, projected upon reality, and regarded as true.

Parallels in the development of Marx's and Nietzsche's mature views of man should now be clear. In opposition to German idealism, both turn to Left Hegelian and romantic conceptions of natural man: Marx praises Feuerbach for his understanding of man as a sensuous being; Nietzsche renounces Wagner when he abandons his previous Feuerbachian sensuality. However, both ultimately criticize Left Hegelianism and romanticism for their ahistoricity. Left Hegelians and romantics may deny traditional theology by affirming natural man, but they introduce a new, albeit naturalistic, theology. This appears in the Left Hegelians' conceptions of "Man's" species-consciousness as the transcendence of alienation. It is also seen in the romantics' advocacy of ascetic or aesthetic ideals as escapes from life as suffering. Feuerbach does not understand "sensuous human activity, practice" and "relapses into idealism" when confronted with alienating social conditions.[83] Wagner analogously denies life as becoming and ends "as romantics end, as *Christians*" when confronted with life as suffering.[84] Marx and Nietzsche move past Left Hegelianism and romanticism, going on to examine the conditions which frustrate natural, historical man.

Natural, Historical Man

In overcoming the limitations of their origins, Marx and Nietzsche reject not only idealist but also empiricist conceptions of humanity. The former they associate with Continental philosophers, specifically Kant and Hegel, but the latter they portray as predominantly English, i.e., the product of Bacon, Hobbes, and Locke. Whereas idealism is too abstract and apologetic, empiricism is too ahistorical and atomistic. Marx does qualify this critique somewhat. He recognizes the positive influence of the

English materialists upon their French counterparts. French materialism has a revolutionary potential (one Feuerbach failed fully to realize) which links it to socialism.[85] Nietzsche, however, associates materialism per se with empiricism, a disagreement with Marx to which I return. In any case, they characterize their conceptions of man as transcending both idealism and empiricism. In speaking of his method, Marx says,

> Its premises are men, not in any fantastic isolation and rigidity, but in their actual, empirically perceptible process of development under definite conditions. As soon as this active life-process is described, history ceases to be a collection of dead facts as it is with the empiricists (themselves still abstract), or an imagined activity of imagined subjects, as with the idealists.[86]

Nietzsche says somewhat more speculatively,

> Suppose nothing else were "given" as real except our world of desires and passions, and we could not get down, or up, to any other "reality" besides the reality of our drives.... Is it not permitted to make the experiment and to ask the question whether this "given" would not be *sufficient* for also understanding ... the so-called mechanistic (or "material") world?[87]

These passages confirm that both understand man as a natural and a historical being. What, though, is he like? What is his "life-process" or the "reality of his drives"? How does he create himself historically? To answer these questions, I examine first their views of man as a being who externalizes himself historically and, second, their understanding of man's externalization, of his creative activity and his creations.

Externalization

When Marx and Nietzsche reject idealist and empiricist conceptions of man, they do not reject all conceptions of man's essence or nature. Both still speak of essential or natural man, but both argue that what man is is inextricably bound up with his historical relations to nature and to other men. In fact, man's nature or essence *is* to externalize himself in changing ways and forms.

Marx describes this human essence when he calls man an "objective being." By this he means that man creates himself in and is conditioned by external objects. To take the latter first, as a part of nature man depends upon external objects to survive and to express himself.

> As a natural, corporeal, sensuous, objective being he is a *suffering*, conditioned and limited being, like animals and plants. That is to say, the *objects* of his drives exist outside him as *objects* independent of him; but these objects are objects of his *need*, essential objects, indispensable to the exercise and confirmation of his essential powers.[88]

Man's drives are directed outward toward these external objects, and by giving himself objective form in them, he meets his subsistence needs and expresses himself. "To say that man is a *corporeal*, living, real, sensuous objective being with natural powers means that he has *real, sensuous objects* as the object of his being and of his vital expression, or that he can only *express* his life in real, sensuous objects."[89]

Marx argues that production or labor is the activity in which men objectify themselves: "As individuals express their life, so they are. What they are, therefore, coincides with their production, both with *what* they produce and with *how* they produce."[90] As men produce and change nature, they also change. Conditioned by their productive activity and the objects they produce, they develop new powers of production and express themselves in new products.

> Labour is, in the first place, a process in which both man and Nature participate, and in which man of his own accord starts, regulates, and controls the material reactions between himself and Nature. . . . By thus acting on the external world and changing it, he at the same time changes his own nature. He develops his slumbering powers and compels them to act in obedience to his sway.[91]

History is the process of development of man's productive powers, a process in which man is simultaneously creator and creature of external objects. For Marx, history is the history of the expansion of man's essential objectifying productive powers: "The history of *industry* and the *objective* existence of industry as it has developed is the *open* book of the essential powers of man."[92]

Although Nietzsche does not understand the external world or man's creations as objects, he too understands man's life activity as a creative and created process of externalization. Again to take the latter first, arguing against both free will and determinism, Nietzsche states that man simply is his manifold relations as a part of the whole. He says,

> That no one *gives* man his qualities—neither God, nor society, nor his parents and ancestors, nor he himself.... No one is responsible for man's being there at all, for his being such-and-such, or for his being in these circumstances or in this environment. The fatality of his essence is not to be disentangled from the fatality of all that has been and will be....
>
> One is necessary, one is a piece of fatefulness, one belongs to the whole, one is in the whole.[93]

As creator, man directs his will to power—what he is—outward. He meets his needs and expresses himself by projecting what he is upon reality.

> Man projects his drive to truth, his "goal" in a certain sense, outside himself as a world that has being, as a metaphysical world, as a "thing-in-itself," as a world already in existence. His needs as creator invent the world upon which he works, anticipate it; this anticipation (this "belief" in truth) is his support.[94]

As he projects his drives upon reality he, like Marxian man, develops. However, the developmental activity which most concerns Nietzsche is sociopsychological, not socioeconomic. As men obey the past creations of their wills to power, they reorder their basic drives, repressing some instincts, developing others, and expanding their power. As their strength increases, they also overcome their past creations, i.e., the previous philosophical and moral systems which expressed the strength and order of their previous drives. "And life itself confided this secret to me: 'Behold,' it said, 'I am *that which must always overcome itself.*'"[95] For Nietzsche, history has been the history of the expansion of the will to power: "Man, become master over the forces of nature, master over his own savagery and licentiousness (the desires have learned to obey and be useful)—man, in comparison with a pre-man—represents a tremendous quantum of *power—not* an increase in 'happiness'!"[96]

Although Marx and Nietzsche describe general characteristics of man's life activity, they argue that neither production nor the will to power exists in general. Man's productive and willing capacities develop historically, taking different forms at different times. Marx says: "Whenever we speak of production, then, what is meant is always production at a definite stage of social development—production by social individuals.... However, all epochs of production have certain common traits, common characteristics."[97] Nietzsche, during a critique of Schopenhauer, similarly denies that the will to power can be understood independently of its particular historical forms:

My proposition is: that the will of psychology hitherto is an unjustified generalization, that this will *does not exist at all*, that instead of grasping the idea of the development of one definite will into many forms, one has eliminated the character of the will by subtracting from it its content, its "whither?"[98]

In chapter 3, I compare Marx's historical materialist conception of history as the development of man's productive forces and Nietzsche's genealogical conception of history as man's self-overcoming. There I also discuss why each identifies either production or willing as man's basic life activity. For now, I only want initially to establish that Marx and Nietzsche agree that man externalizes himself in historical relations. In fact, in strikingly similar statements, both say that a being without such relations is a non-being:

The properties of a thing are effects on other things; if one removes other things then a thing has no properties, i.e., there is no thing without other things, i.e., there is nothing in itself.

A being which has no object outside itself is not an objective being. A being which is not itself an object for a third being has no being for its *object*, i.e., it has no objective relationships and its existence is not objective.
A non-objective being is a *non-being*.[99]

Contrary to existentialist interpretations of Nietzschean man as the self-creating subject and mechanistic interpretations of Marxian man as the mere product of his productive forces, both Marx and Nietzsche understand man as creator and creature of his relations to the world. To develop this point more fully, I examine those relations to nature and to other men in greater detail.

Relations to Nature

THE NATURAL WORLD

Before examining production and willing in relation to nature, I must discuss how Marx and Nietzsche understand nature itself, since their views of nature shape their conceptions of man's relations to it.

For Marx, the natural world is the world of material objects perceived by the senses. Men labor upon these material objects which nature provides and adapt them to human wants. Nature spontaneously provides some objects of labor, e.g., fish, water, timber, and labor merely separates them from immediate connection with their environment. Others require labor to transform them into raw material, e.g., ore, extracted and ready for washing. Yet others are objects of labor to be fashioned into instruments of labor: "As the earth is his original larder, so too it is his original tool house."[100] Marx often refers to these basic material objects as "means of production": "If we examine the whole process from the point of view of its result, the product, it is plain that both the instruments and the subject of labour, are means of production, and that the labour itself is productive labour."[101] As man develops historically and expands his productive powers, the products of his previous labor become means of production for his subsequent labor. This entire process of development is, however, contingent upon the presence of a material substratum in nature.

Nietzsche, as a critic of materialism per se, has a more extreme conception of becoming than Marx. While Marx maintains that a natural, material substratum exists, Nietzsche questions both our sensory experience of material objects and their very existence:

> As for materialistic atomism, it is one of the best refuted theories there are ... thanks chiefly to the Dalmatian Boscovich: he and the Pole Copernicus have been the greatest and most successful opponents of visual evidence so far. For while Copernicus has persuaded us to believe, contrary to all the senses, that the earth does *not* stand fast, Boscovich has taught us to abjure the belief in the last part of the earth that "stood fast"—the belief in "substance," in "matter," in the earth-residuum and particle-atom: it is the greatest triumph over the senses that has been gained on earth so far.[102]

Nietzsche argues that materialist atomism, like the thing-in-itself, imposes a false conception of "being" on the world. What Nietzsche does is to hypothesize that will affects will wherever effects are recognized; he tries to explain all mechanical occurrences as "will force," "effects of will." This means that in the world as will to power, as he puts it, "no things remain but only dynamic quanta, in a relation of tension to all other dynamic quanta: their essence lies in their relation to all other quanta, in their 'effect' upon the same."[103] It is in this context that he speaks of the will to power as "not a becoming, but a *pathos*—the most elemental fact from which a becoming and effecting first emerge."[104] *Pathos* means that which happens to a person or thing and what one has experienced, good or bad. It also refers to the incidents of things. Etymologically, it is associated with *paschein* which means to suffer, to endure, to undergo, to be born along, to be in some manner shaped or turned. Here, Nietzsche seems to say that the experiential, contextual component of willing is most basic, more basic than the existence of subjects or objects.

Man as subject, then, is not related to objects in the Marxian sense, but only to other interrelated "dynamic quanta": "The subject alone is demonstrable; hypothesis that only subjects exist—that "object" is only a kind of effect produced by a subject upon a subject— a *modus* of *the subject*."[105] Even the subject does not exist as an entity—whether ego or actor. Nietzsche supplants both thinking ego and acting subject and situates the self in the manifold sensory experiences of the body. He describes the body, as we have seen, as a "plurality" of which consciousness is only a small part. This plurality does, however, have "one self." The self creates itself as a self; it is a *centered* plurality of *ordered* drives which discharges its will in relation to other such pluralities. This "subject" Nietzsche describes as "no subject, but an action, a positing, creative, no 'causes and effects'."[106] The world within which it creates itself, the world viewed from inside—the only perspective from which one can view it—"it would be 'will to power' and nothing else."[107]

From the perspective of life as will to power, subject and object, cause and effect, become "mere semiotics and nothing real."[108] Such constructs do permit communication and facilitate action by organizing experience, but they do not correspond to reality. Thus, although Marx and Nietzsche question "given" realities, Nietzsche would probably argue that Marx does not question them radically enough. By accepting subject and object, even dialectically constituted, as "given," Marx retains semiotic fictions—the notion of subjects who affect objects—which, Nietzsche would argue, deny becoming and which make the "thing-in-itself" cognitively possible:

> When one has grasped that the "subject" is not something that creates effects, but only a fiction, much follows.
> It is only after the model of the subject that we have invented the reality of things and projected them into the medley of sensations. If we no longer believe in the effective subject, then belief also disappears in effective things, in reciprocation, cause and effect between those phenomena that we call things.
> There also disappears, of course, the world of effective atoms: the assumption of which always depended upon the supposition that one needed subjects.
> At last, the "thing-in-itself" also disappears, because this

is fundamentally the conception of a "subject-in-itself." But we have grasped that the subject is a fiction. The antithesis "thing-in-itself" and "appearance" is untenable; with that, however, the concept "appearance" also disappears.[109]

Elsewhere, Nietzsche argues that socialists, who retain Hegel's metaphysical language, also retain his faith in the existence of a true world accessible to reason. Marx may "invert" Hegel, but he only substitutes scientific metaphysics for theological metaphysics; they are equally untenable in a world without truth.[110]

LABORING UPON NATURE

According to Marx, man relates to nature by objectifying his labor in natural objects and thereby transforming them.

In the labour process, ... man's activity, with the help of the instruments of labour, effects an alteration, designed from the commencement, in the material worked upon. The process disappears in the product; the latter is a use-value, Nature's material adapted by a change of form to the wants of man. Labour has incorporated itself with its subject: the former is materialized, the latter transformed.[111]

Marx describes this process as man's mastery and appropriation of nature. Through labor, man subjects natural objects to his needs and makes those objects his. Marx discusses man's appropriation of nature in Lockean language as the creation of property, however, not necessarily of private property:

All production is appropriation of nature on the part of an individual within and through a specific form of society. In this sense, it is a tautology to say that property (appropriation) is a precondition of production. But it is altogether ridiculous to leap from that to a specific form of property, e.g., private property [as Locke does].[112]

Locke's notion of private property is predicated upon man's private ownership of his body, his labor (an extension of his body), and its products (an extension of his labor).[113] In contrast, Marx understands man as a social being, and labor as a social activity which produces social products: "So the *social* character is the general character of the whole movement; *just as* society itself produces *man* as *man*, so it is *produced* by him. Activity and consumption, both in their content and in their *mode of existence*, are *social* activity and *social* consumption."[114] As I will presently discuss, private property in capitalist society conceals the social character of man's productive activity and perverts his appropriation of nature, i.e., man's mastery of nature increases, but under social relations which prevent him from controlling his products and his productive activity.

Man's labor is first directed to producing means of subsistence, e.g., food for the hungry, shelter for the cold, etc. Man's first historical act is to satisfy these physical needs. However, animals also produce to satisfy physical needs, and Marx has said that men "begin to distinguish themselves from animals as soon as they begin to *produce*."[115] What distinguishes human from animal production?

Marx addresses this issue in the *Economic and Philosophical Manuscripts*. There he says:

> It is true that animals also produce. They build nests and dwellings, like the bee, the beaver, the ant, etc. But they produce only their own immediate needs or those of their young; they produce one-sidedly, while man produces universally; they produce only when immediate physical need compels them to do so, while man produces even when he is free from physical need and truly produces only in freedom from such need.[116]

Unlike animals, men do not labor only from compulsion to meet immediate physical needs. They expand their needs historically: "The satisfaction of the first need (the action of satisfying, and the instrument of satisfaction which has been acquired) leads to new needs."[117] As they expand their needs, they also expand their powers to satisfy those needs: "With his development this realm of physical necessity expands as a result of his wants; but at the same time, the forces of production which satisfy these wants also increase."[118] This means that men can potentially satisfy their expanded physical needs and can potentially move beyond compelled to free production.

Freedom as a result of meeting expanded physical needs, however, is not yet true freedom. According to Marx, true freedom only begins "where labour which is determined by necessity and mundane considerations ceases."[119] Although Marx is generally most concerned with material objects of production, he describes this truly free, and hence truly human, appropriation of the natural world as "beyond the sphere of actual material production."[120] It involves man's total, i.e., universal, appropriation of the natural world through all of his senses.

> Man appropriates his integral essence in an integral way, as a total man. All his *human* relations to the world—seeing, hearing, smelling, tasting, feeling, thinking, contemplating, sensing, wanting, acting, loving—in short, all the organs of his individuality, like the organs which are directly communal in form, are in their *objective* approach or in their *approach to the object* the appropriation of that object. This appropriation of *human* reality, their approach to the object, is the *confirmation of human reality.*[121]

History is the development of man's essential, i.e., objectifying, powers, the progressive actualization of man's unique potential to labor freely and universally.

But why do men, unlike animals, have this potential to labor freely and universally? According to Marx, men, unlike animals who are one with their life activity, are distinct from and conscious of that life activity.

> The animal is immediately one with its life activity. It is not distinct from that activity; it *is* that activity. Man makes his life activity itself an object of his will and consciousness. He has conscious life activity. It is not a determination with which he directly merges. Conscious life activity directly distinguishes man from animal life activity.[122]

In other words, men can consciously control their productive activity and therefore can potentially produce universally and freely. In addition, it is because men are conscious of and distinct from their life activity that they can express themselves in their appropriations of nature. "This mode of production must not be considered simply as being the production of the physical existence of the individuals. Rather it is a definite form of activity of these individuals, a definite form of expressing their life, a definite *mode of life* on their part."[123] In his productive activity, then, man not only appropriates nature, but also expresses his essence as an objective being, i.e., he is conscious of his appropriations as objectifications of himself and can potentially create products to confirm, affirm, or realize his essence.[124]

Marx says that man's consciousness of his life activity is a product of his nature as a species-being or herd animal: "He is a conscious being, i.e., his own life is an object for him, only because he is a species-being,"[125] and "Consciousness is . . . from the very beginning a social product."[126] I analyze man's social relations after discussing Nietzsche's will to power and nature.

INTERPRETING CHAOS

Nietzsche would agree with Marx that man's essential life activity is not the pursuit of self-preservation or even of material comfort. Both argue that when either becomes the end of life, man becomes less than human. This is because both understand man's life activity as a creative process which requires constant striving to destroy what has gone before. When men live to preserve themselves, as they do in modern society, Marx says that a means to life is falsely proclaimed as its end. Nietzsche analogously argues that under such circumstances a result of expanding life is falsely proclaimed as its goal. This suggests that both would despise the last man (whom Nietzsche may inappropriately intend as a portrayal of man in socialist society) as a man who has made self-preservation and material comfort his goal and no longer creates. Beyond this agreement on man's continual creativity, however, disagreements appear in their conceptions of his needs and his relations to nature.

Earlier, I quoted Nietzsche's statement "His [man's] needs as creator invent the world upon which he works."[127] Those needs which concern Nietzsche are primarily psychological, not material. (In fact, as we will see in chapter 6, Nietzsche stigmatizes those who emphasize material needs as "under-nourished.") Although the experiential aspect of willing, the will to power as a *pathos*, is most basic, it does not exhaust the phenomena of willing. For in order to create, men must organize and direct their manifold experiences. Their greatest need is a "metaphysical need" for certainty, for a stable world with fixed boundaries in which to act. Otherwise, they will be paralyzed by the chaos of experience, by seeing "becoming" everywhere. As Nietzsche puts it,

> This is a universal law: a living thing can only be healthy, strong, and productive with a certain horizon; if it is incapable of drawing one round itself ... it will come to an untimely end. Cheerfulness, a good conscience, belief in the future, the joyful deed—all depend, in the individual as well as the nation, on there being a line that divides the visible and clear from the vague and shadowy.[128]

The semiotic fictions discussed earlier and the philosophical/ moral systems expressed in such metaphysical language are horizons. They are interpretations men create and impose upon reality to meet their need for certainty. Nietzsche speaks of such interpretations as the highest manifestations of the will to power: "To impose upon becoming the character of being—that is the supreme will to power."[129]

Such interpretations express the will to power of their creator, how he has ordered his drives. Nietzsche does not believe that a "drive to knowledge" is the impetus for philosophizing, but rather that philosophies express other drives. He says,

> Anyone who considers the basic drives of man ... will find that all of them have done philosophy at some time—and that every single one of them would like only too well to represent just *itself* as the ultimate purpose of existence and the legitimate *master* of all the other drives. For every drive wants to be master—and it attempts to philosophize in *that* spirit....
>
> In the philosopher ... there is nothing whatever that is impersonal; and above all, his morality bears decided and decisive witness to *who he is*—that is, to what order of rank the innermost drives of his nature stand in relation to each other.[130]

Like Marx, Nietzsche sees man's expressions as appropriations: by giving form to the world man changes it and, in a sense, makes it his. Nietzsche also concurs with Marx that this process of appropriation is the mastery, even exploitation, of nature: man subjects it to his will. However, contrary to Marx, Nietzsche argues that when man masters nature, he also masters himself and other men. The creator imposes his creations not only on the natural world, but also upon his own drives and those of other men; he and they obey the philosophical and moral systems he creates.

Marx, who criticizes psychology for abstracting from human labor, for treating it as a "vulgar need" (Nietzsche is rather vulnerable here), does not examine the process of self-mastery undergone by his social producers. Marx also argues that men cooperate to master nature and that exploitative social relations are historically specific forms which conceal and/or pervert man's cooperative character. In contrast, Nietzsche regards man's relations to nature and society as equally and essentially exploitative: "Life itself is *essentially* appropriation, injury, overpowering of what is alien and weaker; suppression, hardness, imposition of one's own forms, incorporation and at least, at its mildest, exploitation—"[131] Commanding and obeying, oneself or others, are the nature of life. Zarathustra says:

> Wherever I found the living, there I heard also the speech on obedience. Whatever lives, obeys.
> And this is the second point: he who cannot obey himself is commanded. That is the nature of the living.
> This, however, is the third point that I heard: that commanding is harder than obeying; and not only because he who commands must carry the burden of all who obey, and because this burden may easily crush him. An experiment and hazard appeared to me to be in all commanding; and whenever the living commands, it hazards itself. Indeed, even when it commands *itself*, it must still pay for its commanding. It must become the judge, the avenger, and the victim of its own law.[132]

Since Nietzsche's creators impose interpretations upon the world and do not produce material objects, Marx might argue that Nietzsche (like Hegel) mistakenly understands history as the history of ideas and that Nietzsche's creators, who neither create nor relate to objects, are non-beings. Yet Nietzsche agrees with Marx that consciousness is derivative of more basic historical forces, though he does not agree on what those forces are and how they are structured. For both, interpretations of reality are historically contingent. In addition, Nietzsche argues that men shape more than consciousness when they impose their interpretations upon reality. The creations of the will to power, by changing man's internal ordering of his drives and his relations to the external world, create the conditions for his future activities. Man's condition in modern society exemplifies this. Nietzsche argues that

> the fight against Plato or, to speak more clearly and for "the people," the fight against the Christian-ecclesiastical pressure of millennia—for Christianity is Platonism for "the people"—has created in Europe a magnificent tension of the spirit the like of which has never yet existed on earth: with so tense a bow we can now shoot for the most distant goals.[133]

I will examine how modern society conditions the possibilities of willing later; now I only want to establish that such an effect exists. Man may not be an "objective" being for Nietzsche, but he is nonetheless a being whose creative activities are historically conditioned.

History, according to Nietzsche, is a succession of attempts by man to master nature, himself, and other men. But if all of life is will to power, what, if anything, distinguishes human from animal willing? Nietzsche describes "man in comparison with pre-man" as "a tremendous quantum of *power*."[134] For Nietzsche, as for Marx, man differs in that he wills with greater freedom and scope than pre-man. In a passage which also foreshadows the overman, Nietzsche distinguishes man as a sovereign individual from pre-man:

> This emancipated individual, with the actual *right* to make promises, this master of a *free* will, this sovereign man—how should he not be aware of his superiority over all those who lack the right to make promises and stand as their own guarantors, of how much trust, how much fear, how much

reverence he arouses ... and of how this mastery over himself also necessarily gives him mastery over circumstances, over nature, and over more short-willed and unreliable creatures.[135]

Nietzsche argues, again like Marx, that man wills more freely and more broadly than pre-man because he is distinct from and therefore can direct his willing. In *The Use and Abuse of History*, Nietzsche distinguishes between animals and men, saying that the former forget everything and live in the moment, while the latter remember the past. Memory requires a separation of the self from immediate experience and opens up the possibility of directing one's actions.[136] Elsewhere, Nietzsche says that man is separate from and able to direct his willing because he is conscious:

To ordain the future in advance ... man must first have learned to distinguish necessary events from chance ones, to think causally, to see and anticipate distant eventualities as if they belong to the present, to decide with certainty what is the goal and what the means to it, and in general be able to calculate and compute. Man himself must first of all have become *calculable, regular, necessary*.[137]

Like Marx, Nietzsche understands man's consciousness as a social product: "It was only as a social animal that man acquired self-consciousness—which he is still in the process of doing, more and more."[138]

Although Marx and Nietzsche criticize German idealists for understanding man in terms of his consciousness, both do argue that consciousness distinguishes human from animal activity. However, neither understands consciousness itself as man's essence. Nietzsche describes consciousness as a means to the enhancement of power: "We have no right whatever to posit this piece of consciousness as the aim and wherefore of this total phenomenon of life: becoming conscious is obviously only one more means toward the unfolding and extension of the power of life."[139] Marx says that consciousness is only a means to the objectification of man's species-life: "Conscious life activity directly distinguishes man from animal life activity. Only because of that is he a species-being. Or rather, he is a conscious being, i.e.

his own life is an object for him, only because he is a species-being. Only because of that is his activity free activity."[140] Both agree that man develops his distinctive capacity for conscious activity through social relations. What are those social relations? How do they contribute to the development of consciousness?

Relations to Society

SOCIAL PRODUCTION

Marx describes man as a "species-being" or "herd animal." By this he means, first, that men have a "materialistic connection" to one another "determined by their needs."[141] In order to appropriate natural objects, men cooperate with one another; their relations to nature are simultaneously social relations. Marx says,

> The production of life, both of one's own in labour and of fresh life in procreation, now appears as a double relationship: on the one hand as a natural, on the other as a social relationship. By social we understand the co-operation of several individuals, no matter under what conditions, in what manner and to what end. It follows from this that a certain mode of production, or industrial stage, is always combined with a certain mode of cooperation, or social stage.[142]

Man is able to relate to nature and to other men because, unlike animals, who are one with their life activity, his "instinct is a conscious one." However, man's consciousness is initially barely distinct from animal instinct; it is best described as a potential which must be developed.

> Man's consciousness of the necessity of associating with individuals around him is the beginning of the consciousness that he is living in society at all. This beginning is as animal as social life itself at this stage. It is mere herd-consciousness, and at this point man is only distinguished from sheep by the fact that with him consciousness takes the place of instinct or that his instinct is a conscious one.[143]

Man develops his consciousness as he expands his natural and social relations. Marx says, "This sheep-like or tribal consciousness receives its further development and extension through increased productivity, the increase of needs, and, what is fundamental to both of these, the increase of population."[144] Here Marx not only says that man begins with a "conscious instinct" (a potential), but also that "consciousness [the result of its actualization] is from the very beginning a social product."[145] Thus, when Marx describes man as a species-being, he means secondly that man is aware of and comes to awareness of himself through his relations to other men.

Marx stresses that man's consciousness is practical, not pure, consciousness; it is the product of social relations formed to meet material needs. Only after the division of material and mental labor appears can consciousness feign independence of matter:

> Division of labour only becomes truly such from the moment when a division of material and mental labour appears. (The first form of ideologists, *priests*, is concurrent.) From this moment onwards consciousness *can* really flatter itself that it is something other than consciousness of existing practice, that it *really* represents something without representing something real; from now on consciousness is in a position to emancipate itself from the world and to proceed to the formation of "pure" theory, theology, philosophy, ethics, etc.[146]

In reality, consciousness continues to express man's natural and social relations.

It is because man is a species-being whose life activity is conscious that he can make his life activity the object of his will. That is, he can purposively expand his productive powers to satisfy his expanding needs, ultimately to free and universal production. Marx, who understands man's historical development as the expansion of his productive powers also refers to it as the objectification of his essential species-powers. "It can be seen how the history of *industry* and the *objective* existence of industry as it has developed is the *open* book of the essential powers of man . . . as the reality of man's essential powers and as *man's species-activity*."[147]

Marx's description of man as a species-being also conveys a third idea, that not only the process but also the goal of man's productive activity is social. Marx says that man makes the species his object. By this he means that the individual and society are not separate forces which merge to produce and then separate, but are inextricably linked.

> The individual *is* the *social being*. His vital expression ... is therefore an expression and confirmation of *social life*. Man's individual and species-life are not two *distinct things*, however much—and this is necessarily so—the mode of existence of individual life is a more *particular* or a more *general* mode of the species-life, or species-life a more *particular* or more *general* individual life.[148]

Man's production only fulfills his human essence when activity and consumption, process and goal, are social:

> Activity and consumption, both in their content and in their *mode of existence*, are *social* activity and *social* consumption. The *human* essence of nature exists only for *social* man; for only here does nature exist for him as a *bond* with other *men*, as his existence for others and their existence for him, as the vital element of human reality.[149]

INTERNALIZATION

Nietzsche also describes man as a "species-being" or "herd animal," but not because he possesses a "conscious instinct," a potential to relate to others, which distinguishes him from animals. Instead, he says, *"Consciousness has developed only under the pressure of the need for communication."*[150] Man is merely a weak and vulnerable animal—"the most endangered animal"—and he needs the protection of his peers. Such protection could only be forthcoming once he had learned to express his distress, and that required consciousness.

> Consciousness is really only a net of communication between human beings; it is only as such that it had to develop; a solitary human being who lived like a beast of prey would not have needed it. That our actions, thoughts, feelings, and

movements enter our own consciousness—at least part of them—that is the result of a "must" that for a terribly long time lorded it over man. As the most endangered animal he *needed* help and protection, he needed his peers, he had to learn to express his distress and to make himself understood; and for all of this he needed "consciousness" first of all.[151]

However, as language requires consciousness, so consciousness requires language: conscious thinking takes the form of words. Nietzsche confronts a conundrum here typical for those who begin with man as an isolated individual. If consciousness requires association *and* association requires consciousness, how did man "know" that he needed his kind in the *first* place? Here Marx, as we have seen, resorts to a distinctively human "conscious" instinct. Nietzsche, however, maintains that "the development of language and the development of consciousness (*not* of reason but merely of the way reason enters consciousness) go hand in hand."[152] In this passage, Nietzsche distinguishes between reason and consciousness. A remark from the *Will to Power* clarifies the distinction: "the misunderstanding of passion and reason, as if the latter were an independent entity and not rather a system of relations between various passions and desires; and as if every passion did not possess its quantum of reason—"[153] He seems to argue that reason as a particular ordering of the passions exists unconsciously. This reason persists in social man, resembling in some respects the Freudian unconscious: "Man, like every living being, thinks continually without knowing it; the thinking that rises to *consciousness* is only the smallest part of all this."[154]

This preconscious reason may incline man toward society, but the development of consciousness itself is neither peaceful nor cooperative. According to Nietzsche, man becomes conscious through violence and coercion. A conqueror and master race forms him:

The welding of a hitherto unchecked and shapeless populace into a firm form was not only instituted by an act of violence but also carried to its conclusion by nothing but acts of violence—that the oldest "state" thus appeared as a fearful tyranny, as an oppressive and remorseless machine, and went on working until this raw material of people and semi-animals was at last not only thoroughly kneaded and pliant but also *formed*.[155]

Their cruel punishments for disobedience to social norms, e.g., stoning, breaking on the wheel, etc., taught men to remember. It is with the aid of such images and procedures, Nietzsche says, that "one finally remembers five or six 'I will not's,' in regard to which one had given one's *promise* so as to participate in the advantages of society—and it was indeed with the aid of this kind of memory that one at last came 'to reason!'" He concludes that "reason, seriousness, mastery over the affects, all these prerogatives and showpieces of man" have been "dearly bought."[156]

As man came to reason, he turned his instincts which he could no longer discharge outward inward, back against himself:

> All instincts that do not discharge themselves outwardly *turn inward*—this is what I call the *internalization* of man: thus it was that man first developed what was later called his "soul." The entire inner world, originally as thin as if it were stretched between two membranes, expanded and extended itself, acquired depth, breadth, and height, in the same measure as outward discharge was *inhibited*. Those fearful bulwarks with which the political organization protected itself against the old instincts of freedom ... brought about that all those instincts of wild, free, prowling man turned backward *against man himself*.[157]

Man created and obeyed moral systems in order to control his instincts. Nietzsche says that all societies create such systems which express the wills to power of their creators: "A tablet of the good hangs over every people. Behold, it is the tablet of their overcomings; behold, it is the voice of their will to power."[158] All such systems of good and evil are projections of the will to power which also dictate repression of the will to power; they are nature turned against nature, man turned against man.

However, man's internalization of his instincts takes different forms. Nietzsche distinguishes between "two basic types": master and slave morality. These terms designate something akin to

Weberian ideal types. That is, they characterize the dominant nature of a historical period, and also of an individual, although they are usually found "mixed" together or "alongside each other," even in a "*single* soul." They describe "one basic difference," a difference in how one relates to other men: masters are predominantly active, slaves predominantly reactive. Masters posit themselves, their distinctive qualities, as good and the qualities of their opposites as bad. Nietzsche describes their creative activity: "The noble type of man experiences *itself* as determining values; it does not need approval; it judges 'what is harmful to me is harmful in itself'; it knows itself to be that which first accords honor to things; it is *value-creating*."[159]

In contrast, slaves begin by defining their opposite—the master who oppresses them—as evil and react by positing their own qualities which help them endure (patience, industry, humility, etc.) as good. "Here," Nietzsche says, "is the place for the origin of that famous opposition of 'good' and 'evil': into evil one's feelings project power and dangerousness, a certain terribleness, subtlety, and strength that does not permit contempt to develop."[160] He characterizes the contrast between masters' and slaves' moral systems: "According to slave morality, those who are 'evil' thus inspire fear; according to master morality it is precisely those who are 'good' that inspire, and wish to inspire, fear, while the 'bad' are felt to be contemptible."[161]

Nietzsche's distinction between active and reactive types has been interpreted as a difference in the *direction* of willing, with masters willing outward and slaves willing inward.[162] This oversimplifies the difference between action and reaction. Internalization of the instincts exists in different forms in both types. Masters and slaves are conscious, social beings with all of the mechanisms of self-control that implies. Once "a conqueror and master race"—they *were* unconscious, instinctive artists—created political bulwarks, man developed psychological ones as well. However, the internalization of master moralities creates the conscience, the power of the sovereign individual over his drives which makes him calculable, regular, necessary. Nietzsche says that "in a certain sense, the whole of asceticism belongs here."[163] But only in a certain sense. He distinguishes the conscience from "that other 'somber thing,' the consciousness of guilt, the 'bad conscience.'"[164]

Man's initial internalization of his instincts provides the potential for the bad conscience—Nietzsche even calls it the "origin of the 'bad conscience'"—but this potential must be actualized. Nietzsche says that after man was imprisoned in the "state" he "became the inventor of the 'bad conscience.'"[165] The *bad* conscience is the form of internalization characteristic of slave morality. It is the invention of ascetic priests, espoused in truly ascetic ideals. Note the development implicit in the following passage:

> Its [guilt's] origin has been briefly suggested . . . as a piece of animal psychology, no more: there we encountered the sense of guilt in its raw state, so to speak. It was only in the hands of the priest, that artist in guilt feelings, that it achieved form—oh, what a form! "Sin"—for this is the priestly name for the animal's "bad conscience" (cruelty directed backward)—has been the greatest event so far in the history of the sick soul: we possess in it the most dangerous and fateful artifice of religious interpretation.[166]

Human history, according to Nietzsche, involves the successive triumphs of slave morality, triumphs ironically made possible by the conqueror and master race which first imprisoned man in society. Gradually, masters have learned not only to control their instincts, but also to feel guilty over precisely what slaves deem "evil" in them. This process of self-denial, one we will examine in detail, culminates in modern society, promising either the last man or the overman.

Although Nietzsche agrees with Marx that man develops consciousness, his distinctive human capacity in society, he clearly sees this as the result of chance, not the realization of some human potential. In fact, pre-man is not recognizably human. He had to be "forcibly sundered" from his animal existence, though he may have had inklings that he needed his peers. Only after man is enclosed in society, after he becomes ascetic, i.e., begins to take sides against himself, does human development begin. Nietzsche describes this process:

From now on, man is *included* among the most un-
expected and exciting lucky throws in the dice game of
Heraclitus' "great child," be he called Zeus or chance; he
gives rise to an interest, a tension, a hope, almost a certainty,
as if with him something were announcing and preparing
itself, as if man were not a goal but only a way, an episode, a
bridge, a great promise—[167]

With these remarks we approach Nietzsche's notion of
genealogy. It will be examined in detail in the next chapter, but
some preliminary, cautionary remarks are in order here.
Nietzsche's reference to chance does not mean that the development of man from pre-man or overman from man is totally
random. What it does mean is that neither human history nor
individual activity is purposive in the usual sense of the term.
Nietzsche speaks of goals as "relatively random, arbitrary, almost
indifferent in relation to the tremendous quantum of energy that
presses . . . to be used up somehow." He contrasts this view with
the common one: "People are accustomed to consider the
goal . . . as the *driving force* . . . but it is merely the *directing* force—
one has mistaken the helmsman for the steam."[168]

History is random because it is not "goal-oriented," i.e.,
driven by a goal. It is only relatively random because in all events
the will to power operates, striving to expand its strength. This
"steam" (to continue Nietzsche's metaphor) builds up pressure
under past experiences and shapes future ones: its condition
limits where we can choose to go, and the power of our choice.
Beyond such constraints, the direction chosen—whether the
"helmsman" steers toward man from pre-man or toward the
overman from man—is random, left to chance. Man makes his
own history, but (to paraphrase Marx) not just as he wills.

As society, including its preconditions of consciousness and
communication, was not the "goal" of pre-man, so it is not man's
"goal." Man becomes human, he strengthens his will to power,
developing his ability consciously to control his instincts and
achieving a certain freedom in society. However, again contrary to
Marx, Nietzsche views society not as an end, but as a means to
individuals: "*Basic error*: to place the goal in the herd and not in
single individuals! The herd is a means, no more!"[169] Society exists
not for its own sake, but "only as the foundation and scaffolding

on which a choice type of being is able to raise itself to its higher task and to a higher state of *being*."[170] For Nietzsche, man enclosed in society and turned against himself is the sick animal. A higher state of being requires removing the idiosyncrasies of society (guilt, punishment, justice, etc.) from existence.[171]

Although differences in Marx's and Nietzsche's views of man, some of which have already appeared, will become increasingly apparent, it is appropriate here to summarize some fundamental similarities. Both understand man as a natural historical being, as a being who creates himself historically through his relations to nature and society. Both also understand history as the expansion of his human activity, as the development of increased productive capacities or of a stronger will to power. Further, both argue that man's life activity, his labor or his willing, frustrates itself in modern society: Marx describes modern man as alienated; Nietzsche describes him as sick. According to Marx, although man's productive capacity expands tremendously in capitalist society, potentially allowing men to meet their needs and to produce freely and universally, they are alienated from human production. According to Nietzsche, although man is stronger than pre-man, his conscious creations in modern society are ascetic ideals which undermine his instincts and deny life as will to power. Marx and Nietzsche agree that the means to overcome alienation and ascetic ideals exist in modern society. Their metaphors for this coincide: Nietzsche speaks of man's sickness as an illness in the sense that *pregnancy* is an illness; Marx describes contradictions which will give *birth* to the revolutionary proletariat. Yet before turning to their critiques of modern society, I must further examine their basis for them. To do so, I explore their historical methods, how they criticize societies in light of man's potential powers.

CHAPTER THREE

DIALECTICAL HISTORY

Their history is ... the history of the evolving productive forces taken over by each new generation, and is, therefore, the history of the development of the forces of the individuals themselves. (Marx and Engels, *The German Ideology*, p. 87)

Put briefly: perhaps the entire evolution of the spirit is a question of the body; it is the history of the development of a higher body that emerges into our sensibility. (Nietzsche, *The Will to Power*, aphorism #676)

Marx's and Nietzsche's views of man undermine the traditional dichotomy between nature and history. For both, man's nature is to create himself historically through his relations to other beings and things. Both also expose seemingly natural social institutions and values as man's historical creations. By breaking down this dichotomy between nature and history, Marx and Nietzsche weaken other dichotomies as well. Epistemologically, they blur the line between objective realities and subjective preferences, since men can no longer pretend to detach themselves, as observers, from the world they observe. Ethically, they also make it difficult to distinguish between morality and power or between justice and interest.

This means that my analysis so far of Marx's and Nietzsche's views of man begs several questions. If man is as he creates himself historically, if his natural essence is his historical existence, why would Marx and Nietzsche criticize modern (or for that matter any) society? Why not let what is be or, more accurately, let what is becoming become? Further, once Marx and Nietzsche explain social structures, including conceptions of morality and justice, historically, how can they evaluate them? Upon what can they base their critiques?

To answer these questions, I examine Marx's and Nietzsche's theories of history in greater detail, comparing how they explain and evaluate societies in light of man's creative powers. I focus upon Marx's historical materialist and Nietzsche's genealogical analyses of how man's tendency to expand his powers historically determines the development (rise, functioning, and fall) of particular societies. I do not attempt the awesome, perhaps impossible, task of assessing the empirical validity of Marx's and Nietzsche's theories of history. Instead, I explore substantive similarities between the general types of historical analysis each employs. Later, I will examine differences between Marx's historical materialist and Nietzsche's genealogical analyses of how a specific society, modern society, frustrates man's life activity.

Before I proceed, one cautionary note is in order. By discussing historical materialism and genealogy as general types of historical analysis, I do not mean to imply that either is a formal method which is independent of history and which scientists must superimpose upon it. On the contrary, both are attempts to convey in thought the way history is structured. Although both are properly regarded as structural hypotheses, Marx and Nietzsche do occasionally refer to historical materialism and genealogy as methods. However, they do so because they think that one must examine history in a particular way in order to convey its structure in thought. Marx and Nietzsche also refer to their methods as scientific. This terminology highlights the differences between formal scientific method and their structural ones. It also emphasizes their critiques of positivism: both argue that science is properly explanatory and evaluative.[1]

I organize my examination of historical materialist and genealogical analysis in four main sections: what historical materialism and genealogy are not; expanding production and increasing strength as the determinant historical tendencies; societies as systems of domination organized by those tendencies; dialectical history and overcoming.

What Historical Materialism and Genealogy Are Not

Numerous conflicting interpretations of how Marx and Nietzsche explain and evaluate historical developments exist. I will begin my discussion by warning against interpretations of historical materialism and genealogy as (a) transcendent or immanent teleologies; (b) economic or physiological determinisms; (c) incoherent histories. At present, I will only indicate the major problems with such interpretations. As an alternative interpretation, this chapter is a response to them.

Interpretations of historical materialism and genealogy as teleological do, as I argue later, illuminate some aspects of those theories of history. However, teleological interpretations may also mislead by implicitly suggesting, if they do not explicitly state, that Marx or Nietzsche posits a *telos*, an end, present as potential in the origin, at which history aims.[2] They mislead in this way because teleological systems are generally characterized as "goal-oriented."[3] Teleologists, then, are commonly thought to explain historical development as the progressive actualization of transcendent or immanent, conscious or unconscious, ends, goals, or purposes.

Marx and Nietzsche attacked the ascription of transcendent goals to history by using Feuerbach's transformative method to invert Hegel's theology. Both criticize Hegel's notion of history as the autogenesis of spirit. They respectively argue that Hegel confuses subject and predicate or negates life by positing a transcendent spirit, even though that spirit actualizes itself in particulars. Nietzsche maintains that no one wants to exemplify anything through man. He asks, "What alone can be *our* doctrine?" and answers:

That no one *gives* man his qualities—neither God, nor society, nor his parents and ancestors, nor he himself. . . . No one is responsible for man's being there at all, for his being such and such, . . . The fatality of his essence is not to be disentangled from the fatality of all that has been and will be. Man is not the effect of some special purpose, of a will, and end.[4]

Marx similarly denies the existence of transcendent historical purposes. In a reference to the increasing interdependence of nations with the development of trade, he makes this more general point about historical method:

> This transformation of history into world history is not indeed a mere abstract act on the part of the "self-consciousness," the world spirit, or of any other metaphysical spectre, but a quite material, empirically verifiable act, an act the proof of which every individual furnishes as he comes and goes, eats, drinks and clothes himself.[5]

Both reject Hegel's metaphysical pantheism because, as a teleological explanation of history as the autogenesis of spirit, it denies that history is explicable solely in terms of man's natural, historical life processes or drives.

According to Marx and Nietzsche, not only transcendent but also immanent goals are absent from history. In the continuation of the previous quotation, Nietzsche absolves history of anthropological as well as theological ends. He says, "Nor is he [Man] the object of an attempt to attain an 'ideal of humanity' or an 'ideal of happiness' or an 'ideal of morality.' It is absurd to wish to devolve one's essence on some end or other. We have invented the concept of 'end': in reality there is no end."[6] Nietzsche caricatures the ascription of ends to history: "A man is as he *ought* to be: that sounds to us as insipid as 'a tree is as it ought to be.'"[7] He thinks that men, like trees, have characteristic tendencies and characteristic forms of organization, but this does not imply that men, any more than trees, can or should pursue goals.

Nietzsche argues that moralists and theologians, the proponents of immanent and/or transcendent goals, mistakenly and dangerously invert cause and effect with their formula: "Do this and that, refrain from this and that—then you will be happy! Otherwise...." By presuming that happiness will ensue if men pursue particular ends, moralists and theologians erroneously argue that a consequent—moral and/or religious virtue—creates its antecedent. Nietzsche revalues this distortion of individual and human development, saying:

> In my mouth, this formula is changed into its opposite—first example of my "revaluation of all values": a well-turned-out human being, a "happy one," *must* perform certain actions and shrinks instinctively from other actions; he carries the order, which he represents physiologically, into his relations with other human beings and things.[8]

Such inversions are dangerous and must be revalued because they negate life: they deny its innocence by arguing that man could or should become something other than what he is. Nietzsche describes theologians' and moralists' mistake:

> Let us finally consider how naive it is altogether to say: "Man *ought* to be such and such!" Reality shows us an enchanting wealth of types, the abundance of a lavish play and change of forms—and some wretched loafer of a moralist comments: "No! Man ought to be different." ... But even when the moralist addresses himself only to the single human being and says to him, "You ought to be such and such!" he does not cease to make himself ridiculous. The single human being is a piece of *fatum* from the front and from the rear, one law more, one necessity more for all that is yet to come and to be. To say to him, "Change yourself!" is to demand that everything be changed, even retroactively. And indeed there have been consistent moralists who wanted man to be different, that is, virtuous—they wanted him remade in their own image, as a prig: to that end, they *negated* the world![9]

History, according to Nietzsche, develops through a sequence of combinations of force, each of which conditions subsequent and is conditioned by antecedent combinations; it does not contain a transcendent or immanent *telos*.

When Marx moves beyond his early inversion of Hegel's history as the autogenesis of spirit to an understanding of history as the autogenesis of man, he also denies that immanent historical goals exist. As he develops the premises of historical materialism, he parodies the Left Hegelians' views, and by association his own previous ones, on this issue:

> The individuals, who are no longer subject to the division of labour, have been conceived by the philosophers as an ideal, under the name "Man." They have conceived the whole process ... as the evolutionary process of "Man," so that at every historical stage "Man" was substituted for the individuals and shown as the motive force of history. The whole process was thus conceived as a process of the self-estrangement of "Man," and this was essentially due to the

fact that the average individual of the later stage was always foisted on to the earlier stage, and the consciousness of a later age on to the individuals of an earlier.[10]

This criticism of Left Hegelian histories of "Man" parallels Nietzsche's criticism of moral-religious formulas, and implies what Marx explicitly says elsewhere, that communist society is not an anthropological ideal. Marx argues that the Left Hegelians, by presuming that a later historical goal—an ideal of man—causes earlier history, invert cause and effect, making a consequent the cause of its antecedent. He refers to such teleological explanations as speculative distortions of historical development:

> This [historical development] can be speculatively distorted so that later history is made the goal of earlier history, e.g. the goal ascribed to the discovery of America is to further the eruption of the French Revolution. Thereby history receives its own special aims and becomes "a person ranking with other persons" (to wit: "Self-consciousness, Criticism, the Unique," etc.), while what is designated with the words "destiny," "goal," "germ," or "idea" of earlier history is nothing more than an abstraction formed from later history, from the active influence which earlier history exercises on later history.[11]

In contrast to theological and anthropological teleological interpretations of history, Marx says, "History is nothing but the succession of the separate generations, each of which exploits the materials, the capital funds, the productive forces handed down to it by all preceding generations."[12] It is the successive development of the productive forces, not a transcendent or immanent *telos*, which gives history coherence:

> Because of this simple fact that every succeeding generation finds itself in possession of the productive forces acquired by the previous generation, which serve it as the raw material for new production, a coherence arises in human history, a history of humanity takes shape which is all the more a history of humanity as the productive forces of man and therefore his social relations have been more developed.[13]

Nonetheless, Nietzsche's overman and Marx's communist society are often regarded as immanent historical goals. Nietzsche contributes to this misinterpretation of his philosophy himself. Although he specifically denies the existence of theological and anthropological goals, he does refer to the values men create as "goals in a certain sense."[14] In addition, he paradoxically calls the overman a goal—"Not 'mankind' but *overman* is the goal!"[15]—and denies that the overman is a goal: "In the end there appears a man, a monster of energy, who demands a monster of a task. For it is our energy that disposes of us; and the wretched spiritual game of goals and intentions and motives is only a foreground— even though weak eyes may take them for the matter itself."[16] He also says that the overman is not a goal in any ordinary sense: the world is "without goal, unless the joy of the circle is itself a goal."[17] These remarks provisionally indicate that, whatever kind of a goal the overman is, he is not an "end" goal (a circle has no beginning or end) or an "idealistic type" at which man aims (he is not a human type at all).[18] Nietzsche also suggests here that goals can serve a purpose; they may prevent despair over the meaning-lessness of life. By taking them for the matter itself, the weak may find solace.

Marx's remarks that communism is "the solution of the riddle of history"[19] and is begotten by capitalist production, "the negation of negation," with "the inexorability of a law of Nature"[20] have been similarly regarded as references to an immanent historical goal. In fact, Nietzsche views socialism as such a goal. He sees it as a fatalistic—

> *history* with an immanent spirit and a goal within, so one can entrust oneself to it. One wants to get around the will, the willing of a goal, the risk of positing a goal *for oneself*; one wants to rid oneself of the responsibility (one would accept fatalism)[21]—

and anthropological—

> One attempts a kind of this-worldly solution [to the death of God], but in the same sense—that of the eventual triumph of truth, love, and justice (socialism: "equality of the person")[22]—

substitute for Christianity. He criticizes socialism because such secular ideals, like the religious formula they replace, invert cause and effect, posit an "end" state when overcoming will cease, and negate life as will to power.

Marx's and Nietzsche's images of the future do differ, but in more profound ways than these superficial Nietzschean criticisms of socialism convey. Marx agrees with Nietzsche's condemnation of end goals: creativity will differ, but it will persist and flourish after the current motive force of historical development, class conflict, ceases.[23] Further, by arguing that communist society results from contradictions in capitalist society and resolves them, Marx argues neither that communist society is a goal within history, nor that it creates its capitalist antecedent. Elsewhere, Marx and Engels explicitly deny that communist society is an anthropological ideal: "Communism is for us not a *state of affairs* which is to be established, an *ideal* to which reality [will] have to adjust itself. We call communism the *real* movement which abolishes the present state of things. The conditions of this movement result from the premises now in existence."[24] Engels also distinguishes Marx's dialectic from speculative idealist distortions of historical development which would declare that "the negation of the negation has to serve . . . as the mid-wife to deliver the future from the womb of the past." He says,

> In characterizing the process as the negation of the negation . . . Marx does not dream of attempting to prove by this that the process was historically necessary. On the contrary: after he has proved from history that in fact the process has partially already occurred, and partially must occur in the future, he then also characterizes it as a process which develops in accordance with a definite dialectical law. That is all.[25]

Marx and Engels agree with Nietzsche that whatever tendencies and forms of organization characterize historical development, history does not aim at a transcendent or an immanent *telos*. Neither explains or evaluates modern society in terms of progress toward such theological or anthropological goals.

Marx and Nietzsche not only argue that history lacks transcendent and immanent goals, but also maintain that those who posit such goals mistakenly presume that consciousness determines historical development. By suggesting that history aims at an ideal of "Man," the Left Hegelians not only invert cause and effect, but also make it "possible to transform the whole of history into an evolutionary process of consciousness."[26] Nietzsche similarly says that in their ideals moralists and theologians posit spirit as the cause of coordination and unity.[27] In opposition to both, Marx and Nietzsche regard consciousness merely as a means to the expansion of man's creative powers. It is derivative, not determinant.

Yet when Marx and Nietzsche reject teleological explanations of history as caused by transcendent or immanent ends present as potential in the origin, do they simply substitute current economics and physiology, respectively, as causally determinant? Nietzsche's statement that "he [man] carries the order, which he represents physiologically, into his relations with other human beings and things"[28] and Marx's statement that "the mode of production of material life conditions the general process of social, political and intellectual life"[29] have been so interpreted. Problems quickly appear, however, in interpretations which present historical materialism as an economic determinism or genealogy as a physiological one.

Far from substituting physiological causal determinism for religious and/or moral causes, Nietzsche questions causality itself. Earlier I argued that Nietzsche, with his notion of the will to power as a pathos, denies the existence of discrete subjects and objects. He maintains that "if we no longer believe in the effective subject, then belief also disappears in effective things, in reciprocation, cause and effect between those phenomena that we call things."[30] When Nietzsche says that a man must perform certain actions and shrinks instinctively from others, he does not mean that physiology causally determines activity. Rather he means that men, as particular quanta of force within a particular society at a particular time, order themselves in particular ways. They carry this order into their interactions with other beings and things. These interactions are coherent, but not because of teleological ends or deterministic necessities. Nietzsche criticizes both as examples of causality:

Against apparent *"necessity"*:—this is only an expression for the fact that a force is not also something else.

Against apparent *"purposiveness"*:—the latter only an expression for an order of spheres of power and their interplay.[31]

According to Nietzsche, man's actions are neither potentially purposive as religious and/or moral teleologies presume, nor necessary as mechanistic causality presumes. Instead, man simply is or, more accurately, man becomes what he is by actualizing his constantly changing will to power as a constantly changing part within a constantly changing whole. Given this interplay of forces, numerous events interact to shape any historical moment.

Although Marx and Engels admit that subjects and objects exist, they also criticize causal determinists' assumption that a cause is a discrete entity which impinges upon a second discrete entity and creates a third discrete effect. When he argued that Marx, in characterizing capitalist development as the "negation of the negation," did not "dream of attempting to prove by this that the process was historically necessary," Engels suggested that historical materialism is not an economic causal determinist explanation of history. Elsewhere, Engels indicates that historical materialism is an explanation of history as the product of reciprocal interactions, not of discrete causes which create discrete effects:

> Hanging together with this [misinterpretations of historical materialism as economic causal determinism] is the fatuous notion of the ideologists that because we deny an independent historical development to the various ideological spheres which play a part in history we also deny them any *effect upon history*. The basis of this is the common undialectical conception of cause and effect as rigidly opposite poles, the total disregarding of interaction. These gentlemen often almost deliberately forget that once a historic element has been brought into the world by other, ultimately economic causes, it reacts, can react on its environment and even on the causes that have given rise to it.[32]

Engels, like Nietzsche, describes history as made by the convergence of numerous forces:

History is made in such a way that the final result always arises from conflicts between many individual wills, of which each again has been made what it is by a host of particular conditions of life. Thus there are innumerable intersecting forces, an infinite series of parallelograms of forces which give rise to one resultant—the historical event.[33]

Economic production is the ultimate element which determines historical development, but it is not the only one.

It is sometimes said that Engels reinterpreted historical materialism in these passages to save Marx from himself and his critics. However, Marx also repeatedly refers to reciprocal historical interactions between economic and superstructural forces. In fact, he says historical materialism depends upon such interactions:

This conception of history depends on our ability to expound the real process of production, starting out from the material production of life itself, and to comprehend the form of intercourse connected with this and created by this mode of production ... as the basis of all history; and to show it in its action as State, to explain all the different theoretical products and forms of consciousness, religion, philosophy, ethics, etc. etc. and trace their origins and growth from that basis; *by which means, of course, the whole thing can be depicted in its totality (and therefore, too, the reciprocal action of these various sides on one another).*[34]

However, if history is the interaction of numerous forces, why does Marx attribute explanatory priority to economics and Nietzsche attribute it to physiology? In other words, if reciprocal influences exist, why does each explain man's relations to nature and to society as determined by a particular influence? One answer might be that Marx and Nietzsche invoke such determinisms merely to stress their opposition to the prevailing idealist conception of history as spirit. Engels does admit that he and Marx are themselves "partly to blame for the fact that the younger people sometimes lay more stress on the economic side than is due to it." He continues, "We had to emphasize the main principle vis-à-vis our adversaries, who denied it, and we had not always the time, the place or the opportunity to allow the other elements involved in the interactions to come into their rights."[35]

Walter Kaufmann similarly defends Nietzsche's professed physiologism, saying, "What concerns us is that Nietzsche's occasional insistence on a reversal of cause and effect, which would seem to imply a deprecation of consciousness, must be understood as a polemical antithesis against current prejudices."[36] Still, such apologies for Marx's supposed economic reductionism and Nietzsche's analogous biologism do not explain how either could regard history as the interaction of numerous forces and still say that one force determines it.

Such apologies also open the door to a final misinterpretation. If economics and physiology aren't really determinant (Engels and Kaufmann do stop short of saying this), then Marx and Nietzsche may be reinterpreted as denying any historical determinant at all. Louis Althusser (who understands dialectics as causal determinism by a simple, internal contradiction) criticizes economistic Marxists for merely inverting Hegel's dialectic and substituting Capital/Labor for master/slave as the causally determinant historical contradiction. Althusser correctly maintains that Marx and Engels think that numerous contradictions converge to create any historical development and that superstructures have relative autonomy. But, unlike Marx and Engels, he concludes that this "overdetermination" is incompatible with economic determinism in the last instance. With this, Althusser implicitly rejects historical materialist dialectics.[37]

Michel Foucault's interpretation of Nietzsche's genealogy is analogous. Foucault argues that, in rejecting history as the "slow exposure of meaning hidden in an origin" (teleology) or continuous development (causal determinism), Nietzsche regards history as the "hazardous play of dominations" or as a "profusion of tangled events."[38] Althusser and Foucault do not explicitly deny coherence to historical development, but descriptions of history as "overdetermined" and as a "profusion of tangled events" raise doubts about what that coherence could possibly be. Althusser does not account for Marx's references to economics, nor does Foucault account for Nietzsche's references to physiology, as historically determinant.

Marx and Nietzsche do not regard incoherence as the only alternative to causality and teleology in historical development. Both admit that chance has played a major role in history so far. Still, chance rules primarily because men have not understood history as their creation and hence have not consciously created it. By demystifying history, by exposing its coherence as man's creation, Nietzsche and Marx would potentially increase man's control of it. Nietzsche argues that his historical method fundamentally opposes "the now prevalent instinct and taste which would rather be reconciled even to the absolute fortuitousness, even the mechanistic senselessness of all events than to the theory that in all events a *will to power* is operating."[39] Marx says that "the mode of production of material life conditions the general process of social, political, and intellectual life."[40] Since men must understand their historical creations in order to control them, it seems crucial to examine how Marx and Nietzsche explain and evaluate the determination of those creations.

Historical Materialism and Genealogy

Marx and Nietzsche deny that history possesses and progresses toward a *telos*, but other aspects of teleological explanation do illuminate their theories of history.[41] Teleologists analyze characteristic tendencies of organized wholes and explain the component parts of those wholes functionally, that is, they explain the parts in terms of their contribution to the tendencies of the whole. The characteristic tendencies need not aim at a transcendent or an immanent end; they can simply be tendencies toward expansion in a particular direction. Teleological explanations in history also need not be static or conservative analyses of how parts preserve a social whole; they can be explanations not only of how parts maintain the whole at any given moment, but also of how parts contribute to man's tendency to expand his powers by transcending or overcoming previous wholes. Marx's historical materialism and Nietzsche's genealogy are attempts to provide such explanations. I discuss what each regards as the determinant historical tendency, how that tendency functionally organizes social wholes, and why that tendency explains the historical development of those wholes.

Determinant Historical Tendencies

In chapter 2, when I compared Marx's and Nietzsche's views of man, I said that each would provide empirical evidence that he had correctly identified man's characteristic activity. After reviewing why such evidence is needed, I examine how each would provide it. Historical materialism is an attempt to show that man's productive activity is the determinant historical tendency. With his genealogy, Nietzsche hypothesizes that man's value-creating powers constitute that tendency.

In *The German Ideology*, Marx describes production as man's first historical act. This raises the questions: First, in what sense? And, why production? Man's inability to survive without producing means of subsistence immediately suggests that production may be first by necessity, chronology, or both. Yet these suggestions quickly appear insufficient. With regard to necessity, Marx recognizes that men must not only produce but also consume what they produce in order to survive. In addition, animals produce means of subsistence, and Marx says that production distinguishes men from animals. In fact, truly human production begins only *after* necessity ceases in the realm of freedom. Production is first not because it is a necessary means to man's existence, but because it is man's essential life activity:

> This mode of production must not be considered simply as being the production of the physical existence of the individuals. Rather it is a definite form of activity of these individuals, a definite form of expressing their life, a definite *mode of life* on their part. As individuals express their life, so they are.[42]

With regard to chronology one might say that although men must eventually consume what they produce, they must produce it first. But Marx says that production and consumption are simultaneous moments; production is productive consumption and consumption is consumptive production. "Without production no consumption; without consumption, no production."[43] Production is first not because it occurs first, but because it is determinant:

> They [production, distribution, exchange, consumption] all form the members of a totality, distinctions within a unity. Production predominates not only over itself . . . but over the other moments as well. The process always returns to production to begin anew. . . . A definite production thus determines a definite consumption, distribution and exchange as well as *definite relations between these different moments.*[44]

Neither necessity nor chronology, then, explains why Marx thinks production is man's essential determinant life activity.

Nietzsche's analysis of the will to power poses analogous problems. Nietzsche hypothesizes that "the world viewed from inside, the world defined and determined according to its 'intelligible' character—it would be 'will to power' and nothing else."[45] Yet although all of life is will to power, man's imposition of values upon nature, himself, and other men is somehow distinctive. Man proudly distinguishes himself from animals as "the creature that measures values, evaluates and measures . . . the 'valuating animal as such.'"[46] Nietzsche also regards man's will to power as somehow determinant: "He [man] carries the order, which he represents physiologically, into his relations with other human beings and things."[47] His values express what he is, how he has ordered his drives in relation to other drives.

But why does Marx posit producing or Nietzsche posit value-creating as man's life activity? Why doesn't Marx argue as Nietzsche does that production is a means to willing and hence is explained by it? "A living thing seeks above all to *discharge* its strength—life itself is *will to power*; self-preservation is only one of the indirect and most frequent *results*."[48] Why doesn't Nietzsche argue as Marx does that values (and the social and political relationships which both agree enforce them) are created to further and hence are explained by particular modes of production? "The ruling ideas are nothing more than the ideal expression of the dominant material relationships, the dominant material relationships grasped as ideas; hence of the relationships which make the one class the ruling one, therefore, the ideas of its dominance."[49]

Each so identifies man's life activity because each regards history as the expansion of those human powers over nature. According to Nietzsche, men tend to strengthen the will to power historically:

> Put briefly: perhaps the entire evolution of the spirit is a question of the body; it is the history of the development of a higher body that emerges into our sensibility. The organic is rising to yet higher levels. Our lust for knowledge of nature is a means through which the body desires to perfect itself.[50]

Marx argues analogously that men expand their productive powers historically:

> Since these conditions [production relations] correspond at every stage to the simultaneous development of the productive forces, their history is at the same time the history of the evolving productive forces taken over by each new generation, and is, therefore, the history of the development of the forces of the individuals themselves.[51]

Each regards this tendency to expand as a specifically human capacity; man's unique consciousness of his life activity allows his powers to expand. Each also argues that consciousness arose in order to allow those powers to expand. This explanation of how consciousness originates and functions further illustrates that man is not determined by economic or physiological tendencies. Instead, his productive or willing tendencies are functionally determinant.

Marx and Nietzsche identify these determinant historical tendencies through empirical observation, not from faith in a transcendent or an immanent *telos*. Marx's historical materialism provides empirical evidence that man is a producing animal, that he expands his productive powers historically, and that this expansion is sufficiently regular to constitute a tendency. Nietzsche's genealogy provides analogous evidence for man's value-creating powers. Each will, however, think that the other observes ideologically and hence inaccurately identifies man's life activity.

Assessing the empirical evidence each provides to support his hypothesized tendency is a task far beyond the scope of this chapter. More in accord with my purpose, to examine how Marx and Nietzsche criticize modern society in light of man's creative powers, both do regard man's life activity in modern society as evidence of this tendency. In speaking of the development of capitalist from feudal society, Marx says:

> We see then: the means of production and of exchange, on whose foundation the bourgeoisie built itself up, were generated in feudal society. At a certain stage in the development of these means of production and of exchange, the conditions under which feudal society produced and exchanged ... became no longer compatible with the already developed productive forces; they became so many fetters. They had to be burst asunder; they were burst asunder.[52]

Nietzsche says of the spiritualization of asceticism since primitive societies:

> Its [guilt's] origin has been briefly suggested ... as a piece of animal psychology, no more: there we encountered the sense of guilt in its raw state, so to speak. It was only in the hands of the priest, that artist in guilt feelings, that it achieved form—oh, what a form! "Sin"—for this is the priestly name for the animal's "bad conscience" (cruelty directed backward)—has been the greatest event so far in the history of the sick soul: we possess in it the most dangerous and fateful artifice of religious interpretation.[53]

Marx's bourgeoisie, as well as Nietzsche's ascetic priests, increase man's domination of nature:

> The bourgeoisie, during its rule of scarce one hundred years, has created more massive and more colossal productive forces than have all preceding generations together. Subjection of Nature's forces to man.... What earlier

century had even a presentiment that such productive forces slumbered in the lap of social labor?[54]

You will see my point: this ascetic priest, this apparent enemy of life, this *denier*—precisely he is among the greatest *conserving* and yes-creating forces of life.[55]

By hypothesizing that man's powers *tend* to expand, neither Marx nor Nietzsche means that history is uniformly or constantly progressive. Marx says that since history has evolved "naturally," i.e., without a general plan, societies and the individuals within them have developed independently, unevenly, and slowly:

[Evolution] proceeds from various localities, tribes, nations, branches of labour, etc. each of which to start with develops independently of the others and only gradually enters into relations with the others. Furthermore, it takes place only very slowly; the various stages and interests are never completely overcome, but only subordinated to the prevailing interest and trail along beside the latter for centuries afterwards. It follows from this that within a nation itself the individuals, even apart from their pecuniary circumstances, have quite different developments.[56]

As long as productive forces evolve "naturally," advances may even be lost for later development:

As long as there exists no commerce transcending the immediate neighbourhood, every invention must be made separately in each locality, and mere chances such as irruptions of barbaric peoples, even ordinary wars are sufficient to cause a country with advanced productive forces and needs to have to start right over again from the beginning.[57]

Nietzsche also argues that ages and peoples develop independently: they represent pieces and fragments of man. He further agrees that man's development is uneven. "Types" achieved can be lost. Still, man does evolve, and "milestone men" appear here and there to tell him how far he has come. Nietzsche characterizes this process in the following passage:

Most men represent pieces and fragments of man: one has to add them up for a complete man to appear. Whole ages, whole peoples are in this sense somewhat fragmentary; it is perhaps part of the economy of human evolution that man should evolve piece by piece. But that should not make one forget for a moment that the real issue is the production of the synthetic man; that lower men, the tremendous majority, are merely preludes and rehearsals out of whose medley the whole man appears here and there, the milestone man who indicates how far humanity has advanced so far. It does *not* advance in a single straight line; often a type once achieved is lost again.[58]

Unlike Marx, however, Nietzsche argues that humanity is both progressing and regressing. That is, even "with all the tensions of the past three hundred years, for example, we have not yet reattained the man of the Renaissance, and the man of the Renaissance, in turn, is inferior to the man of antiquity."[59] Although Marx, because he regards history as endless, must support his hypothesized tendency by showing general (if not uniform or constant) historical progress, Nietzsche can argue both that modern man descends and man ascends because he regards history as neither finite (with an end), nor infinite (endless), but as a circle.

This introduces Nietzsche's controversial concept of eternal recurrence. Nietzsche offers numerous suggestions about its meaning and import. At times, he presents it as a scientific hypothesis, asserting that "the law of the conservation of energy demands *eternal recurrence.*"[60] In this context, he argues that the world lacks both an end state—"If the world had a goal, it must have been reached"—and eternal novelty—"we forbid ourselves the concept of an infinite force as incompatible with the concept 'force.'"[61] The world is a certain definite quantity of force and a certain definite number of centers of force which pass through a calculable number of combinations an infinite number of times. He concludes:

And since between every combination and its next recurrence all other possible combinations would have to take place, and each of these combinations conditions the entire sequence of combinations in the same series, a circular movement of absolutely identical series is thus demonstrated: the world as a circular movement that has already repeated itself infinitely often and plays its game *in infinitum.*[62]

At other times, eternal recurrence apears to be a test of strength, of one's ability not merely to endure life, but also to embrace it by willing that it infinitely repeat itself. Here, the scientific truth of the idea matters less than its impact upon human nature. Nietzsche refers to it as a "counter-myth" and stresses its role as "the great *cultivating* idea" and "*selective* principle."[63] Nietzsche clearly regarded both of these approaches to eternal recurrence— the "proof of the doctrine" and the "probable consequences of its being believed"—as extremely important.[64] However, since I focus upon his critique of modern society rather than his alternative to it (except, of course, as the latter impinges on the former), I will examine eternal recurrence from a rather different angle.

The compatibility of eternal recurrence with historical development is the crucial issue here, since cycles are arguably nonprogressive. Nietzsche addresses this issue when he characterizes his Dionysian world as a "sea of forces flowing and rushing together . . . with tremendous years of recurrence, with an ebb and a flood of its forms; out of the simplest forms striving toward the most complex . . . and then again returning home to the simple out of this abundance."[65] Historical development appears here as a basic feature of eternal recurrence, not as something incompatible with it. The development which occurs does not continue indefinitely, nor is it movement toward a stable condition. Nietzsche rejects such linear conceptions of history, in part because of their association with religious and moralistic teleologies. Nonetheless, recurrence involves a kind of progress. The world as will to power develops toward a "high tide" of complexity and strength which is followed by an "ebb tide" of simplicity and weakness, and then by repetition of the cycle. Strictly speaking, development occurs only on the ascending half of the cycle. Yet even the descending half may be seen as developmental in a less strict sense. If history is a circle, every moment of which follows from and leads to every other moment, then every moment— including the sick, all too human moments of modern society—is potentially a means to the overman; every moment is potentially progressive. Even repetition of the cycle does not preclude development. Progress is periodic, not constant, but no less genuine. So interpreted, Nietzsche's concept of eternal recurrence is compatible with the notion that man's will to power expands historically.

Marx and Nietzsche agree, then, that the tendency of man's powers to expand historically operates neither constantly nor uniformly. They also agree that historical progress does not depend upon any particular individual's actions. Both understand individuals functionally, that is, in terms of their roles within a historically determined social order. Since individuals do not freely choose their social relations, they should not be held responsible for them. Marx makes this point in the preface to *Capital*:

> I paint the capitalist and the landlord in no sense the *couleur de rose*. But here individuals are dealt with only in so far as they are the personifications of economic categories, embodiments of particular class-relations and class-inter-ests. My standpoint, from which the evolution of the eco-nomic formation of society is viewed as a process of natural history, can less than any other make the individual respons-ible for relations whose creature he socially remains, how-ever much he may subjectively raise himself above them.[66]

It is less frequently recognized that Nietzsche also understands individuals functionally. Perhaps this is because, whereas Marx considers individuals in terms of man's historical development, Nietzsche portrays man's historical development through indi-viduals. Nonetheless, Nietzsche explains his "milestone men" in terms of determinant historical tendencies; they are significant as signposts on the road to the synthetic man.

Finally, although human powers can expand because men have a capacity to act consciously, Marx and Nietzsche agree that men do not consciously further this historical tendency. It is absurd to think that men decide to produce socially in order to become conscious so that they eventually can develop the capacity for unalienated production. Social production relations develop because man's "instinct is a conscious one" which gives him the initial capacity to enter into those relations that further develop his capacities.[67] Nor do men consciously decide to impose values in order to internalize their wills to power so that they eventually can develop the strength to overcome ascetic ideals. Nietzsche describes the work of the master race which initially created consciousness by imposing social values on a formless population as "an instinctive creation and imposition of forms." This race was "the most involuntary, unconscious artists there are."[68] Men developed social customs because they have an instinct to dominate; those customs by creating consciousness then furthered the expansion of the will to power. Only ideologists reify conscious purposes, separating consciousness as a "cause" of history from the forces which functionally determine it.

In modern society, the bourgeoisie, who consciously create production relations which further their economic interests, thereby "involuntarily promote" the forces leading to their own demise and the continued advance of industry. Marx says that "the development of Modern Industry . . . cuts from under its feet the very foundation on which the bourgeoisie produces and appropriates products. What the bourgeoisie . . . produces, above all, is its own grave-diggers. Its fall and the victory of the proletariat are equally inevitable."[69] Similarly, ascetic priests, who consciously deny life through ascetic ideals which further their psychological interests, unconsciously preserve the will and create the conditions for their own overcoming:

> All great things bring about their own destruction through an act of self-overcoming. . . . In this way Christianity *as a dogma* [faith in God] was destroyed by its own morality [truthfulness]; in the same way Christianity *as morality* must now perish too: we stand on the threshold of *this* event. After Christian truthfulness has drawn one inference after another, it must end by drawing its *most striking inference*, its inference *against* itself; this will happen, however, when it poses the question *"What is the meaning of all will to truth?"*[70]

Again, only ideologists would mistakenly regard capitalism and asceticism as "givens," as social structures which are independent of man's developing powers and are, therefore, eternal.

By viewing history as determined by man's tendency to expand his powers, Marx and Nietzsche would explain why particular societies develop historically. In *Capital*, shortly after Marx proposes to "lay bare the economic law of motion of modern society," he characterizes his standpoint as one "from which the evolution of the economic formation of society is viewed as a process of natural history."[71] He contrasts his approach with that of the political economists. Although they discover that value originates in labor, they "never once ask the question why labour is represented by the value of its product and labour-time by the magnitude of that value."[72] Instead, they treat commodity fetishes as self-evident truths, as necessities akin to productive labor itself. Where they analyze appearances, Marx penetrates to reality and reveals that commodity fetishes do not express production itself, but a historical mode of production, i.e., capitalist production.

Nietzsche analogously says, "It is my purpose here to bring to light, not what this [the ascetic] ideal has *done*, but simply what it *means*; what it indicates; what lies hidden behind it, beneath it, in it; of what it is the provisional, indistinct expression."[73] He criticizes past psychologists, as Marx criticizes past economists, for diagnosing and treating symptoms, for failing to explore the deeper origins of man's sickness in his developing powers. Nietzsche's "method" is distinctive as a form of backward inference: "the backward inference from the work to the maker, from the deed to the doer, from the ideal to those who *need it*, from every way of thinking and valuing to the commanding need behind it."[74] He explains ascetic ideals, as Marx explains class relations, in terms of their function for specific forms of social organization which express historically dominant interests.

By examining the historical origins of societies, Marx and Nietzsche not only open previously unquestioned and presumably unquestionable "given" realities to question, but also reveal a basis from which to question: Is that society still functional for men's expanding powers? Yet how does man's tendency to expand his powers functionally determine and hence explain the development of societies? How do Marx and Nietzsche question societies from this basis? In order to answer these questions, I examine how man's tendency to expand his powers determines and hence explains societies at any given moment. Then I discuss how that tendency determines and hence explains their rise and fall. My distinction between synchronic and diachronic determinism is merely analytical, however. The same tendency of man's powers to expand functionally determines the conditions of man's life activity at any given moment and when those conditions become fetters upon his activity and must be overturned.

Societies as Ordered Wholes

THE WHOLES

Marx and Nietzsche are able to explain the structure of particular societies because they regard societies as wholes, whose component parts are ordered by man's powers. Both criticize those who fail to recognize this ordering tendency and dismember social organisms. Marx accuses political economists of dislocating social limbs: "In constructing the edifice of an ideological system by means of the categories of political economy, the limbs of the social system are dislocated. The different limbs of society are converted into so many separate societies, following one upon the other."[75] Nietzsche similarly attacks scientific historians because their quest for truth undermines the horizons which have unified societies and have guided individuals in ordering their drives. He depicts modern man as the repository of "an enormous heap of indigestible knowledge stones." There is little coherence to his internal life and little correspondence between it and the external world. Nietzsche concludes that "our modern culture is for that reason not a living one. . . . It is not a real culture but a kind of knowledge about culture, a complex of various thoughts and feelings about it, from which no decision as to its direction can come."[76]

Political economists and scientific historians, who dissociate social parts, cannot see the tendencies which determine and therefore cannot explain or evaluate social wholes. They can only describe given realities as eternal; they are the most virulent positivists. Marx says:

Economists express the relations of bourgeois production, the division of labour, credit, money, etc., as fixed,
immutable, eternal categories....

Economists explain how production takes place in the
above-mentioned relations, but what they do not explain is
how these relations themselves are produced, that is, the
historical movement which gave them birth.[77]

Nietzsche, who warns against *"superfluous* teleological principles," criticizes modern historiography for rejecting all teleology:

Its noblest claim nowadays is that it is a mirror; it rejects all
teleology; it no longer wishes to "prove" anything; it disdains
to play the judge and considers this a sign of good taste—it
affirms as little as it denies; it ascertains, it "describes."[78]

Marx and Nietzsche agree that this inability to perceive
societies as ordered wholes and the related inability to explain or
to evaluate them in terms of man's expanding powers reflect real
dislocations in modern society. Marx says this rupture of social
parts made its way from reality—the subjection of individuals to
the vicissitudes of the market—to the textbooks, not the reverse.[79]
Nietzsche depicts modern life, which scientific historians mirror,
as fragmented, without "horizons," aims, unity, or truth. Yet both
argue that those who conclude from this modern condition that
societies are pluralities and historical movement is non-existent
or inexplicable mistake modern chaos for nature.

In laying bare the "economic laws of motion of modern
society," Marx penetrates beneath the dislocations of modern
society and reveals that even they are determined by production.
To do so, he illuminates the mutual interactions within the
different moments of the social whole, interactions determined by
production.

They [production, distribution, exchange, consumption] all
form the members of a totality, distinctions within a unity.
Production predominates not only over itself... but over the
other moments as well.... A definite production thus deter-

mines a definite consumption, distribution and exchange as well as *definite relations between these different moments.* . . . Mutual interaction takes place between the different moments. This is the case with every organic whole.[80]

Nietzsche denies that the world is a comprehensive whole: "The total character of the world . . . is in all eternity chaos—in the sense not of a lack of necessity but of a lack of order, arrangement, form, beauty, wisdom, and whatever other names there are for our aesthetic anthropomorphisms."[81] However, he regards organic life as a fortuitous exception to this chaos. Man's mistake is to project "the natural expediency of the organic"—himself— onto the universe and to view it as a purposive, valuable whole. Nietzsche cautions us:

> —Let us beware of thinking that the world is a living being. Where should it expand? On what should it feed? How could it grow and multiply? We have some notion of the nature of the organic; and we should not reinterpret the exceedingly derivative, late, rare, accidental, that we perceive only on the crust of the earth and make of it something essential, universal, and eternal, which is what those people do who call the universe an organism.[82]

Although no cosmic whole exists (men have unconsciously created cosmologies to give their lives meaning within the universe), individuals and societies are organic wholes with characteristic tendencies and typical patterns of organization. As we have seen, the historical tendency which Nietzsche identifies does not operate in Hegelian or Aristotelian fashion. History is not "absolutely fortuitous," but Nietzsche denies that demonstrable purposes explain origins. "The cause of the origin of a thing and its eventual utility, its actual employment and place in a system of purposes, lie worlds apart; whatever exists, having somehow come into being, is again and again reinterpreted to new ends, taken over, transformed, and redirected by some power superior to it."[83] Still, evolution occurs as things assume successive functions because in all events the will to power operates, endeavoring to expand its power. Nietzsche says that "all events in the organic world are a subduing, a *becoming master.*"[84] As a process of mastery, life has a developmental tendency: "And life itself confided this secret to me: 'Behold,' it said, 'I am *that which must always overcome itself.' "*[85]

Individuals and societies are organized by the expanding will to power. Unlike the world which observes no laws, life has a "moral imperative of nature": " 'You shall obey—someone and for a long time: *else* you will perish and lose the last respect for your self.' "*[86] Nietzsche describes the body as a "social structure composed of many souls" and willing as "a question of commanding and obeying" on the basis of this social structure. From this, he concludes that "a philosopher should claim the right to include willing as such within the sphere of morals—morals being understood as the doctrine of the relations of supremacy under which the phenomenon of 'life' comes to be."[87] He also draws an analogy between the body and the "well-constructed and happy commonwealth." Societies, like individuals, are neither unities nor pluralities, but patterns of organization or disorganization. As Nietzsche puts it: "All unity is unity only as organization and cooperation—just as a human community is a unity—as opposed to an atomistic anarchy, as a pattern of domination that *signifies* a unity but *is* not a unity."[88]

Part of the problem in modern society is that individuals and communities no longer organize themselves as unities. Zarathustra says that he walks "among men as among the fragments and limbs of men," that man is "in ruins and scattered over a battlefield or butcherfield."[89] Zarathustra also laments the death of "peoples" and the birth of states. The former were genuine cultures unified by "tablets of the good"; the latter are "new idols" who tell "lies in all the tongues of good and evil."[90]

According to Nietzsche, the chaos of modern life is not a natural organic condition. Rather, it reflects the unnatural unwillingness and/or inability of the will to power to command. Nietzsche describes the "now prevalent instinct and taste" which prefers even the "absolute fortuitousness" of events to "the theory that in all events *a will to power* is operating" as a "democratic idiosyncrasy." He criticizes it because, by opposing "everything that dominates and wants to dominate," it robs life of "*activity.*"[91] He also laments the fact that modern man, in his despair over the death of God, has assumed that without Him the world and man are valueless. This means that just now when man can and must consciously create his own individual and social order, he most doubts his ability to do so. He continues to seek truth, instead of creating it, even though his reason tells him that it is not to be found. Nietzsche says, "Just now when the greatest strength of will would be necessary, it is weakest and least confident. Absolute mistrust regarding the organizing strength of the will for the whole."[92] Nietzsche would no doubt criticize contemporary attacks upon totality, critiques which ironically often draw upon him, as symptoms of democratic proclivities and/or nihilistic despair. He says that it is a measure of strength "to what extent one can endure to live in a meaningless world *because one organizes a small portion of it oneself.*"[93]

Marx and Nietzsche agree then that societies are organic wholes whose parts are ordered by man's expanding powers. What, however, are the parts of the whole and how does man's determinant historical tendency order them? To answer these questions, I examine Marx's and Nietzsche's conceptions of society independently and in greater detail.

HISTORICAL MATERIALISM: THE "SIDES" OF THE "TOTALITY"

Marx's most famous statement of his historical materialist conception of society appears in the "Preface to *A Contribution to the Critique of Political Economy.*" There he says,

> In the social production of their existence, men inevitably enter into definite relations, which are independent of their will, namely, relations of production appropriate to a given stage in the development of their material forces of production. The totality of these relations of production constitutes the economic structure of society, the real foundation on which arises a legal and political superstructure and to which correspond definite forms of social consciousness. The mode of production of material life conditions the general process of social, political, and intellectual life.[94]

I will analyze the component parts of society and the relationships between them described here, beginning with the mode of production of material life and, then, turning to the social, political, and intellectual life it determines.

In a passage quoted earlier, Marx makes it clear that the material productive forces are not only raw materials and technology, but also the human powers which create and use them: "The history of the evolving productive forces taken over by each new generation . . . is . . . the history of the development of the forces of the individuals themselves."[95] To repeat: productive forces don't determine men; men's productive forces are determinant. In creating and applying their productive forces to nature, men enter into certain material production relations.

> The production of life, both of one's own in labour and of fresh life in procreation, now appears as a double relationship: on the one hand as a natural, on the other as a social relationship. By social we understand the co-operation of several individuals, no matter under what conditions, in what manner and to what end. It follows from this that a certain mode of production, or industrial stage, is always combined with a certain mode of co-operation, or social stage, and this mode of co-operation is itself a "productive force."[96]

In the continuation of this quotation, Marx says that the "multitude of productive forces [productive forces per se and the mode of cooperation they determine] determines the nature of society." He distinguishes in this passage and elsewhere between men's material production relations (modes of cooperation) and social production relations (society) which they determine. For example, he says,

> Assume a particular state of development in the productive forces of man and you will get a particular form of commerce and consumption [material production relations]. Assume particular stages of development in production, commerce and consumption [material production relations] and you will have . . . a corresponding civil society [social production relations].[97]

And,

> Social relations are closely bound up with productive forces. In acquiring new productive forces men change their mode

of production [material production relations]; and in changing their mode of production, in changing the way of earning their living, they change all their social relations [social production relations]. The handmill gives you society with the feudal lord; the steam-mill, society with the industrial capitalist.[98]

Marx's distinction between material and social production relations is neither clear nor consistent. Yet he seems to separate the division of labor, the way men cooperate to master nature, from the property relations, the way men master one another in doing so, which it determines. He explicitly makes this distinction in *The German Ideology*:

The various stages of development in the division of labour are just so many different forms of ownership, i.e., the existing stage in the division of labour determines also the relations of individuals to one another with reference to the material, instrument, and product of labour.[99]

These forms of ownership are the power relations, that is, the class relations, in societies. They determine the control individuals have over their productive activity and their products. For example, both the serf and the free laborer cooperate with others in order to produce and neither owns his means of production, but whether they labor for a feudal lord or for an industrial capitalist changes how their productive activity and their products are alienated.

In the "Preface," when Marx refers to the "relations of production" as the "economic structure of society," he means these class relations. The productive forces themselves are not economic categories: "Machinery is no more an economic category than the bullock that draws the plough."[100] The way machinery is applied, the division of labor, which is also a material "productive force," is also not part of this economic structure. Class relations are the economic structure of society, the real foundation on which arise the legal, political, and ideological superstructure. Class relations determine particular legal and political forms, i.e., the laws enforced by the state which make ownership *de facto* ownership *de jure*. Marx refers to the executive of the modern state as "but a committee for managing the common affairs of the whole bourgeoisie."[101] They also determine ideological forms:

> The class which has the means of material production at its disposal, has control at the same time over the means of mental production, so that thereby, generally speaking, the ideas of those who lack the means of mental production are subject to it. The ruling ideas are nothing more than the ideal expression of the dominant material relationships.[102]

By looking ahead for a moment, we can summarize these relations between the social parts with a specific example from capitalist society: the development of the productive forces requires certain material production relations (factory production and commercial agriculture); these require certain social production relations (a class of free laborers, who do not own means of production and who must sell their labor power, and a capitalist class, whose members own means of production and appropriate surplus value); these form the economic basis which requires certain laws (protecting private property); these require a certain state for their enforcement (the liberal state); this requires a certain ideology to legitimate itself (possessive individualism).

Man's productive forces do not causally determine these other parts within the social organism. Instead, his productive forces functionally determine them. Particular classes, laws, states, and ideologies exist because they are required by, because they are functional for, in order to further, etc., the tendency of man's productive forces to expand. This functional determinism requires (and hence explains how Marx could speak of) reciprocal interactions between the parts of society; it also requires (and hence explains how Engels could speak of) ideological "effects upon history." That is, functional determinism by the expanding productive forces requires classes, laws, states, and ideologies which *cause* those productive forces to expand. Marx and Engels do not need to show that these social parts are without causal effects, but only that those effects are functionally determined by man's productive forces. Both say that only ideologists mistakenly think that these social parts develop independently of this determinant tendency.

Division of labour only becomes truly such from the moment when a division of material and mental labour appears. (The first form of ideologists, *priests*, is concurrent.) From this moment onwards consciousness *can* really flatter itself that it is something other than consciousness of existing practice, that it *really* represents something without representing something real; from now on consciousness is in a position to emancipate itself from the world and to proceed to the formation of "pure" theory, theology, philosophy, ethics, etc. But even if this theory, theology, philosophy, ethics, etc. comes into contradiction with the existing relations, this can only occur because existing social relations have come into contradiction with existing forces of production.[103]

Marx would agree with Engels that, in spite of the numerous reciprocal interactions which create any historical event, "the economic movement finally asserts itself as necessary." Among the conditions under which we make our history, "the economic [ones] are ultimately decisive."[104]

GENEALOGY: ORDERS OF RANK

Nietzsche also thinks that a basic tendency—the tendency of man's will to power to become stronger—orders social and individual organisms. It is that tendency which appears as an order of means and ends or one of causes and effects:

That the apparent "purposiveness" ... is merely the consequence of the will to power manifest in all events; that becoming stronger involves an ordering process which looks like a sketchy purposiveness; that apparent ends are not intentional but, as soon as dominion is established over a lesser power and the latter operates as a function of the greater power, an order of rank, of organization is bound to produce the appearance of an order of means and ends.[105]

However, Nietzsche's denial of causality and his related hypothesis that all of life is will to power make it difficult to determine not only what the parts of the whole are, but also how they are ordered. He says that greater powers command, specifically, impose the character of a function upon, lesser powers.

What does he mean? Nietzsche explains these interrelated individual and social ordering processes in the *Genealogy of Morals*. Since my interpretation of his argument there differs in some respects from prevailing views, I develop it with reference to the most prominent of those, that of Giles Deleuze.[106]

In his analysis of the *Genealogy of Morals*, Deleuze distinguishes between masters' and slaves' self-creative activity. The master's syllogism—"I am good, therefore you are bad"—involves an active self-affirmation. Reaction to the slave and negation of the slave follow from positive premises and serve only to reinforce them. Difference, the master's principle of self-definition, is the principle of "generic culture," of man's species-activity. Deleuze distinguishes difference from dialectics, a distinction to which I return, calling the latter the syllogism of the slave. As a dialectician, the slave depends upon reaction to masters and negation of them to define himself. The slave's syllogism is: "You are evil. I am the opposite of what you are; therefore I am good." Deleuze argues that master and slave relate dialectically only within slave morality, and that dialectic is the historical perversion of culture. He depicts the themes of the three books of the *Genealogy*, i.e., *ressentiment*, the bad conscience, and ascetic ideals, as successive stages in the master-slave dialectic. Their cumulative consequence is to make active forces reactive, to make masters slavely moral.

Deleuze's argument that masters only define themselves dialectically within slave morality allows him to affirm mastery as a creative play of forces without confronting the related issue of masters' power over slaves.[107] This interpretation of master morality may be attractive, but it is not entirely accurate. We have already seen that Nietzsche regards a non-objective being as a non-being. In the *Genealogy*, difference too depends upon that from which it differs to establish itself. Nietzsche says that nobility established itself as good in "contradistinction" to the common and plebian: "It was out of this *pathos of distance* that they first seized the right to create values and to coin names for values."[108] Nietzsche frequently describes a relationship between masters and slaves before slave morality. Its characteristics include many which Deleuze associates with slave morality, e.g., guilt, internalization, and asceticism. Nietzsche speaks of the "blond beasts" who first mastered a formless population as the creators of "guilt" in its "raw state."[109] By imposing social values (and torturing those who disobeyed them), they forced men to internalize their instincts and created the "bad conscience": "Hostility, cruelty, joy in persecuting, in attacking, in change, in destruction—all this turned against the possessors of such instincts: *that* is the origin of the 'bad conscience.' "[110] He explains the "bad conscience" in terms of an exchange *coterminous* with civilization:

> The feeling of guilt, of personal obligation, had its origin . . . in the oldest and most primitive personal relationship, that between buyer and seller, creditor and debtor: it was here that one person first encountered another person, that one person first *measured himself* against another. No grade of civilization, however low, has yet been discovered in which something of this relationship has not been noticeable.[111]

Guilt [*Schuld*] originates in the "material concept" that an individual has debts [*Schulden*] to the community in exchange for the advantages of membership. Crime and punishment rest upon this principle of equivalence: if an individual defaults on his obligation, the community receives recompense through the pleasure of exercising its instinct for cruelty, its will to power, by inflicting external (torture) or internal (guilt) pain upon him. Although slave moralists later spiritualized cruelty and further developed the conscience, Nietzsche says that "in a certain sense, the whole of asceticism belongs" with the "few primitive demands of social existence."[112] In the first essay of the *Genealogy*, where Deleuze's master-slave dialectic begins, Nietzsche already speaks of good and evil as an "inversion" and a "deepening" of the "antithetical valuations of good and bad."[113] All of this suggests that culture itself, not merely degenerating culture, involves a dialectic between master and slave.

According to Nietzsche, those who create and impose values order the social organism, and reason which forces the passions to obey those values orders the individual organism. However, a society's value creators and an individual's reason (the "causes" of those orders) are themselves functionally determined and hence explained by the will to power. How and to what extent a people organize the world, e.g., how and to what extent they spiritualize cruelty, reflects their will to power: "A tablet of the good hangs over every people. Behold, it is the tablet of their overcomings; behold, it is the voice of their will to power."[114] How and to what extent reason controls a passion reflects another, stronger passion: "The will to combat the violence of a craving is beyond our power, equally with the method we adopt and the success we may have in applying it. In all this process our intellect is rather merely the blind instrument of another rival craving."[115]

What has happened with slave morality is that the dialectic of good and bad has been inverted: good has become evil. The operative will to power has also been transmuted: active forces have become reactive forces. This reveals a parallel between Nietzschean and Marxian history: the dialectic between master and slave *within* slave morality, like that between bourgeoisie and proletariat *within* capitalist society, expresses the current level of man's creative powers.[116] There is another parallel between Nietzsche's explanation of dominant values (including slave moralists') and Marx's explanation of ruling classes (including the bourgeoisie) as means for the expansion of man's power. Ascetic ideals are artifices for preserving the will: they give man a reason to will if only a will to nothingness. "Becoming conscious"— capable of confirming to such ideals—"is obviously only one more means toward the unfolding and extension of the power of life."[117] The problem in modern society is that ascetic ideals and conscious conformity to them which—akin to capitalist production—are mere means to the expansion of man's life activity have been mistaken for his end. Nietzsche says, "This is my *basic objection* to all philosophic-moralistic cosmologies and theodicies, to all *wherefores* and *highest values* in philosophy and theology hitherto. One kind of means has been misunderstood as an end; conversely, life and the enhancement of its power has been debased to a means."[118]

Marx and Nietzsche, then, would penetrate beneath the "given" structures (capitalist production relations and ascetic ideals, respectively) of modern society, and would expose those "givens" as historical products. They are parts of a social whole, functionally determined by the current level of man's life activity. But Marx and Nietzsche not only explain the functioning of existing societies, they also explain their rise and fall in terms of man's determinant tendency to expand his powers. Now, I turn to their explanations of historical development.

Dialectics and Overcoming

Although there is confusion over exactly what it means, Marx's historical materialism is generally regarded as a dialectical theory of history. However, as we have begun to see, disagreements exist about whether Nietzsche's genealogy is also dialectical. Walter Kaufmann calls Nietzsche a "dialectical monist," and Giles Deleuze says Nietzsche's philosophy "forms an absolute anti-dialectics."[119] Such controversy arises in part because Nietzsche criticizes a specific conception of dialectics as if it were dialectics per se. After examining Nietzsche's critique of dialectics, I will suggest how he agrees with Marx that history develops dialectically.

Nietzsche associates dialectics with faith in rationality, in particular with the Socratic notion that reality is rational and that individuals achieve virtue and happiness when reason orders their passions in conformity with it. Nietzsche criticizes Socratism because, as I have discussed, rational systems (including any virtuous or happy order reason may impose on the passions) are not "reality," but historical creations functionally determined by the will to power. In fact, Nietzsche associates dialectical reason with distance from reality. He says of dialecticians, "One approaches reality, 'real being,' through dialectic; one distances oneself from it through the instincts, senses, mechanism."[120] He refers to this "approach" as the denaturalization of moral judgments: they are torn from their conditionality. He regards its practitioners as degenerate: "the scarecrow of the ancient philosopher" is "a plant removed from all soil; a humanity without any particular regulating instincts; a virtue that 'proves' itself with reasons."[121]

Man's ordering of reality by truth and of passion by reason must in the case of dialectics (as in other cases) be understood as a means to life, not as its end. Dialectic is a tool: "Trust in reason and its categories, in dialectic, therefore the valuation of logic, proves only their usefulness for life, proved by experience—*not* that something is true."[122] The dialecticians' faith in the inherent rationality of individuals and events reflects the present inability of the will to power consciously to create, i.e., its need to believe that it has discovered social and individual order. As Nietzsche succinctly puts it: "Wherever authority still forms part of good bearing, where one does not give reasons but commands, the dialectician is a kind of buffoon." "One chooses dialectic only when one has no other means."[123]

Nietzsche's primary target in these passages—a target to which he refers as dialectics per se—is a dialectic of reason. This target he shares to some extent with Marx: both attack the notion that reality is determined by reason. Nietzsche criticizes Socrates' dialectic for mistaking reason and its categories for reality as Marx criticizes Hegel's dialectic for conceiving the real as the process of thought concentrating itself. Neither critique precludes the adoption of a different, both would probably say demystified, hypothesis that history is dialectically ordered by man's determinant tendency to expand his productive forces or his will to power.[124]

But what would Marx or Nietzsche mean by saying that history is dialectically ordered, whether by productive forces or the will to power? Although they are often criticized because they are regarded as formal scientific laws, not structural hypotheses, and because they apply to nature as well as history, Engels' three basic laws nonetheless provide a clear, concise characterization of dialectics. These laws are: the transformation of quantity into quality and vice versa; the interpenetration of opposites; the negation of the negation.[125] I will suggest how each applies to Nietzsche's genealogy as well as to Marx's historical materialism.

First, my discussion of man's determinant historical tendencies implied that Marx and Nietzsche understand quantitative as qualitative changes and vice versa. Both argue that quantitative changes in man's powers functionally determine qualitatively new forms of man's life activity, i.e., men change their natural and social relations as their powers increase quantitatively. Neither Marx nor Nietzsche specifies at what exact point quantitative changes become qualitative changes, or the reverse; they cannot do so because history changes unevenly and continually, not sequentially. But both speak of characteristics, i.e., classes and values, which qualitatively distinguish societies from one another. Communist society is qualitatively different from capitalist society, though the point at which the transformation occurs— when the dictatorship of the proletariat begins and ends— remains obscure. Similarly, the overman differs qualitatively from man, though he also overlaps with a transitional type, the higher man. Nietzsche specifically suggests: "Might all quantities not be signs of qualities? A greater power implies a different consciousness, feeling, desiring, a different perspective; growth itself is a desire to be more; the desire for an increase in quantum grows from a *quale*."[126] He also insists, denying a crude biologism, that the association of quantitative and qualitative change is not some sort of reduction of the latter to the former; they accompany one another.

Second, my discussion of their historical methods has implied that Marx and Nietzsche think that opposites interpenetrate. In particular, neither accepts the notion that discrete causes oppose discrete objects to create a third discrete effect. This is evident in their insistence that theological or anthropological essences/natures do not oppose man's concrete existence/ history, i.e., that man is a natural, historical being. It also appears in their conceptions of societies as organisms whose parts are functionally interrelated. Both explain such theological or anthropological moralities, which allow, even encourage, man's powers to expand, as themselves functions of his determinant tendencies. Both think that morality becomes immorality when the continued expansion of man's powers functionally determines the development of new social and individual orders. For both, then, nothing exists beyond or behind man's historical existence. There are only numerous historical forces which create historical events by interrelating in ways which are ultimately functionally determined by man's powers. Again, Nietzsche specifically criticizes "the fundamental faith of the metaphysicians ... the faith in opposite values."[127]

Third, both explain historical development in terms of the negation of the negation. In other words, both think that organisms develop to qualitatively new interrelations of their parts through contradictions. According to Marx and Engels, development occurs when class relations become contradictory or dysfunctional for man's expanding productive forces:

> At a certain stage of their development [when quantitative changes have accumulated to the point of becoming qualitative changes] the material productive forces of society come into conflict with the existing relations of production. . . . From forms of development of the productive forces these relations turn into their fetters. Then begins an epoch of social revolution. The changes in the economic foundation lead sooner or later to the transformation of the whole immense superstructure.[128]

According to Nietzsche, history develops because values become contradictory or dysfunctional for man's expanding will to power: "Whatever I create and however much I love it—soon [when quantitative changes have accumulated to the point of becoming qualitative changes] I must oppose it and my love; thus my will wills it."[129]

There is, then, a contradiction which develops in societies between the order which preserves the current level of man's powers and the tendency of those powers to continue to expand. At some point, that contradiction becomes so intense that man's determinant tendency forces the development of new social structures. Marx and Nietzsche think that such a contradiction is developing in modern society. Both explain its rise and fall in such terms. To repeat, Marx says of capitalist class relations: "What the bourgeoisie . . . produces, above all, is its own grave-diggers. Its fall and the victory of the proletariat are equally inevitable."[130] Nietzsche's remarks on ascetic ideals are analogous: "After Christian truthfulness has drawn one inference after another, it must end by drawing its *most striking inference*, its inference *against* itself; this will happen, however, when it poses the question '*what is the meaning of all will to truth?*' "[131]

It is this third dialectical law, the so-called "labor of the negative," which is most often questioned with reference to Nietzsche. Kaufmann defends its applicability, citing Nietzsche's use of *aufheben* and stressing the etymological association of Nietzsche's preferred Latin term, *sublimieren*, with the German *aufheben.*[132] Still, Kaufmann does not address what Deleuze regards as the crucial issue. Deleuze distinguishes between dialectical negation and differential affirmation. Regarding this distinction, he argues that for the affirmation of difference dialectics substitutes negation of what differs, for the affirmation of self it substitutes negation of the other, and for the affirmation of affirmation it substitutes negation of the negation. What I argue is that Deleuze's distinction between dialectics and difference, at least with respect to Nietzsche's philosophy, breaks down.

Regarding negation of the other as affirmation of self, we have already seen that for Nietzsche and Marx, a non-objective being is a non-being. Although Deleuze initially argues that notions of struggle, war, rivalry, even comparison, are foreign to Nietzsche, he later acknowledges that difference too requires opposition and domination.[133] He persists, however, in distinguishing *kinds* of opposition and domination. The crucial distinction is whether negation is the consequence of affirmation or the obverse: "To the famous positivity of the negative Nietzsche opposes his own discovery: the negativity of the positive."[134] But even this distinction disappears once Deleuze admits that the positive develops in opposition to the conditions which would negate it, i.e., becoming-reactive overcomes itself and becomes active. The crucial distinction becomes not negation or affirmation, or even negation from affirmation or affirmation from negation, but whether negation is active or reactive. Deleuze again: "We know what transmutation or transvaluation means for Nietzsche: not a change of values, but a change in the element from which the value of values derives."[135]

Deleuze is correct that, for Nietzsche, it is not enough simply to invert the dialectic to affirm reality. The inversion from slave to master morality must be accompanied by a qualitative change of force. Such a change is necessary not, as Deleuze argues, because both terms of the master-slave dialectic are slavely moral. The inversion establishes master morality. A further change is necessary because master *and* slave morality, as forms of culture, are ascetic. Here it becomes convenient that Deleuze's dialecticians are Hegel and Feuerbach, not Marx. For Marx, as his critique of Feurbach reveals, agrees with Nietzsche that affirmation requires more than an inversion of existing relations. This suggests another parallel between Marx's dictatorship of the proletariat and Nietzsche's higher men. One can, I think, regard the dictatorship of the proletariat as an inversion of capitalist society. The proletariat rules but over a society "still stamped with the birthmarks of the old society from whose womb it emerges," e.g., wage labor, equal right, and the state.[136] Similarly, Nietzsche's higher men are new masters, a kind of cultural elite, who want to respond to the burdens of nihilism. But their response, their new morality, is also an inversion: they respond to the will to nothingness with the Yea-Yuh of the ass who affirms everything.

Communist society and the overman involve more than these inversions. Communist society crosses the narrow horizon of bourgeois right "in its entirety" and inscribes on its banner: "From each according to his ability, to each according to his needs!"[137] The overman does not create a new morality, but negates this idiosyncrasy of society altogether and lives an "autonomous" and "supra-moral" existence. For these reasons, communism and the overman differ qualitatively from what precedes them. Their difference in quality develops from active negation, not passive affirmation, even of inverted social relations. This negation is not so much rejection as transfiguration. Here, the transformation of quantity into quality becomes important again. Communist society requires the productive forces built up under capitalism, and the overman's "conscious innocence" requires the strength of the will to power built up under ascetic ideals. It is the quality of the active force within the dialectic, the force which transfigures not merely inverts, over which Marx and Nietzsche disagree. That disagreement exists independently of their agreement that history develops dialectically.

Still, Nietzsche's dialectical monism prevents him from delineating with the same clarity as Marx what exactly the parts of life as will to power are and what exactly contradicts and overcomes what. Unlike Marx's bourgeoisie, ascetic priests appear "regularly" and "universally" in almost every age. The history of asceticism parallels history as class conflict in this respect, i.e., asceticism like exploitation takes different forms, Jewish, Christian, scientific, in different ages. Yet the will to power does not order societies in the same way production relations do. It does not operate through a determinant, dominant group. The ascetic priest "belongs to no one race; he prospers everywhere; he emerges from every class of society."[138] Instead, ascetic priests are generated by the stage of society as a whole to treat its sicknesses. Their techniques are many, some innocent (anesthetization, mechanical activity, petty pleasure, neighborly love, herd organization), some guilty (torture, sin, now nihilism), and all limited to treating symptoms. Because ascetic priests are not characteristic of a specific group and are not characterized by a specific technique, Nietzsche cannot specify a specific contradiction, like that between productive forces and production relations, that develops and precipitates the overcoming of previous orders: "Life itself confided this secret to me: 'Behold,' it said, 'I am *that which must always overcome itself.*' "[139]

This vagueness limits the utility of the will to power for social psychology. How does one operationalize a principle which is everything? It may also encourage interpretations of Nietzsche's philosophy as method without substance or method separable from substance. Such interpretations of Nietzsche's genealogy as method facilitate syntheses with Marx's historical materialism. Nietzsche can be interpreted as negating, not affirming, or as deconstructing, not constructing. I have argued elsewhere that negating and deconstructing have substantive implications, specifically practical, if not theoretical, acceptance of the status quo.[140] My concern here is to show that, although Marx and Nietzsche understand man as a being who externalizes himself, identify his functionally determinant historical tendencies, and think those tendencies operate dialectically—similarities which could be read as similarities in method, thereby allowing a synthesis of their work—their so-called methods are really structural hypotheses. Marx and Nietzsche presume that one must view history in similar ways in order to convey its structure in thought, but they do not think that structure is the same. In fact, their views of that structure differ significantly.

Nietzsche would presumably attribute Marx's emphasis on production to his psychological need to believe in the Enlightenment—science conquering nature—and in Christian humanitarianism—postscarcity "equality of the person"—in a world without God. Both, he would argue, reflect the same overestimation of truth by an impoverished life.

This pair, science and the ascetic ideal, both rest on the same foundation . . . on the same overestimation of truth (more exactly: on the same belief that truth is inestimable and cannot be criticized). Therefore they are *necessarily* allies, so that if they are to be fought they can only be fought and called in question together. A depreciation of the ascetic ideal unavoidably involves a depreciation of science.[141]

Marx would presumably attribute Nietzsche's emphasis on creating values—which Nietzsche understands as contractual relations between creditors and debtors—to his bourgeois context:

For the bourgeois it is so much the easier to prove on the basis of his language, the identity of commercial and individual, or even universal, human relations, since this language itself is a product of the bourgeoisie, and therefore in actuality as in language the relations of buying and selling have been made the basis of all others. For example *propriété*—property [*Eigentum*] . . . —all of which are used both for commercial relations and for features and mutual relations of individuals as such.[142]

Each would explain the other's view of history as functionally determined by the will to power or production; each would think that the other had merely elevated a "given"—ascetic or bourgeois—life activity to man's essence. The differences in their structural hypotheses and the problems they potentially pose for syntheses of their critiques of modern society will appear in their specific critiques of modern society.

Finally, I can now discuss how Marx and Nietzsche criticize societies, in particular modern society, in terms of man's creative powers. Both explain the origins and functioning of modern society as functionally determined by man's tendency to expand his productive forces or will to power. Capitalist production relations and ascetic ideals vastly increase man's domination of nature. Both criticize modern society as dysfunctional for the continued expansion of those tendencies: man's essence—to expand his powers—contradicts his existence—which frustrates them—in modern society. Marx's communism is not an ideal opposed to reality, but rather "the *real* movement which abolishes the present state of things."[143] Similarly, Nietzsche's "objective measure of value" for individuals and societies is "the quantum of enhanced and organized power."[144]

Although both describe man's creative powers as frustrated, neither thinks that this frustration begins in modern society, rather, it assumes a new form there. Marx argues that man's producing powers have been alienated as long as classes have existed, that is, since primitive communism; Nietzsche argues that man's will to power has been sick as long as ascetic ideals have existed, that is, since the morality of mores. This alienation or sickness has been a necessary condition for man's life activity; the domination of classes or truths was functional for man's expanding producing or willing powers. The bourgeoisie "created more massive and more colossal productive forces than have all preceding generations together." Ascetic priests preserved the will by giving life a goal; *"a will to nothingness . . . is and remains a will! . . . man would rather will nothingness than not will."*[145]

Alienation and sickness were necessary until now. But Marx and Nietzsche now criticize capitalist class relations and ascetic ideals, respectively, not only because they have become dysfunctional for the continued expansion of man's powers, but also because the scope of man's powers now exceeds the limits of classes or truths per se. Man's life activity no longer needs to frustrate itself. As the proletariat sweeps away the old conditions of production, it will, "along with these conditions, have swept away the conditions for the existence of class antagonisms and of classes generally."[146] Similarly, in drawing its inference against itself, Christianity will pose the question *"What is the meaning of all will to truth?"*[147]

I now turn to Marx's and Nietzsche's analyses of how modern society frustrates man's life activity. While I have previously emphasized structural similarities in their general views of man and history, substantive differences in their specific critiques of modern society now become increasingly important. Marx and Nietzsche hypothesize dialectical histories: they agree that men create themselves historically by expanding their powers over nature, and that man's expanding powers functionally determine the order of social organisms and when that order will be overcome. However, although both have dialectical histories, they have different historical dialectics. That is, each understands man's powers differently and each criticizes modern society as dysfunctional for those powers from a different perspective. Marx criticizes capitalist production and its superstructure because the former alienates and the latter expresses the alienation of man's productive powers. Nietzsche criticizes ascetic psychology in modern ideology, politics, and economics because all deny man's will to power. As I examine their perspectives upon modern society, I will suggest not only how they differ, but also how each perspective is incomplete, and finally how their incomplete perspectives are contradictory, not complementary.

CHAPTER FOUR

SCIENCE VERSUS SKEPTICISM: IDEOLOGY AS ILLUSION

Once upon a time a valiant fellow had the idea that men were drowned in water only because they were possessed with the idea of gravity. If they were to knock this notion out of their heads, say by stating it to be a superstition, a religious concept, they would be sublimely proof against any danger from water. His whole life long he fought against the illusion of gravity, of whose harmful results all statistics brought him new and manifold evidence. (Marx and Engels, *The German Ideology*, preface)

He who will one day teach men to fly will have moved all boundary stones; the boundary stones themselves will fly up into the air before him, and he will rebaptize the earth—"the light one."
    The ostrich runs faster than the fastest horse, but even he buries his head gravely in the grave earth; even so, the man who has not yet learned to fly. Earth and life seem grave to him; and thus the spirit of gravity wants it. But whoever would become light and a bird must love himself: thus *I* teach. (Nietzsche, *Thus Spoke Zarathustra*, p. 304)

Marx's and Nietzsche's opposition to modern ideology is rooted in the idea of fetishism. Both maintain that modern man represents his own creations as the natural order of things, as a world beyond his control. According to Marx, men produce commodities which they buy and sell on the market, believing that it is natural for market forces, not human labor, to establish values. Nietzsche analogously argues that truths, man's creations which enable him to act in a chaotic world, become idols when he mistakes them for reality. Marx and Nietzsche agree that modern man creates fetishes because truth is distorted in modern society, because society frustrates his powers. Both demystify modern ideologies because until man correctly perceives his life as his creation, he cannot hope to control it or to fulfill himself in it.

Numerous twentieth-century social theorists concerned with the relationship between economic and psychological determinants of consciousness, and encouraged by parallels between Nietzsche's notion of idols and Marx's concept of ideology, have tried to synthesize their critiques.[1] In this chapter, I examine how Marx's and Nietzsche's critiques of modern ideology diverge and converge, suggesting and subverting such syntheses. First, I compare Marx's historical materialist and Nietzsche's genealogical concepts of ideology, focusing upon their agreement about its basic features and disagreement over its origins. Second, I turn to their critiques of modern ideology, that is, Christian and scientific metaphysics. I show that they demystify these ideologies as fetishes of exchange relations among egoistic individuals from different perspectives which correspond to their different views on how ideologies originate. Third, I maintain that their different perspectives are contradictory, not complementary. Marx and Nietzsche agree that modern ideologies portray a means for developing man's powers as his end. Yet they view these ideologies as means to very different ends: Marx would reveal the truth beneath illusions, and Nietzsche would reveal truth as an illusion. For Marx, Nietzschean skepticism and for Nietzsche, Marxian science merely fetishize man's frustrated powers. I conclude by considering what effects this contradiction between science and skepticism has on synthesizers' attempts to interpret and to change the world.

What Is Ideology?

Unlike Marx, Nietzsche seldom speaks of ideologies, referring instead to idols, illusions, ideals, and horizons. Still, these various terms have a systematic meaning in his philosophy akin to the Marxian term. As I examine Marx's and Nietzsche's conception of ideology, I illustrate the applicability of the term to both philosophies. Marx and Nietzsche agree that ideologies possess the following characteristics: they are (a) social; (b) functionally determined; and (c) illusory forms of consciousness. Where they disagree is over the theory of truth by which ideologies can be explained and evaluated. The sources of that disagreement emerge as I examine the basic features of ideology.

First, ideology is a social form of consciousness. As I argued in chapter 2, Marx and Nietzsche maintain that consciousness originates in and remains the product of man's social relations; there is no presocial or asocial consciousness. Marx says "Consciousness is . . . from the very beginning a social product, and remains so as long as men exist at all."[2] Nietzsche argues:

> It was only as a social animal that man acquired self-consciousness. . . . Consciousness does not really belong to man's individual existence but rather to his social or herd nature. . . . Our thoughts themselves are continually governed by the character of consciousness—by the "genius of the species" that commands it—and translated back into the perspective of the herd.[3]

They not only agree that consciousness develops in society, but also that each society develops a consciousness, an ideology, suited to its historical conditions. For Marx, "The ideas of the ruling class are in every epoch the ruling ideas, i.e. the class which is the ruling *material* force of society, is at the same time its ruling *intellectual* force."[4] According to Nietzsche, "A tablet of the good hangs over every people. Behold, it is the tablet of their overcomings; behold, it is the voice of their will to power."[5]

They disagree about how man's social consciousness develops, however. Marx argues that man as a species-being possesses a conscious instinct which allows him to relate to others and, through those relationships, to develop fully human consciousness. Nietzschean man lacks this conscious instinct. Nietzsche says that consciousness was "dearly bought" through cruel punishments for disobedience to social norms. The artists who formed man exchanged the creditor's psychic pleasure in inflicting pain for the debtor's infractions of the communal contract. Punishment draws its power "in the contractual [exchange] relationship between *creditor* and *debtor*, which is as old as the idea of 'legal subjects' and in turn points back to the fundamental forms of buying, selling, barter, trade and traffic."[6]

Man projects his identity as a social subject, his equivalence to an internalized communal contract, outward in his attempts to make reality equivalent to reason. Consciousness does not represent the release of man's species-being; it expresses his repression as a social subject. This suggests that Nietzsche regards truth as an ideology and foreshadows his disagreement with Marx. That disagreement becomes clearer as I examine the remaining features of ideology.

Second, as I indicated in chapter 3, Marx and Nietzsche argue that man's ideologies, as social forms of consciousness, are functionally determined. As there is no presocial or asocial consciousness, so there is no independent consciousness. Marx argues that a certain stage in the development of man's productive powers functionally determines corresponding class relations. These class relations are "the economic structure of society . . . to which correspond definite forms of social consciousness."[7] When Marx calls morality, religion, philosophy, and art ideology, he means that they can be explained in relation to the economic structure of society. These materialist explanations imply that ideas "no longer retain the semblance of independence. They have no history, no development; but men, developing their material production and their material intercourse, alter, along with this their real existence, their thinking and the products of their thinking."[8] However, as we have seen, Marx only denies that ideology develops independently, not that it plays a part in history. Ideology performs a function, but that function is determined by man's productive powers. To explain how ideologies function, I look more closely at Marx's concepts of class and class consciousness.

Marx thinks that classes generally consist of individuals who have similar relationships—relationships of ownership and control—to the means of production. These individuals have common class interests opposed to other classes because of those similar relationships. Yet class interests are not necessarily identical with the individual interests of class members. Divisions exist within classes, e.g., between mental and manual laborers, between members of competing industries, and between competing members of the same industry.[9] Individuals can also be unaware of their similar relationships to the productive forces and hence of their common class interests. Marx describes such a situation among the French peasants:

In so far as millions of families live under economic conditions of existence that divide their mode of life, their interests and their culture from those of the other classes, and put them in hostile contrast to the latter, they form a class. In so far as there is merely a local interconnection among these small peasants, and the identity of their interests begets no unity, no national union and no political organization, they do not form a class.[10]

Although the French peasants share a common situation and common interests, they are at most a class potentially or in itself. Until they become conscious of their common situation and organize to promote their common interests, they are not an actual class or a class in itself. Ideologies function by promoting class consciousness. They operate in a similar manner for ruling and non-ruling classes. In both cases, they legitimate particular class interests by portraying them as general human interests. But, in each case, they function with different results. They reinforce the domination of ruling classes and encourage the opposition of non-ruling ones.

According to this characterization, ideologies necessarily function as forms of false consciousness. Marx's and Engels' efforts to distinguish their scientific socialism from ideological viewpoints contribute to this interpretation of ideology. However, although Marx and Engels rarely describe their views as ideological, references to "proletarian ideology" are not necessarily inappropriate. The fact that an ideology is functional does not necessitate that it be false; science and ideology need not be mutually exclusive. For example, one might argue that historical materialism is becoming widely known because it serves the class interests of the proletariat, that those interests are also human interests, and that, for that reason, historical materialism is true, not false, consciousness. This, I think, is how Marx explains his historical materialism. Again, disagreement with Nietzsche seems imminent, since Marx maintains the possibility of truth.

Nietzsche does agree with Marx that ideology has a practical foundation. (We can even call it a material foundation as long as we remember his reservations about matter.) However, Nietzsche's psychological foundation determines ideals differently than Marx's economic interests do. According to Nietzsche, ascetics appear in most ages and emerge from many races and classes. Ascetic ideals are functions not of a specific group, but of society as a whole. They order reality and encourage action for a particular people with a particular psychological order. They are morphologies of the will to power of an individual and/or a society; they manifest its form.[11] The morphological character of ideals appears in Nietzsche's reference to a people's "tablet of the good" as "the tablet of their overcomings." It is also evident in his comment that a philosophy reveals who a philosopher is: "In the philosopher . . . there is nothing whatever that is impersonal; and above all, his morality bears decided and decisive witness to *who he is*—that is, in what order of rank the innermost drives of his nature stand in relation to each other."[12]

According to these remarks, the will to power does not *underlie* ideals for Nietzsche; they are its organization, not its expression. Yet, in these same passages, Nietzsche also refers to "peoples" as "creators" and to their "tablets" as the "voice of their will to power." He says as well that each of man's drives "would like only too well to represent just *itself* as the ultimate purpose of existence and the legitimate *master* of all the other drives."[13] And he argues that the ascetic possesses in his truth "not only his faith but also his will, his power, his interest."[14] Here, his argument seems closer to Marx's functional one, i.e., that ideologies arise to serve groups formed around common interests arising from a common situation.

Nietzsche's problem is how to explain the relationship between morphology and function without such a group. He says that philosophers' innermost drives are ordered in relation to society, but he does not say how they create that society. He only implies that their combined individual value creations "add up to" an expression of a social will to power. He refers to truth as

a mobile army of metaphors, metonymies, anthropomorphisms: in short a *sum* of human relations which become poetically and rhetorically intensified, metamorphosed, adorned and after long usage seem to a nation fixed, canonic, and binding.[15]

Perhaps those who command a society by creating its dominant values can, because their drives are similarly ordered in relation to similar norms, be thought of as "groups in themselves." Nietzsche does not deny that they sometimes, somehow, realize and organize to promote their similar interests, but he does seem to think that even if they never become groups for themselves— even if they never transcend "the simple addition of homologous multitudes"—they nonetheless functionally determine a ruling ideology. That ideology functions for them by portraying their interests as universal interests. This legitimates their "cumulative" domination.

Third, although Marx wants to exclude historical materialism, he agrees with Nietzsche that ideologies are illusions. Both argue that ideological consciousness is ignorant of its own material base and social function. Such ignorance contributes to mystification of the beliefs involved. People who are ignorant of the historically dominant interests an ideology serves often fetishize those beliefs. Ideologies function as illusions: they legitimate historical relations which represent ruling interests by mystifying their historical origins, by portraying them as natural relations which represent human interests. In short, they portray social relations which are functionally determined by the current level of man's powers as relations beyond his control. Nietzsche's *"basic objection* to all philosophic-moralistic cosmologies and theodicies, to all *wherefores* and *highest values* in philosophy and theology hitherto" is that "one kind of means has been misunderstood as an end; conversely, life and the enhancement of its power has been debased to a means."[16] Marx describes an analogous process of reification:

> Each new class which puts itself in the place of one ruling before it, is compelled, merely in order to carry through its aim, to represent its interests as the common interest of all the members of society, that is, expressed in ideal form: it has to give its ideas the form of universality, and represent them as the only rational, universally valid ones.[17]

Marx and Nietzsche concede that rulers' interests converge historically to an extent with human interests. According to Marx, a "new class" which portrays its interests as the "common interest" does represent all non-ruling classes against the presently ruling class. When they overthrew feudal aristocrats, the bourgeoisie did emancipate man politically and economically: they expanded freedom and production. Similarly, when Nietzsche's philosophers and theologians portray the order of their wills to power as the meaning of life, they satisfy man's need for horizons. He says, "A living thing can only be healthy, strong, and productive within a certain horizon."[18] Truth is the kind of error without which men cannot live; it fulfills "physiological demands for the preservation of a certain type of life."[19] Ascetics offered man truth: "It [truth] was the only meaning offered so far; any meaning is better than none at all."[20]

However, Marx maintains that the class interests of the new class ultimately deny human interests: non-rulers can benefit from the revolution only if they too can become rulers, only if they too can join the "new class."[21] The bourgeoisie expand freedom and production, but they do so through social relations which alienate men. Nietzsche's argument is analogous: the ascetic possesses in his truth "not only his faith but also his will, his power, his interest."[22] His faith gives life meaning, but that meaning furthers his interests. It preserves and spreads his sick will to power.

Capitalist and ascetic ideologies are means for expanding man's powers which must not be mistaken for man's end. But this is precisely the problem in modern society. Capitalists fetishize their class rule which alienates men:

> The aim is . . . to present production . . . as encased in eternal natural laws independent of history, at which opportunity *bourgeois* relations are then quietly smuggled in as the inviolable natural laws on which society in the abstract is founded.[23]

Ascetics fetishize their will to power which sickens men:

Morality in Europe today is herd animal morality—in other words, as we understand it, merely *one* type of human morality beside which, before which, and after which many other types, above all, *higher* moralities are, or ought to be, possible. But this morality resists such a "possibility," such and "ought" with all its power: it says stubbornly and inexorably, "I am morality itself, and nothing besides is morality."[24]

Marx and Nietzsche demystify these modern ideologies. They reveal the historical origins not only of modern man's consciousness but also of the social relations which make that consciousness necessary. Each criticizes the ideology which distorts reality and the distorted reality which requires it. Marx attacks the economic alienation which requires commodity fetishes, and Nietzsche exposes the psychological sickness which needs idols.

Neither thinks that criticism alone can overcome these social conditions. Nietzsche distinguishes between critics and philosophers: "*Genuine philosophers . . . are commanders and legislators*: they say, '*thus* it *shall* be!' . . . Their 'knowing' is *creating*, their creating is a legislation, their will to truth is—*will to power.*"[25] Marx says, "Clearly the weapon of criticism cannot replace the criticism of weapons, and material force must be overthrown by material force."[26] Nonetheless, while stressing the necessity of practice, both recognize the importance of theory. Nietzsche regards critics as "instruments of the philosopher."[27] Marx says that "theory also becomes a material force once it has gripped the masses."[28] Critics must demystify modern ideologies by exposing them as fetishes of man's social relations before man can hope to overcome those relations. Specifically, Marx and Nietzsche demystify Christianity and science as fetishes of the social relations—exchange relations among egoistic individuals—which frustrate modern man. However, as we have already begun to see, they do so from different perspectives, ones which correspond to their differences over the origins of ideology. Marx would expose the truth of species-life beneath capitalist economic illusions. Nietzsche would expose truth as an ascetic psychological illusion.

Christianity and Modern Science

The Christian God

Marx's and Nietzsche's demystifications of Christianity begin where Feuerbach's ended, that is, with the realization that God is a human creation. Feuerbach "reduced theology to anthropology" by explaining the Christian God as "nothing else than a product and reflex of the supernatural human mind."[29] Marx concurs: *"Man makes religion*, religion does not make man."[30] Nietzsche similarly asks, "What? Is man merely a mistake of God's? Or God merely a mistake of man's?"[31] Both quickly move beyond these descriptions of God's anthropological nature to explanations of man's historical conditions which require Him. They understand those historical conditions as exchange relations among egoistic individuals, but each identifies a different kind of exchange.

According to Marx, religions express human suffering: "Religion is the sigh of the oppressed creature, the heart of a heartless world and the soul of soulless conditions. It is the *opium* of the people."[32] That suffering is caused by economic exchange relations. In his young Hegelian language, Marx says that Christianity expresses the suffering caused by the separation of modern man's egoistic life in civil society from his species-life in political community. In his mature historical materialist language, Marx discusses the relations of civil society as class relations between bourgeoisie and proletariat: the member of the proletariat, who does not own means of production, sells his labor power to the capitalist, who owns means of production and purchases wage labor. This exchange allows the laborer to earn a wage equal to the value of his labor power and allows the capitalist to extract surplus value, the difference between the value and the productivity of that labor power. It also "leave[s] no other nexus between man and man than naked self-interest, than callous 'cash payment,'" "resolve[s] personal worth into exchange value," and "substitute[s] naked, shameless, direct, brutal exploitation" for "exploitation, veiled by religious and political illusions."[33]

Marx argues that modern man superimposes a species-life in

political community upon his egoistic life in civil society: "He lives in the *political community*, where he regards himself as a *communal being*, and in *civil society*, where he is active as a *private individual*, regards other men as means, debases himself to a means and becomes a plaything of alien powers."[34] His communal life comforts him, but it remains an abstraction: "The relationship of the political state to civil society is just as spiritual as the relationship of heaven to earth."[35]

Christianity—especially Protestant Christianity with its emphasis upon the individual alone before God—expresses man's suffering due to this double life.

> The members of the political state are religious because of the dualism between individual life and species-life, between the life of civil society and political life. They are religious inasmuch as man considers political life, which is far removed from his actual individuality, to be his true life and inasmuch as religion is here the spirit of civil society and the expression of the separation and distance of man from man.[36]

Christianity not only expresses, but also reinforces this double life by portraying bourgeois man (the egoistic individual of civil society), not "true" man (species-man), as "actual" man on earth. Marx suggests that

> only under the rule of Christianity, which makes *all* national, natural, moral and theoretical relationships *external* to man, could civil society separate itself completely from political life, tear apart all the species-bonds of man, substitute egoism and selfish need for those bonds and dissolve the human world into a world of atomistic individuals confronting each other in enmity.[37]

By accepting bourgeois man on earth and fetishizing species-man in heaven, Christianity mystifies the historical origins of the capitalist class relations of civil society and thereby reinforces them. Marx exposes the historical origins of Christianity in man's double life in modern society, and reveals that Christianity is only a fetish of man's alienated powers. With this, he moves beyond criticism of Christian illusions to criticism of the alienating socioeconomic conditions—exchange relations among egoistic individuals—which require them.

Nietzsche also thinks that religions express suffering, but suffering of a different sort. According to Nietzsche, man suffers because he is a sickly animal; he suffers of himself, from the internalization of his instincts which accompanies social existence. But his primary problem is not this suffering itself. For Nietzsche, suffering is a part of life which cannot be abolished and must be affirmed. What man suffers from is the meaninglessness of his existence, especially of his suffering, the absence of answers to the questions "Why man at all?" and *"Why* do I suffer?" Ascetic ideals, Christianity among them, meant "that something was *lacking*, that man was surrounded by a fearful void—he did not know how to justify, to account for, to affirm himself; he *suffered* from the problem of his meaning."[38] Ascetic ideals have provided such meaning. Nietzsche says, "The meaninglessness of suffering, *not* suffering itself, was the curse that lay over mankind so far— *and the ascetic ideal offered man meaning!"*[39]

Ascetics' interpretations of suffering brought more suffering with them, however, by placing suffering under the perspective of guilt. We have already seen how guilt originates in the "very material concept of debts," a concept coterminous with society. Although the whole of asceticism in a certain sense belongs here, later ascetics spiritualized cruelty and deepened suffering. As Nietzsche puts it, they exploited the sense of guilt. The internalization of the instincts of animal man created "the sense of guilt in its raw state," as a "piece of animal psychology," but "it was only in the hands of the priest, that artist in guilt feelings, that it achieved form—oh, What a form! 'Sin.' " Nietzsche describes sin, "the priestly name for the animal's 'bad conscience' (cruelty directed backward)," as the "greatest event so far in the history of the sick soul."[40] Ascetic priests teach man that *he* is the cause of his suffering, that suffering is punishment for his actions. It is payment upon a debt (sin) to the ultimate creditor (God) which can never be retired. Christianity is an instrument of self-torture:

> You will have guessed *what* has really happened here,
> *beneath* all this: that will to self-tormenting, that repressed

cruelty of the animal-man made inward and scared back into himself, the creature imprisoned in the "state" so as to be tamed, who invented the bad conscience in order to hurt himself after the *more natural* vent for this desire to hurt had been blocked—this man of the bad conscience has seized upon the presupposition of religion so as to drive his self-torture to its most gruesome pitch of severity and rigor. Guilt before *God*: this thought becomes an instrument of torture to him.[41]

The errors involved in Christianity are by now familiar ones. In *Twilight of the Idols*, Nietzsche describes them as the "Four Great Errors."[42] The first is the confusion of cause and effect. Theology and morality so far, not just Christianity, have mistakenly argued that if men are virtuous, then they will be happy. Nietzsche argues instead that men, whose will to power establishes their relations in the world, must act in certain ways. This means that if they are virtuous, it is the effect of their happiness, of their healthy, well-ordered body.

A second error, the error of a false causality, underlies even Nietzsche's polemical reversal of cause and effect. The notion of sin, according to Nietzsche, presumes the existence of three "inner facts" which seemingly guarantee causality. They are the existence of consciousness ("spirit" or "being") and of ego and will (attributes of the "subject") as causes. According to Nietzsche, an "ancient and enduring psychology is at work here." Will, spirit, and ego are fetishes of man's sickness in society, of his suffering as an egoistic individual. "It was out of himself that man projected his three 'inner facts'—that in which he believed most firmly, the will, the spirit, the ego."[43] Even the concept of being arises from the concept of the ego: "He posited 'things' as 'being,' in his image, in accordance with his concept of the ego as a cause." This includes the metaphysicians' "thing-in-itself," of which Nietzsche says, "The error of the spirit as cause [is] mistaken for reality! And made the very measure of reality! And called God!"[44]

Man's third error is to cling to these imaginary causes which "explain" his unpleasant condition. The psychology behind this is that any explanation is better than none, and that familiar explanations are more comforting than strange ones. Eventually, one kind of positing of causes predominates more and more, becomes a system, and precludes other explanations. "Sin" as an explanation for physiological discomfort is precisely such an imaginary cause, one which conceals the historical origins of man's discomfort.

The fourth error builds upon the previous three: it is the error of free will. The notion of sin presumes that men are subjects who, because they can choose how they act, can be held responsible for their actions to God. Nietzsche argues instead that men are never so separate from the world in which they act as to have (or not to have) free will. Neither then are they in a position to assume its responsibilities, to be guilty and sinful.

Ascetic priests' ideals—God and subject—are fetishes of social man's sick will to power. They function for it by making suffering meaningful, by giving man a reason to continue willing and preventing a suicidal nihilism. But they also exploit man's sickness; they spread the contagion of slave morality. Nietzsche suggests that the history of culture is the spiritualization of cruelty; revenge against life as will to power is a means to culture. The ascetics who wield that instrument do not themselves represent culture, however. Rather, they express the will to power of sick herd men. The truths they create—the subject responsible to God—fetishize man's sickness as an egoistic individual. According to Nietzsche, there is no actor—no subject who could be responsible—but only action in the world as will to power. As there is no actor, so there is no being—no God to whom the subject is responsible—but only becoming. All of these errors poison the innocence of becoming.

The ascetic priest spreads this sickness because his internalized revenge is simultaneously externalized *ressentiment* against healthy men. With the notion of the subject responsible to God, slaves suggest that masters can and should be other than they are. They represent their sickness—their social virtues which deny life—as health. Nietzsche says,

> The subject (or, to use a more popular expression, the *soul*) has perhaps been believed in hitherto more firmly than anything else on earth because it makes possible to the majority of mortals, the weak and oppressed of every kind, the sublime self-deception that interprets weakness as freedom, and their being thus-and-thus as *merit*.[45]

Christianity—especially Protestant Christianity with its emphasis upon individual responsibility before God—protects the herd by portraying all men, creditors as well as debtors, as guilty. Nietzsche says that Christianity attempts to "break the strong... poison and sicken the noble instincts... until the strong perish through orgies of self-contempt and self-abuse."[46]

By fetishizing man as a subject responsible to God, Christianity mystifies its origins in a sick will to power and the origins of that sickness in the conditions of man's social existence, conditions slave moralists exploit. Whereas Marx exposes Christianity as a fetish of economic exchange relations which alienate species-man, Nietzsche exposes it as a fetish of psychological exchange relations which sicken individuals.

Scientific Truth

Marx and Nietzsche agree that although Christianity is dead in theory it lives on in practice. Nietzsche quotes the "free spirit" of his age on this issue: "It is the church, and not its poison, that repels us.—Apart from the church, we, too, love the poison."[47] Marx recognizes that a secularized Christian principle, the Protestant work ethic, continues to serve as the opium of the people. Christianity lives on because the historical conditions which require it persist. Even its theoretical successor—scientific metaphysics—is only its atheistic analogue. Modern science expresses and fetishizes the persistent historical conditions which functionally determined Christianity. With it, man only substitutes the domination of things for the domination of God.

It is important to note, however, that neither Marx nor Nietzsche criticizes science qua science as ideology. Marx's socialist science and Nietzsche's gay science are, as their names suggest, demystified scientific forms. For this reason, I examine their critiques of scientific metaphysics along with their demystified alternatives to it.

As scientific socialists, Marx and Engels posit a particular relationship between knowing and being. In *Ludwig Feuerbach and the Age of Classical German Philosophy* Engels asks, "Are we able in our ideas and notions of the real world to produce a correct reflection of reality?" His answer is an infamous "Yes."[48] A review of the component parts of dialectical materialism reveals how Marx concurs with this answer.

We saw that, as a materialist, Marx argues that a material world exists objectively, that is, exists independently of knowing subjects. Like Engels, Marx argues that it is this objective world which our sensations reflect. He explicitly refers to the ideal as "the material world reflected by the human mind and translated into forms of thought," and to ideology as the "reflex," "echo," or "sublimate" of material life.[49] Still, although Marx explicitly maintains that matter exists in itself to be reflected by our senses, he bypasses philosophical arguments to this effect. The premises of dialectical materialism are to be neither understood nor defended abstractly. It is a "real, positive science," where "real" and "positive" mean sensuously ascertained. Consequently, when Marx rejects the Kantian (as Engels later rejects the neo-Katian) incomprehensible "thing-in-itself" and the accompanying distinction between appearance and reality, he does so practically, not theoretically. As Engels succinctly says, "If we are able to prove the correctness of our conception of a natural process by making it ourselves, bringing it into being out of its conditions and using it for our own purposes in the bargain, then there is an end of the Kantian incomprehensible 'thing-in-itself.' "[50]

In accord with this emphasis upon practical activity, Marx criticizes previous materialists as metaphysicians. Theirs is merely a metaphysics of matter, not of mind. Engels characterizes a metaphysician: "For him a thing either exists or does not exist; a thing cannot at the same time be itself and something else." Unlike metaphysicians, dialecticians "comprehend things and their representations, ideas, in their essential connection, con-catenation, motion, origin, and ending."[51] As dialecticians, Marx and Engels examine how man's conceptual and productive relations develop historically. They demonstrate that neither objects nor the consciousness reflective of them is immutable.

Marx's critique of previous scientific concepts illustrates how consciousness develops.[52] He criticizes scientific materialism and its social scientific analogue, political economy, in their capitalist forms. Contemplative materialists expressed the standpoint of civil society: "The highest point reached by contemplative materialism, i.e., materialism which does not comprehend sensuousness as practical activity, is the contemplation of single individuals and of civil society."[53] Political economy analogously "does no more than interpret, systematize, and defend in doctrinaire fashion the conceptions of the agents of bourgeois production who are entrapped in bourgeois production relations."[54] Socialist science takes a "new standpoint," that of "social humanity," to expose how these scientists distort reality.[55]

Marx focuses his critique of modern science upon the political economists' fetishism of commodities. He shows how the commodity fetishes of political economy, like Christianity, express man's double life in modern society. Under capitalist class relations man is alienated from his productive activity, his products, and his fellow men. Political economists objectify each aspect of man's alienated social production in a corresponding commodity fetish.

First, men are alienated from their productive activity. The reality here is that laborers sell their labor power to capitalists who control whether or not and the conditions under which they may work. The corresponding commodity fetish is that all sorts of human labor have a quantitative equivalent form or exchange value. This fetish obscures the qualitatively different social utility of various sorts of labor.

Second, men are alienated from their products. The reality here is that private laborers produce, private capitalists appropriate, and all men exchange products. The corresponding commodity fetish is that, given the equality of all sorts of human labor, all products have a quantitative equivalent form or exchange value equal to the labor power required to produce them. This fetish obscures the qualitatively different social use value of various commodities.

Third, men are alienated from their fellow men. The reality here is that men interact only in exchange. The corresponding commodity fetish is that "the mutual relations of the producers, within which the social character of their labour affirms itself, take the form of a social relation between the products."[56] This fetish obscures the social character of human labor.

When Marx demystifies these fetishes of political economy by exposing their origins in capitalist class relations, his point is not that political economists—or their philosophical compatriots—

fail to reflect reality. They *do* reflect it. More precisely, the appearances they portray are distortions only because reality is itself distorted. Their concepts simply reflect and hence are limited by their historical context. From a different, more advanced standpoint scientific socialists can demystify those concepts.

Marx demystifies commodity fetishes, as he demystifies Christianity, by revealing their historical origins in capitalist class relations. He says,

> They are forms of thought expressing with social validity the conditions and relations of a definite, historically determined mode of production, viz., the production of commodities. The whole mystery of commodities, all the magic and necromancy that surrounds the products of labour as long as they take the form of commodities, vanishes therefore, so soon as we come to other forms of production.[57]

He criticizes not only the commodity fetishes, but also the alienating conditions—economic exchange relations among egoistic individuals—which require them.

Nietzsche agrees with Marx that modern science, like Christianity, must be demystified. He also argues that modern science and Christianity rest upon the same foundation:

> This pair, science and the ascetic ideal, both rest on the same foundation . . . on the same overestimation of truth (more exactly: on the same belief that truth is inestimable and cannot be criticized). Therefore they are *necessarily* allies, so that if they are to be fought they can only be fought and called in question together.[58]

His attack upon modern science, like Marx's, is illuminated by his notions of materialism and dialectics.

Again, we have already seen that, although Nietzsche criticizes materialism, he is fundamentally a materialist. He agrees with Marx that we cannot get down or up, to any other "reality," besides the reality of our drives. What Nietzsche criticizes (and also mistakes for materialism per se) is the "materialistic atomism" of modern science. He argues that scientific materialists, like

Christians, fetishize men as egoistic individuals. Unlike Christians, though, they do not fetishize the subject as God, but rather as things about which they discover facts. He says, "The thing itself . . . the concept of thing is a mere reflex of the faith in the ego as cause. And even your atom, my dear mechanists and physicists—how much error, how much rudimentary psychology is still residual in your atom!"[59] Scientific materialists, like the idealists they criticize, are metaphysicians. In their search for "reality," scientific materialists merely descend to things rather than ascend to being. Contrary to both, Nietzsche maintains that "the world viewed from inside, the world defined and determined according to its 'intelligible character'—it would be 'will to power' and nothing else—"[60]

With this concept of "matter," Nietzsche confirms that he is a dialectician, despite his critique of dialectics. His dialectic is simply more radical than those—Marx's materialist dialectic among them—which he criticizes. Marx also rejects "materialist atomism" (which he calls empiricism) and argues that neither subject nor object is an "entity." Yet for Marx the categories of dialectical reason still correspond to reality. In contrast, Nietzsche argues that man as a subject is not related to objects, even in Marx's dialectical sense, but only to other congelations of force: "The subject alone is demonstrable; hypothesis that only subjects exist—that 'object' is only a kind of effect produced by a subject upon a subject—a *modus* of *the subject*."[61] Even the subject does not exist as an entity. Nietzsche describes the subject as "no subject, but an action, a positing, creative, no causes and effects." The subject is merely an ordered plurality of drives which discharges its will in relation to other such pluralities. In the world as will to power, "no things remain but only dynamic quanta in a relation of tension to other dynamic quanta: their essence lies in their relation to all other quanta, in their 'effect' upon the same."[62] This means that, for Nietzsche, the notion of a world structured dialectically is profoundly undialectical; it is a contradiction in terms. A dialectical world lacks subjects and objects, let alone their conceptual correspondence.

Nietzsche argues that, although scientific materialists (Marx among them) kill God by exposing Him as an illusion, they continue to express the very psychology which created Him. Their atheism is not the antithesis, but rather the evolution of the will to truth:

> Unconditional honest atheism ... is ... *not* the antithesis of that ideal, [the will to truth] as it appears to be; it is rather only one of the latest phases of its evolution, one of its terminal forms and inner consequences—it is the awe-inspiring *catastrophe* of two thousand years of training in truthfulness that finally forbids itself the *lie involved in belief in God*.[63]

Scientific materialism also continues man's cruelty toward himself. It reduces successive horizons—illusions men need and love—to objective historical or natural phenomena. Nietzsche says,

> Even the seeker after knowledge forces his spirit to recognize things against the inclination of the spirit, and often enough also against the wishes of his heart—by way of saying No where he would like to say Yes, love, adore—and thus acts as an artist and transfigurer of cruelty. Indeed, any insistence on profundity and thoroughness is a violation, a desire to hurt the basic will of the spirit which unceasingly strives for the apparent and superficial—in all desire to know there is a drop of cruelty.[64]

After destroying man's values, scientists cannot create new ones. Science demystifies metaphysical truths, but retains a metaphysical faith in the value of truth:

> It is still a *metaphysical faith* upon which our faith in science rests—that even we seekers after knowledge today, we godless anti-metaphysicians still take our fire, too, from the flame lit by a faith that is thousands of years old, that Christian faith which was also the faith of Plato, that God is the truth, that truth is divine.[65]

It leaves men with a value—the value of truth—which not only kills his truths, but also declares the resulting world without truth valueless. Christiantiy and science merely express different poles of metaphysicians' mistaken faith in opposite values: the Christian's world is true; the scientist's world is false. Nietzsche argues that the categories of reason are the cause of nihilism:

> Briefly: the categories "aim," "unity," "being" which we used to project some value into the world—we *pull out* again; so the world looks *valueless.* . . .
> Conclusion: The faith in the categories of reason is the cause of nihilism. We have measured the value of the world according to categories *that refer to a purely fictitious world.* . . .
> What we find here is still the *hyperbolic naiveté* of man: positing himself as the meaning and measure of the value of things.[66]

Nietzsche concedes that the scientific pursuit of truth, like other ascetic endeavors, is an active nihilism. It expresses the consummate will to nothingness, but that is and remains a will. Yet science mystifies the origins of its truths—subject, object, and their potential correspondence—in man's sick will to power. Nietzsche's genealogy exposes those origins, revealing that reason is not a criterion of reality but a way man masters reality. He says, "This is the greatest error that has ever been committed, the essential fatality of error on earth: one believed one possessed a criterion of reality in the forms of reason—when in fact one possessed them in order to become master of reality."[67] By exposing the origins of science, Nietzsche criticizes truth as man has known it and man's ascetic psychology which pursues it.

Marx and Nietzsche agree that Christian and scientific metaphysics are means for expanding man's powers. According to Marx, the bourgeoisie, with production relations legitimated by Christianity and political economy, have "created more massive and more colossal productive forces than have all preceding generations together."[68] According to Nietzsche, Christian and scientific ascetics have preserved the will by giving life a goal: "*A will to nothingness* . . . is and remains a *will!*"[69] However, these ideologies portray capitalism and asceticism not as means for expanding man's powers, but as his end. The class rule which alienates men appears "as encased in eternal natural laws independent of history."[70] Herd animal morality, an expression of man's sickness, says stubbornly and inexorably, "I am morality itself and nothing besides is morality."[71] Because man's powers now exceed these means, Marx and Nietzsche demystify modern ideology, revealing the origins of Christianity and science, exposing them as fetishes of a distorted reality where men relate only through exchange.

However, they demystify modern ideologies from different perspectives because they view them as means from different origins to different ends. For Marx, modern ideologies express bourgeois man's economic alienation from his species-life in illusory communities, i.e., the Christian's community with God in heaven and the political economist's community among commodities on earth. According to Nietzsche, Christianity and science express herd man's denial of individuals in respective illusory truths, i.e., the theistic truth of God and the atheistic one of things. Marx's task is to demystify these bourgeois illusions and reveal the truth of man as a species-being. Nietzsche's different purpose is to demystify truth as we have known it, to portray it as an ascetic ideal. This suggests that Marx's economic and Nietzsche's psychological perspectives upon modern ideology contradict, not complement, one another. From Marx's perspective, Nietzsche's skepticism about truth expresses man's alienation under capitalist economics. For Nietzsche, Marx's scientific socialism is another expression of the life-denying will to truth. To illustrate this contradiction, I return in greater detail to how each distinguishes his new science from ideology.

Science Versus Skepticism

Like the ideologies they demystify, Marx's historical materialism and Nietzsche's genealogy are functionally determined by social relations which correspond to man's developing powers. However, they are scientific, not ideological, because they are true forms of consciousness, not false ones.

According to Marx, historical materialism expresses the interests of the proletariat, the class exploited by capitalist production. In contrast to all previous classes, the proletariat does not have particular interests which it portrays as universal ones. Its interests are human interests. It represents "the *total loss* of humanity and . . . can therefore redeem itself only through the *total redemption of humanity.*"[72] For this reason, when Marx asks, "So where is the positive possibility of German emancipation?" he responds:

> *This is our answer.* In the formation of a class with *radical chains,* a class of civil society which is not a class of civil society, a class which is the dissolution of all classes, a sphere which has a universal character because of its universal suffering and which lays claim to no *particular right* because the wrong it suffers is not a *particular wrong* but *wrong in general*; a sphere of society which can no longer lay claim to a *historical* title, but merely to a *human* one . . . and finally a sphere which cannot emancipate itself without emancipating itself from—and thereby emancipating—all the other spheres of society.[73]

Although historical materialism represents proletarian interests, it is still scientific socialism. It does not express the illusion of a "new class," but the truth of this world. That truth is man.[74]

Yet historical materialism only reveals the divergence of appearance and reality in capitalist society, it does not overcome it. The scientific socialist understands that commodity fetishes are distorted appearances of distorted social relations, but those distortions persist. As G. A. Cohen expresses it, "Things do not *seem* different to a worker who knows Marxism. He knows they *are* different from what they continue to seem to be."[75] As long as labor remains alienated, things will not be as they seem. This introduces another, more profound Marxian relation between theory and practice. Man not only knows life through labor and thereby overcomes the "incomprehensible thing-in-itself." Science also can only become true, reason can only correspond to reality, practically, through the creation of a society where things are as they appear to be. This, as I understand it, is Marx's point in the second "Thesis on Feuerbach":

> The question whether objective truth can be attributed to human thinking is not a question of theory, but is a *practical* question. Man must prove the truth, i.e. the reality and power, the this-sidedness of his thinking in practice.[76]

Marx suggests here that the interrelated material and mental separation of subject and object in capitalist society is cause for revolution, not for skepticism. In a socialist society where subject and object correspond materially, they will do so mentally as well. Appearances will no longer distort because reality will no longer be distorted. For now, socialist science is needed to reveal the divergence of appearances from reality. However, after realizing its truth, science will wither away. As Marx puts it, "All science would be superfluous if the outward appearance and the essence of things directly coincided."[77]

Nietzsche's genealogy expresses the sociopsychological interests of new philosohers, of philosophers in whom "the will to truth becomes conscious of itself as a *problem*."[78] As historical materialism functions for the proletariat, so genealogy functions for new philosophers by demystifing the fetishes of modern society. In Nietzsche's case, that fetish is truth. By revealing how truth originates in the constraints of man's social existence, Nietzsche encourages new philosophers to overcome the will to truth and consciously to create new values.

There is also a basis for distinguishing Nietzsche's genealogy from ideology. That basis is not the realization of truth, but the absence of delusion, most important, the absence of the delusion of truth. Nietzsche's new philosophers do not express the truth of this world—"man"—for truth is a fetish of man as he has been, man as an egoistic individual. Instead, they no longer falsify life or man by feigning that either corresponds to the categories of reason. They affirm the non-identity of subjects and objects not only with themselves but also with one another. Nietzsche describes this condition as a "conscious innocence." Since there no longer is a "being" to which life or man could conform, neither can be judged. (Nor is there anyone in a position to judge.) Life cannot be condemned as mere appearance opposed to reality. Man cannot be guilty, for he is no longer a subject of society and its gods. Nietzsche counsels his new philosophers:

> Man is hard to discover—hardest of all for himself: often the spirit lies about the soul. Thus the spirit of gravity [the creator of truth] orders it. He, however, has discovered himself who says, "This is *my* good and evil"; with that he has

reduced to silence the mole and dwarf who say, "good for all, evil for all."[79]

New philosophers consciously create meaning for themselves as innocent moments in the innocence of becoming.

Their "conscious innocence" does not preclude a new notion of truth, however. Nietzsche is a nihilist only to those who would master reality by making it equivalent to reason. What he suggests is how philosophers might revalue truth. In his "gay science" truth becomes a self-conscious, interpretive activity. Values are regarded as relative to forms of life and true as conditions for preserving and enhancing them. Nietzsche intends the will to power as just such an interpretation. It affirms life in a manner appropriate for man's nihilistic condition. In this spirit he says of his notion that life is will to power: "Supposing that this also is only interpretation—and you will be eager enough to make this objection?—well, so much the better."[80]

The differences between this Nietzschean perspective and Marx's position should now be clear. Each illuminates the other's limitations. Nietzsche's genealogy suggests that Marx's critique of capitalist economics not only neglects, but even embraces, aspects of ascetic psychology with its faith in science. Marx's historical materialism illuminates how Nietzsche's genealogy of ascetic psychology fails to explore the potential origins of skepticism in capitalist production relations which separate, even destroy, subjects and objects. However, their incomplete perspectives contradict, not complement, one another. Each succumbs to precisely the exchange relations which the other attacks.

Marx would regard Nietzsche's denial of the correspondence, even the existence, of subjects and objects as bourgeois ideology. Marx agrees with Nietzsche that subject and object do not correspond in modern society. However, Marx thinks that men potentially can perceive and can realize their true existence as social producers. He thinks this, in part, because he regards men as potentially reasonable and reality as potentially rational. He does acknowledge that men's actions may have unintended consequences, e.g., the bourgeoisie while pursuing its class interests involuntarily promotes its own demise. But he assumes that the conscious interests which motivate men's actions are their actual interests. This means that once a class arises whose actual interests are human interests, i.e., the proletariat, they will know those interests and will act to make actual man into true man.

Marx would argue that Nietzsche's skepticism expresses the real separation of subject and object in modern society. Nietzsche, like the political economists, mistakes his "given" reality of exchange relations among egoistic individuals for nature. His skepticism about truth is itself bourgeois ideology, an illusion functionally determined by capitalist class relations which alienate men and which must be overcome. Engels says that what Marx calls the "purely *scholastic* question of skepticism" signals incipient revolution:

> The growing preception that existing social institutions are unreasonable and unjust, that reason has become unreason and right wrong, is only proof that in the modes of production and exchange changes have silently taken place with which the social order, adapted to earlier economic conditions is no longer in keeping.[81]

Nietzsche's denial of truth as equivalence not only expresses, but also reinforces, the separation of subject and object under capitalist class relations. For he denies that that separation and the suffering it causes can be overcome, and then he affirms separation and suffering by affirming life. Unlike Nietzsche, Marx regards man's alienation in modern society as an argument not against truth, but against a life which does not conform to it.

Nietzsche, however, would regard Marx's scientific critique of genealogy as an ascetic ideology because Marx maintains the illusion of truth. Unlike Marx, Nietzsche argues that neither man nor life conforms to the categories of reason. Men may consciously seek truth, but they unconsciously seek illusions: they seek the illusion of truth which gives life meaning. Nietzsche says, "The will to logical truth can be carried through only after a fundamental *falsification* of all events is assumed. From which it follows that a drive rules here that is capable of employing both means, firstly falsification, then the implementation of its own point of view: logic does *not* spring from will to truth."[82]

Nietzsche would regard scientific socialism as such an illusion. Marx's dialectical materialism does demystify metaphysical truths—God, Being, and things—but its subjects, objects, and especially their productive and conceptual correspondence in communist society still express a metaphysical faith in truth. Marx too has mistaken his "given" reality, one of psychological exchange relations among egoistic individuals, for nature. His scientific socialism is an illusion expressive of the ascetic will to truth, a will to power which must be overcome. Nietzsche says of socialism:

> In this way a goal seems to have entered the development of mankind: at any rate, the belief in progress towards the ideal is the only form in which a goal in history is thought of today. *In summa*: one has transferred the arrival of the "kingdom of God" into the future, on earth, in human form—but fundamentally one has held fast to the belief in the *old* ideal.[83]

By denying life because it does not conform to truth, Marx not only expresses but also reinforces the herd's will to power. He condemns life as suffering and gives the herd a new, secular will to nothingness. Nietzsche, unlike Marx, regards man's sickness under ascetic psychology as an argument not against life, but against truth which denies it.

Marx's critique of bourgeois ideology in the name of man's truth contradicts Nietzsche's critique of truth as man's ascetic denial of life. While Marx would teach men their "laws of gravity," Nietzsche would overcome gravity and teach them to fly.

Those who attempt to synthesize their critiques may find themselves caught in this contradiction between Marx's quest for the truth and Nietzsche's attack upon it. This contradiction manifests itself in various forms of "skeptical socialism" which are potentially prey to the limitations of both critiques. As Nietzschean skeptics, such synthesizers reject rationality as the product of man's psychological repression in society. With this, they risk becoming bourgeois. Their problem is that social criticism directed toward social change requires a rational foundation, i.e., language and logic informing action. It also requires concerted collective action. But if rationality and collectivity are coterminous forms of psychological repression, then liberation means the transcendence of both. Although skeptics can reject reality, they deny themselves a basis for criticizing or changing it. Only the speechless, solipsistic individual can be free. Still, as Marxian scientists, such synthesizers want to criticize and even to change reality. They would release a rationality which capitalist economics represses. In this they become ascetic. They continue to use the rationality they have declared repressive. They continue to deny life in the name of truth.[84] This suggests that attempts to combine Marx's and Nietzsche's critiques of modern ideology may escape neither the economics nor the psychology of exchange.

CHAPTER FIVE

SOCIALISM VERSUS INDIVIDUALISM: LIBERAL DEMOCRACY AS OPPRESSION

In place of the old bourgeois society, with its classes and class antagonisms, we shall have an association, in which the free development of each is the condition for the free development of all. (Marx and Engels, *The Communist Manifesto*, p. 491)

Everywhere people are now raving, even under scientific disguises, about coming conditions of society in which "the exploitative aspect" will be removed—which sounds to me as if they promised to invent a way of life that would dispense with all organic functions. (Nietzsche, *Beyond Good and Evil*, aphorism #259)

A comparison of Marx and Nietzsche also reveals two ways of criticizing liberal democracy, each part of a larger tradition. Beginning in the late eighteenth century, aristocrats and democrats criticized the democratization of liberalism. Focusing their anger upon paradigmatic events, such as the French Revolution and the Paris Commune, the former attacked the mass and the latter the class basis of liberal democracy. Aristocrats feared that the egalitarian masses would use their political power to destroy aristocracy, the fount of culture. Democrats' corresponding concern was that liberal democracy would legitimate exploitation of the working poor by the idle rich.[1]

Numerous twentieth-century social theorists concerned with the relationship between class conflict and mass culture have tried to synthesize these critiques in their Marxian and Nietzschean forms.[2] In this chapter, I examine how Marx's radical democratic and Nietzsche's radical aristocratic critiques of liberal democracy converge and diverge, suggesting and subverting such syntheses.[3] First, I compare Marx's historical materialist and Nietzsche's genealogical approaches to the state, examining their agreement upon its features and disagreement about its origins. Second, I contrast their critiques of liberal democracy.[4] Although both criticize political freedom as human oppression, as an illusory identity of individual and social life, they do so from different perspectives corresponding to their different views of the origins of the state. Third, I explain why their different perspectives contradict, not complement, one another. They see liberal democracy as a means from incompatible origins to incompatible ends. As a radical democrat, Marx views it as a means from primitive communism to a free society. As a radical aristocrat, Nietzsche views a free society as a contradiction in terms.

Hence, a comparison of their critiques illustrates that liberalism and totalitarianism do not exhaust our political alternatives, that there are at least two—class and mass—ways of criticizing both, each of which portrays liberalism as potentially totalitarian. Most important, such a comparison suggests how contradictions between Marx's and Nietzsche's critiques of liberal democracy may constrain synthesizers attempts to thwart its totalitarian tendencies.

What Is the State?

Marx and Nietzsche agree that states are: (a) political; (b) functionally determined; (c) illusory communities. This agreement appears in the parallel structure of their analyses of the state: both demystify states by exposing their origins in oppression. Yet they disagree over the nature of that oppression because they understand the origins of the state differently. By examining the substantive characteristics states possess, we can clarify their disagreement.

First, Marx and Nietzsche distinguish states as political powers from the apolitical powers which pre- and postdate them. There have not always been, nor will there always be, states.

Political power is a specific, historical organization of power. In contrast to apolitical powers, states are oppressive forces seemingly independent of the society which creates them.

Marx and Engels differentiate between states as political, and gens as social, organizations of power.[5] Engels describes the differences between the gens (gentile constitution) and the state (political constitution) into which it develops historically. The gens was a community where free, equal individuals communally owned and controlled their products. The historical development of the division of labor and the corresponding development of class divisions shattered this primitive communal unity. Conflict simultaneously arose between individual interests and between individual and social interests. Individuals began to interact with one another by exchanging private property; they began to interact with the community by exchanging individual freedom for social protection. The state arose from these exchange relations which it regulated, but as a power seemingly above them. Engels says,

> In order that these antagonisms, classes with conflicting economic interests, shall not consume themselves and society in fruitless struggle, a power, apparently standing above society, has become necessary to moderate the conflict and keep it within the bounds of "order"; this power, arisen out of society but placing itself above it and increasingly alienating itself from it, is the state.[6]

By regulating exchange through law, the state preserved society, but it did so as an expression of the growing fragmentation of individual and social life. It did so as an independent, i.e., political, power.

Nietzsche also refers to gens, but his usual term for these primitive communities is the "morality of mores."[7] However, Nietzsche argues that man's prepolitical past consisted of unmitigated conflict among individuals, not of communal unity. A "conqueror and master race" formed warring individuals into the "oldest 'state'" through cruel punishments which taught them to conform to social norms. According to Nietzsche, political and social life are coterminous; rulers impose both on the ruled. He says,

The individual can, in conditions preceding the organized state, treat others harshly and cruelly to *intimidate* them, to secure his existence through such intimidating demonstrations of his power. This is how the brutal, powerful man acts, the original founder of a state, who subjects to himself those who are weaker. . . . The ground for all morality can only be prepared when a greater individual or collective individual, as, for example, society or the state, subjects the individuals in it, that is, when it draws them out of their isolatedness and integrates them into a union. *Force* precedes morality; indeed, for a time morality itself is force, to which others acquiesce to avoid unpleasure. Later it becomes custom, and still later free obedience, and finally almost instinct: then it is coupled to pleasure, like all habitual and natural things, and is now called *virtue*.[8]

Like Marx, Nietzsche understands the state's origins in terms of exchange. Social creditors exchange the pleasure of inflicting pain for individual debtors' infractions of social norms. But the exchange is psychological, not economic. Most important, social and political life involve relations of credit and debt. Exchange among individuals and between individuals and society originates, not terminates, man's primitive communities. Nietzsche says,

Buying and selling, together with their psychological appurtenances, are older even than the beginnings of any kind of social forms of organization and alliances; it was rather out of the most rudimentary form of personal legal rights that the budding sense of exchange, contract, guilt, right, obligation, settlement, first *transferred* itself to the coarsest and most elementary social complexes.[9]

Nietzsche's state, which also regulates exchange, simultaneously creates society. It does so as the expression of the original fragmentation of individual and social life. It is an independent, i.e., political, power which accompanies society itself.

Although the state's functional determination and illusory character were implicit in this discussion of its political power, they too deserve explicit examination. Second, then, Marx and

Nietzsche agree that the apparent independence of the state from society corresponds to its actual dependence on a ruling power within society. Marx argues that economic class relations functionally determine the nature of states: "Political power, properly so called, is merely the organized power of one class for oppressing another."[10] Engels explains various states as economic instruments by which one class oppresses another: "The ancient state was ... the state of the slave owners for holding down the slaves, just as the feudal state was the organ of the nobility for holding down the peasant serfs and bondsmen, and the modern representative state is an instrument for exploiting wage labor by capital."[11] In contrast, Nietzsche maintains that the state represents the dominant will to power: "A concept denoting political superiority always resolves itself into a concept denoting superiority of soul."[12] He explains various states in terms of a prevalent psychology:

> Monarchy represents the belief in one man who is utterly superior, a leader, savior, demigod.
> Aristocracy represents the belief in an elite humanity and higher caste.
> Democracy represents the disbelief in great human beings and an elite society: "Everyone is equal to everyone else." "At bottom we are one and all self-seeking cattle and mob."[13]

This suggests why neither Marx nor Nietzsche espouses a theory of natural law or natural right to be embodied in the "just" state. Both expose the social content, the exchange relations expressive of particular powers, beneath all juridical forms. Marx argues that

> the justice of the transactions between agents of production rests on the fact that these arise as natural consequences out of the production relationships. The juristic forms in which these economic transactions appear as wilful acts of the parties concerned ... cannot, being mere forms, determine this content. They merely express it. This content is just wherever it corresponds ... to the mode of production. It is unjust whenever it contradicts that mode.[14]

Nietzsche speaks of the "institution of law" as the "most decisive act" of a supreme power:

> "Just" and "unjust" exist, accordingly, only after the institution of the law . . . to speak of just or unjust *in itself* is quite senseless; *in itself*, of course, no injury, assault, exploitation, destruction can be "unjust," since life operates *essentially* . . . through injury, assault, exploitation, destruction.[15]

Both will criticize liberal democrats' "rights of man" by revealing their social content, by exposing the dominant powers for which they function. Neither will attack liberal democracy as unjust.

Marx's and Nietzsche's disagreement about whether economics or psychology functionally determines the state further illuminates their different views of its origins. Marx explains the apparent primacy of theological and political determinants—indeed, the existence of language itself—as a function of man's economic relations.[16] Nietzsche explains the apparent primacy of economic determinants—indeed, the existence of property itself—as a function of man's psychological relations.[17] Neither suggests that men's economic and psychological relations might develop in relation to one another, and also follow their own independent logic. Marx does not seriously consider the possibility that psychological exchange might pre- (and post-) date the state, and Nietzsche does not seriously consider the possibility that economic communism might pre- (and post-) date the state. Nietzsche explains social and political life as the psychological denial of individuals, and Marx explains political life as the economic alienation of species-man.

Third, both argue that states, as political powers functionally determined by man's social relations, are illusory communities. Marx speaks of the state, unlike the gens, as an " 'external,' *forced,* specious identity" of individual and society.[18] He says,

> And out of this very contradiction between the interest of the individual and that of the community the latter takes an independent form as the *State*, divorced from the real interests of individual and community, and at the same time as an illusory communal life, always based, however, . . . on

the classes, already determined by the division of labour, which in every such mass of men separate out, and of which one dominates all the others.[19]

Although Nietzsche regards society and the state as violently imposed forms, he agrees with Marx that man's early communities unified individual and social life. Whereas Marx argues that the absence of a distinction between rulers and ruled constituted a natural unity, Nietzsche maintains that the presence of such a distinction imposed a unity which became "almost instinct."[20]   Engels and Nietzsche describe men's early communities as revealing this similarity, as well as the other dissimilarities:

> It is the greatness but also the limitation of the gentile constitution that it has no place for ruler and ruled. Within the tribe there is as yet no difference between rights and duties; the question whether participation in public affairs, in blood revenge or atonement, is a right or a duty does not exist . . . ; it would seem . . . just as absurd as the question whether it was a right or a duty to sleep, eat, or hunt.[21]
>
> Once peoples hung a tablet of the good over themselves. Love which would rule and love which would obey have together created such tablets.
>   The delight in the herd is more ancient than the delight in the ego; and as long as the good conscience is identified with the herd, only the bad conscience says: I.
>   Verily, the clever ego, the loveless ego that desires its own profit in the profit of the many—that is not the origin of the herd, but its going under.[22]

Both argue that the unity of these early communities decayed historically. They have been supplanted by increasingly illusory identities of individual and society in successive states.[23]
    Marx and Nietzsche agree that the liberal-democratic state is the apotheosis of the state as an illusory community. Marx distinguishes between the liberal-democratic state as the "real" or "political" state, and ancient and feudal states which preceded it. In contrast to ancient and feudal states which exhibited a "substantive unity between people and state," in the modern state

"the constitution itself develops a particular reality alongside the real life of the people."[24] Citizens of liberal democracies lead double lives, one in political community as abstract species-beings and the other in civil society as concrete egoistic individuals. Marx says,

> Where the political state has attained its full degree of development man leads a double life, a life in heaven and a life on earth, not only in his mind, in his consciousness, but in *reality*. He lives in the *political community*, where he regards himself as a *communal being*, and in *civil society*, where he is active as a *private individual*. . . . The relationship of the political state to civil society is just as spiritual as the relationship of heaven to earth.[25]

Nietzsche similarly distinguishes between the liberal-democratic state as the "death of peoples" or "decay of the state" and man's "oldest states" (the "morality of mores" and "peoples") and "mixed cultures" (feudal aristocracies) which preceded it. For Nietzsche, these earlier states also revealed man's communal life in a "unity of artistic style in every outward expression of the people's life."[26] They were *pia fraus* (according to Nietzsche, all states are) but they were no mere mechanical unity.[27] Nietzsche contrasts these states with the liberal-democratic state, to which he refers (in terms similar to Marx's heaven-earth analogy) as man's "new idol":

> State? What is that? Well then, open your ears to me, for now I shall speak to you about the death of peoples.
> State is the name of the coldest of all cold monsters. Coldly it tells lies too; and this lie crawls out of its mouth: "I, the state, am the people." That is a lie! It was creators who created peoples and hung a faith and a love over them: thus they served life.
> It is annihilators who set traps for the many and call them "state": they hang a sword and a hundred appetites over them.
> Where there is still a people, it does not understand the state and hates it as the evil eye and the sin against customs and rights.[28]

Marx and Nietzsche agree that the state is becoming an increasingly illusory identity of individual and social life. However, they disagree about the character of this illusion. Marx regards this identity as increasingly illusory because as the natural unity of the gens disintegrates, the distance between rulers and ruled expands. He says,

> The contradiction between the *democratic representative state* and *civil society* is the completion of the *classic* contradiction between public *commonweal* and *slavery*. In the modern world each person is *at the same time* a member of slave society and of the public commonweal. Precisely the *slavery of civil society* is *in appearance* the greatest *freedom* because it is in appearance the fully developed *independence* of the individual.[29]

Individuals seem more independent in liberal democracies, but the state actually increasingly masters society:

> Society had created its own organs to look after its common interests, originally through simple division of labour. But these organs, at whose head was the state power, had in the course of time, in pursuance of their own special interests, transformed themselves from the servants of society into the masters of society.[30]

Conversely, Nietzsche argues that this identity is increasingly illusory because, as the imposed unity of peoples dies, the distance between rulers and ruled contracts. He says, "Concept of degeneration in both cases: when the herd starts to acquire the qualities of the solitary, and the latter the qualities of the herd, in short, when they approximate each other."[31] He argues that the state is increasingly the servant of society. Europe today provides evidence of this development in what Nietzsche calls the "moral hypocrisy of those commanding": "They even borrow herd maxims from the herd's way of thinking such as, 'first servants of their people' or 'instruments of the common weal.' "[32] He fears a day is coming when there will be "no shepherd and one herd," when "everybody wants the same" and "everybody is the same," and "whoever feels different goes voluntarily into a madhouse."[33]

Both conclude that the illusory identity of individual and social life in the liberal-democratic state must be demystified. Political emancipation must be seen as human oppression. But they criticize political emancipation from different perspectives which correspond to their different views of the origins of the state. As a radical democrat, Marx exposes the origins of the liberal-democratic state in the economic alienation of species-man. As a radical aristocrat, Nietzsche reveals its origins in the psychological repression of individuals.

The Liberal-Democratic State

Although Marx discusses "pre-capitalist" states and Nietzsche discusses "peoples," each does so primarily to illuminate the distinctive features of their mutual political target: the liberal-democratic state. How does Marx's radical democratic critique differ from Nietzsche's radical aristocratic critique of political emancipation?

Political Emancipation

Both understand political emancipation as the emancipation of private from public life. Although neither knew of it, Tönnies' distinction between *Gemeinschaft* and *Gesellschaft* encapsulates the historical development both describe. Tönnies distinguishes between two ideal types of social relations and their corresponding political associations: "The relationship itself [among human wills], and also the resulting association, is conceived of either as real and organic life—this is the essential character of the *Gemeinschaft* (community) or as imaginary and mechanical structure—this is the concept of *Gesellschaft* (society)."[34] Marx and Nietzsche do not conceive of ancient and feudal states as real, organic communities. According to Marx, only primitive communism was real, organic community. Nietzsche thinks that all communities are greater or lesser *pia fraus*. However, modern man's (Tönnies' among them) conception of previous states as real, organic communities and of the liberal-democratic state as an imaginary, mechanical society expresses real dislocations associated with the development from *Gemeinschaft* to *Gesellschaft*. Most simply, this is the development from a community of personal, status relations to a society of impersonal, contractual relations.

Both view this development as the liberation of exchange relations from theological and political illusions. Previous states seemed organic because private life was public: it was the province of God and king. Liberal democracy seems mechanistic in contrast because private life has been emancipated from public life: exchange has been exposed as the basis of the state. In the famous words of the "Communist Manifesto," Marx says,

> The bourgeoisie . . . has put an end to all feudal, patriarchal, idyllic relations. It has pitilessly torn asunder the motley feudal ties that bound man to his "natural superiors," and has left remaining no other nexus between man and man than naked self-interest, than callous "cash payment." . . . In one word, for exploitation, veiled by religious and political illusions, it has substituted naked, shameless, direct, brutal exploitation.[35]

Nietzsche's less familiar remarks are equally explicit:

> The Middle Ages offers in the Church an institution with a quite universal goal, comprehending all men, and humanity, aimed at their supposedly highest interests; in contrast to it the goals of States and nations, which modern history offers, make a disheartening impression; they appear petty, low, materialistic, and geographically narrow.[36]

They agree that the Protestant Reformation sowed the seeds of man's political emancipation. With its defense of free, equal individuals it suggested that religion was a matter of private, not public, concern. But, Marx regards the Reformation as the liberation of bourgeois class interests, and Nietzsche sees it as the liberation of ascetic herd interests. Engels describes the impact of the Reformation:

A contract requires people who can dispose freely of their persons, actions and possessions and meet each other on the footing of equal rights. To create these "free" and "equal" people was one of the main tasks of capitalist production. Even though at the start it was carried out only half-consciously, and under a religious guise at that, from the time of the Lutheran and Calvinist Reformation the principle was established that man is only fully responsible for his actions when he acts with complete freedom of will.[37]

Nietzsche says of the same development:

"Everyone his own priest"—behind such formulas and their peasant cunning there was hidden in Luther the abysmal hatred against "the higher human being"....

What afterward grew out of his Reformation, *good* as well as bad, might be calculated approximately today.... The European spirit became shallower... *more good-natured.* ...The mobility and restlessness of the spirit, its thirst for independence, its faith in a right to liberty, its "natural-ness"—all this also grew owing to the Reformation.[38]

The seeds of man's political emancipation sown in the Protestant Reformation came to fruition in the French Revolution. Marx and Nietzsche draw a structural analogy between Christianity and liberal democracy as illusory communities, and they also draw a substantive one between liberal-democratic and Christian roots in exchange. Marx depicts the French Revolution as the secularization of the bourgeois class interests expressed in Protestant Christianity. Nietzsche describes it as the naturalization of the ascetic herd instincts manifest in Protestant Christianity. Marx says,

Political democracy is Christian inasmuch as it regards man ... as a *sovereign* and supreme being; but man in his uncultivated, unsocial aspect, man in his contingent existence, man just as he is, man as he has been corrupted, lost to himself, sold, and exposed to the rule of inhuman conditions and elements by the entire organization of our society—in a word, man who is not yet a *true* species-being. The sovereignty of man—but of man as an alien being distinct from actual man—is the fantasy, the dream, the postulate of Christianity, whereas in democracy it is a present and material reality, a secular maxim.[39]

Nietzsche says,

> It is the herd instinct, the mediocre nature . . . which gets its supreme sanction through Christianity. This mediocre nature at last grows so conscious of itself . . . that it arrogates even *political* power to itself—
>
> Democracy is Christianity made natural: a kind of "return to nature" after, on account of its extreme anti-naturalness, it could be overcome by opposite values.— Consequence: the aristocratic ideal henceforth loses its naturalness.[40]

Marx and Nietzsche agree that the French Revolution liberated exchange relations among egoistic individuals, but it did not overcome them. It was only a political revolution, not a social one. As critics of the state, both argue that political revolutions alone cannot emancipate humanity.

The Rights of Man

While domination was overt and exchange was covert in previous states, exchange is overt and domination is covert in the liberal-democratic state. Marx and Nietzsche argue that public life has become the tool of private individuals.[41] They expose the social content, the dominant historical interests, beneath the seemingly natural "rights of man." However, as they differ on whose interests are liberated by man's political emancipation, so they differ on whose interests have been oppressed. Marx argues that political emancipation represents the economic oppression of the proletariat by the bourgeoisie. Nietzsche argues that it expresses the psychological oppression of aristocratic individuals by the herd. Both demystify the "rights of man": freedom is oppression; equality is inequality; and security is insecurity. But they do so from these different perspectives.

First, Marx and Nietzsche discuss liberal-democratic freedom as negative liberty. It is freedom from the interference of others, more specifically, freedom of the individual to dispose of person and property by contract at will. Both demystify this juridical illusion, revealing how rights express particular powers, not universal will. Marx says:

> If power is taken as the basis of right, as Hobbes, etc. do, then right, law, etc. are merely the symptom, the expression of the other relations upon which State power rests. The material life of individuals, which by no means depends merely on their "will" . . . this is the real basis of the State and remains so at all the stages at which division of labour and private property are still necessary, quite independently of the *will* of individuals.[42]

Nietzsche concurs, saying that rights "originate" as "recognized and guaranteed degrees of power": "Where rights prevail, a certain condition and degree of power is being maintained, a diminution and increment warded off. The rights of others constitute a concession on the part of our sense of power to the sense of power of those others."[43] Both conclude that the right to freedom involves oppression, but oppression of differing kinds.

According to Nietzsche, the right to freedom expresses the power of herd morality. Nietzsche described morality as a "check" on freedom and as a "tyranny against nature." One might think from this that he would see liberal democrats' ethic of mutual toleration as liberating. However, Nietzsche argues that *laisser-aller* is itself a morality: it declares domination immoral. In doing so, it expresses the interests of the herd's will to power. He says,

> The herd man in Europe today gives himself the appearance of being the only permissible kind of man and glorifies his attributes, which make him tame, easy to get along with, and useful to the herd, as if they were the truly human virtues: namely, public spirit, benevolence, industriousness, moderation, modesty, indulgence, and pity.[44]

Nietzsche views this morality not as an extension of rights, but as resistance to the rights of aristocratic individuals. He says, "They [herd animals] are at one in their tough resistance to every special claim, every special right and privilege (which means in the last analysis, *every* right: for once all are equal nobody needs 'rights' any more)."[45]

Marx also sees the right to freedom as an expression of power, in his case, of the bourgeoisie over the proletariat. Marx says, "By freedom is meant, under the present bourgeois conditions of production, free trade, free selling and buying."[46] Like Nietzsche, he argues that these exchange relations are only formally free; conquest lies beneath the equivalent form. Marx argues that the violent expropriation of peasants from the land created the free laborer.[47] He is doubly free: "free from the old relation of clientship, villeinage or service, but also free from all goods and chattels, from every real and objective form of existence, *free from all property*."[48] Freed from his means of production, he is forced to sell his labor power to live. The capitalist is correspondingly free to exploit his labor power, by extracting surplus value. Marx says, "capital obtains this surplus-labour without an equivalent, and in essence it always remains forced labour—no matter how much it may seem to result from free contractual agreement."[49]

Second, Marx and Nietzsche agree that liberal-democratic freedom involves a kind of equality, that is, equality of rights. Marx says that "equality . . . simply means equal access to liberty . . . namely that each man is equally considered to be a self-sufficient monad."[50] Nietzsche also associates individual freedom and egalitarianism:

> The modern European is characterized by two apparently opposite traits: individualism and the demand for equal rights; that I have at last come to understand. For the individual is an extremely vulnerable piece of vanity: conscious of how easily it suffers, this vanity demands that every other shall count as its equal, that it should be only *inter pares*.[15]

Both argue that as political freedom is oppression, so political equality is inequality. But they also criticize equal right from different perspectives.

According to Nietzsche, men establish equivalents when they create moralities. " 'Everything has its price; *all* things can be paid

for' " is the "oldest and naivest moral canon of *justice*."[52] Although
no two individuals (or things) are ever equal, Nietzsche tolerates
man's oldest, naivest canons of justice because they established equivalents within orders of rank. He says, "Justice on
this elementary level is the good will among parties of approximately equal power to come to terms with one another, to
reach an 'understanding' by means of a settlement—and to
compel parties of lesser power to reach a settlement among
themselves."[53] He draws the line, however, at liberal-democratic
principles of justice. By making everyone equal, by rejecting
orders of rank altogether, they deny life. Nietzsche describes this
transformation:

> Refraining mutually from injury, violence, and exploitation
> and placing one's will on a par with that of someone else—
> this may become, in a certain rough sense, good manners
> among individuals if the appropriate conditions are present
> (namely, if these men are actually similar in strength and
> value standards and belong together in *one* body). But as
> soon as this principle is extended, and possibly even ac-
> cepted as the *fundamental principle of society*, it immediately
> proves to be what it really is—a will to the *denial* of life, a
> principle of disintegration and decay.[54]

The liberal democrats' principle of equal right subsumes qualitatively different individuals under a common standard. Beneath
its equivalent form lies the inequality of herd morality. Nietzsche
fears that

> "equality of rights" could all too easily be changed into
> equality in violating rights—I mean, into a common war on
> all that is rare, strange, privileged, the higher man, the higher
> soul, the higher duty, the higher responsibility, and the
> abundance of creative power and masterfulness.[55]

Marx also argues that inequality lies beneath the equivalent
form. Like herd morality, capitalist commodity production conceals qualitative differences as quantitative equality. Marx refers
to the commodity form as a born leveler and a cynic.[56] It converts
the qualitatively different use value of particular kinds of labor
and particular products into quantitatively equivalent exchange

values. The laborer who sells his labor power and the capitalist who buys it appear to exchange equivalents. Marx says, "He [the laborer] and the owner of money meet in the market, and deal with each other as on the basis of equal rights, with this difference alone, that one is buyer, the other seller."[57] However, beneath this equivalent form is the inequality of capitalist class relations:

> The exchange of equivalents occurs (but it is merely) the surface layer of a production which rests on the appropriation of other people's labour *without exchange*, but under the *guise of exchange*. This system of exchange has *capital* as its basis. If we consider it in isolation from capital, as it appears on the surface, as an *independent* system, this is mere *illusion*, though a *necessary illusion*.... For the rule of exchange-values and of production producing exchange-values *presupposes* alien labour power as itself an exchange-value. I.e. it presupposes the separation of living labour power from its objective conditions; a relationship to these— or to its own objectivity—as someone else's property; in a word, a relation to them as *capital*.[58]

Third, Marx and Nietzsche discuss the right of free, equal individuals to security. Marx says, "*Security* is the supreme social concept of civil society, the concept of *police*, the concept that the whole of society is there only to guarantee each of its members the conservation of his person, his rights and his property."[59] Nietzsche says, "How much or how little is dangerous to the community, dangerous to equality ... now constitutes the moral perspective."[60] They agree that as freedom is oppression and equality is inequality, so security is insecurity. Again from different perspectives, they argue that liberal democracy secures an alienated existence.

According to Nietzsche, law itself formulates conditions necessary to preserve a community. Justice is intolerance to internal and external enemies.[61] Since life involves accumulation of power, and preservation is only one of its infrequent, indirect results, legal orders should only temporarily restrict life.[62] Previous legal orders did develop the species by demanding that individuals sacrifice themselves to preserve the community. This is no longer the case in liberal democracies, however.[63] The altruism expressed in herd morality is a thinly veiled egoism.

Nietzsche says, "The pleasant feelings with which the good, benevolent, just man inspires us (in contrast to the tension, fear which the great new man arouses) are our own feelings of personal security and equality: the herd animal thus glorifies the herd nature and then it feels comfortable."[64] Security perpetuates the egoism of liberal-democratic non-egos and prevents the development of higher men: "In ordinary 'egoism' it is precisely the 'non-ego', the profoundly average creature, the species man, who desires to preserve himself: if *this* is perceived by rarer, subtler, and less average men, it enrages them. For they judge: 'we are nobler! Our preservation is more important than that of those cattle!' "[65]

Marx argues that the right to security protects egoism of a different sort. It protects the possessive individualism of civil society. He says, "The concept of security does not enable civil society to rise above its egoism. On the contrary, security is the *guarantee* of its egoism."[66] Security preserves capitalists' right to extract surplus value and proletarians' right to sell their labor power. It preserves the class relations which make society a mere means to man's physical existence, not his end.

Marx and Nietzsche agree that political emancipation oppresses not only a specific group, i.e., proletarians or aristocrats, but also all of humanity. Each, to some extent, develops both sides of the dialectic between individuals and society. Nietzsche recognizes that individualism can deny the species, arguing that when the "egoistic" herd oppresses aristocrats it simultaneously denies its own realization. In his world as will to power, freedom is measured by the resistance to be overcome: "The degree of resistance that must be continually overcome in order to remain on top is the measure of freedom, whether for individuals or for societies—freedom understood, that is, as positive power, as will to power."[67] The herd animal becomes free, he realizes his will to power by commanding himself to obey higher men. Nietzsche says, "That the weaker should serve the stronger, to that it is persuaded by its own will, which would be master over what is weaker still."[68] Zarathustra tells herd men that they "threw away their last value when they threw away their servitude."[69]

According to Marx, the class relations which permit the bourgeoisie to exploit the proletariat also preclude their own realization in a free society. Both bourgeoisie and proletariat are subjected to the vicissitudes of the market under liberal laissez-faire economics. Marx says, "in imagination individuals seem freer under the dominance of the bourgeoisie than before, because their conditions of life seem accidental; in reality, of course, they are less free, because they are more subjected to the violence of things."[70] The personal independence of capitalist and proletariat is the objective dependence of both.[71]

Marx and Nietzsche conclude that political emancipation is a means which man has mistaken for his end. Marx says, "the *political community* is reduced by the political emancipators to a mere *means* for the conservation of these so-called rights of man and ... the citizen is therefore proclaimed the servant of egoistic man."[72] Nietzsche says, "*Basic error*: to place the goal in the herd and not in single individuals! The herd is a means, no more!"[73]

Despite his criticisms, each regards liberal democracy as a means toward man's end, toward human emancipation. For Marx and Nietzsche political emancipation is progress, but progress toward very different ends. Marx thinks that liberal democracy, by fostering capitalist economics, allows man to transcend the limitations of the gens. Whereas men in the gens were still subject to nature, capitalist development of man's productive forces allows the elimination of scarcity and, with it, class conflict. The development of man's productive forces also encourages individuality. As man's needs and powers expand, so do his enjoyments and capacities. Once these are freed from their "narrow bourgeois form," individuality can flourish:

... the ancient conception, in which man always appears ... as the aim of production, seems very much more exalted than the modern world, in which production is the aim of man and wealth the aim of production. In fact, however, when the narrow bourgeois form has been peeled away, what is wealth, if not the universality of needs, capacities, enjoyments, productive powers, etc., of individuals, produced in universal exchange?[74]

Liberal democracy even encourages its own transcendence by organizing the proletariat, the class capable of overcoming class

conflict and its representative, the state. Engels says that proletarian demands for equality accompany bourgeois ones. But the
proletarian demands are radically democratic: "The proletarians
took the bourgeoisie at its word: equality must not be merely
apparent, must not apply merely to the sphere of the state, but
must also be real, must also be extended to the social, economic
sphere."[75] Although the proletariat during its contest with the
bourgeoisie may be compelled to organize itself as a ruling
class,

> When, in the course of development, class distinctions
> have disappeared, and all production has been concentrated
> in the hands of a vast association of the whole nation, the
> public power will lose its political character.... In place of
> the old bourgeois society, with its classes and class antagon-
> isms, we shall have an association, in which the free
> development of each is the condition for the free develop-
> ment of all.[76]

For Marx, liberal democracy is a means to a free society where
individuality flourishes precisely because the opposition between
individual and social life has been overcome.

Nietzsche's analogous argument is that liberal democracy
simultaneously transcends "peoples" and fosters nihilism. As a
stage in the self-overcoming of truth, nihilism represents progess.
"The measure of *unbelief*, of permitted 'freedom of the spirit' as
an expression of an increase in power. 'Nihilism' an ideal of the
highest degree of powerfulness of the spirit, the over-richest
life."[77] Whereas "peoples" still needed truths, nihilism indicates
that the will to power is sufficiently developed that a new radical
aristocracy can arise. The herd even fosters its own transcendence
by these radical aristocrats. Nietzsche says, "The very same new
conditions that will on the average lead to the leveling and
mediocritization of man—to a useful, industrious, handy, multi-
purpose herd animal—are likely in the highest degree to give birth
to exceptional human beings of the most dangerous and attractive
quality."[78] These aristocratic individuals will transcend justice, the
herd's revenge against life, and its representative, the state:

The justice which began with, "everything is discharge-able, everything must be discharged," ends by winking and letting those incapable of discharging their debt go free: it ends, as does every good thing on earth, by *overcoming itself*. This self-overcoming of justice: one knows the beautiful name it has given itself—*mercy*; it goes without saying that mercy remains the privilege of the most powerful man, or better, his—beyond the law.[79]

Unlike Marx's proletariat, Nietzsche's aristocratic individuals may not create a new society. Nietzsche presents two visions of the future. In the first, this aristocrat is a charismatic leader who creates new horizons for the herd. In the second, he is a solitary new philosopher who merely coexists with the herd. In both cases, the herd is a means to an individual who overcomes the opposition of individual and social life by overcoming society itself. As Nietzsche puts it, he removes the idiosyncrasies of society (guilt, punishment, justice, honesty, freedom, love, etc.) from existence.[80]

Marx and Nietzsche agree that a future organization of power will overcome the illusory and oppressive identity of individual and social life found in successive states. However, for Marx, this future society is a radical democracy, unified by the overcoming of class distinctions. When men overcome their subjection to nature, they also overcome their subjection to men. For Nietzsche, if a charismatic leader creates a new aristocracy, it will be unified by the imposition of orders of rank. Man's overcoming of nature includes his subjection to men.

Socialism versus Individualism

Marx and Nietzsche both criticize the reality beneath the appearance of the rights of man: security is insecurity, equality is inequality, freedom is oppression. Both conclude that political emancipation is not human emancipation, that the liberal-democratic state is an illusory identity of individual and social life. In developing his critique, each considers both sides of the dialectic between individual and society. Like Marx, Nietzsche criticizes bourgeois individualism because it denies the species. Nietzsche argues that the herd precludes its own realization in a higher being when it denies aristocratic individuals: "society must *not* exist for society's sake but only as the foundation and scaffolding on which a choice type of being is able to raise itself to its higher task and to a higher sate of *being*."[81] Like Nietzsche, Marx criticizes bourgeois society because it denies individuals. For Marx, the bourgeoisie, by exploiting the proletariat, precludes its own realization in a free society. Marx says, "It is only when man's object becomes a *human* object or objective man that man does not lose himself in that object. This is only possible when it becomes a *social* object for him and when he himself becomes a social being for himself, just as society becomes a being for him in this object."[82] However, Marxian individuals realize themselves in a free society, and Nietzschean society realizes itself in transcendent individuals. Where Nietzsche would overcome the psychological repression of aristocratic individuals by the herd, Marx would end the economic exploitation of the proletariat by the bourgeoisie.

Marx's democratic and Nietzsche's aristocratic critiques of the illusory identity of individual and society in liberal-democratic states contradict, not complement, one another. Each critique epitomizes the exchange relations which the other attacks. Nietzsche adopts his "given" economics of exchange to question man's psychological oppression. Marx says,

> For the bourgeois it is so much the easier to prove on the basis of his language, the identity of commercial and individual, or even universal, human relations, since this language itself is a product of the bourgeoisie, and therefore in actuality as in language the relations of buying and selling have been made the basis of all others.[83]

Marx adopts his "given" psychology of exchange to question man's economic oppression. Nietzsche says,

> Hatred of egoism, whether it be one's own (as with Christians) or another's (as with socialists), is . . . revealed as value judgment under the predominating influence of revenge. . . . [84]

They criticize liberal democracy as a means from contradictory origins to contradictory ends.

Nietzsche accuses modern men, who argue that original man was a herd animal, of the "delicacy and even more the tartuffery of tame domestic animals."[85] He argues that the worship of gods and ancestors in man's primitive communities implied "natural orders of rank," saying, "Inasmuch as at all times, as long as there have been human beings, there have also been herds of men (clans, communities, tribes, peoples, states, churches) and always a great many people who obeyed, compared with the small number of those commanding."[86]

Marx, in turn, accuses those who regard original man as an isolated individual of "expressing with social validity the conditions and relations of a definite, historically determined mode of production, viz., the production of commodities."[87] He argues that exchange and individuation develop historically. In a passage which could apply to Nietzsche, he says,

> It is of course easy to imagine a powerful, physically superior person, who first captures animals and then captures men in order to make them catch animals for him; in brief, one who uses man as a naturally occurring condition for his reproduction like any other living natural thing; his own labour being exhausted in the act of domination. But such a view is stupid, though it may be correct from the point of view of a given tribal or communal entity; for it takes the *isolated* man as its starting-point. But man is only individualised through the process of history. He originally appears as a *generic being, a tribal being, a herd animal*— though by no means as a "political animal" in the political sense.[88]

Marx and Nietzsche do acknowledge these limitations of their divergent analyses of the historical origins of the state, but neither solves them. Nietzsche agrees with Marx that men only become individuals in any meaningful sense after they develop consciousness through their social relations. He also admits that exchange first develops, as Marx and Engels argue, only between communities.[89] What is Nietzsche's "conqueror and master race" if not a generic being? If individuality develops in society, how can social *and* political life begin with exchange? In turn, Marx recognizes that orders of rank existed in men's primitive communities. He admits that a "given tribal or communal entity" may originate in the domination of a powerful individual. Who is this individual if not a conqueror? If conquest creates community, how can man be a species-being?

My concern here, however, is neither the accuracy nor the consistency but rather the contradictory emphases of Marx's and Nietzsche's analyses of the origins of the state. (Perhaps the pursuit of origins is always to some extent ideological.) For Nietzsche, who understands original man as an isolated individual, a free society is a contradiction of terms. Whereas Marx, who understands original man as a herd being, thinks freedom is only possible in society.

Liberal democracy, then, is a means not only from contradictory origins, but also to contradictory ends. To illustrate Marx's and Nietzsche's contradictory ends, it is worth quoting their respective remarks on the Paris Commune at length. Marx hailed the Commune as a triumph for international socialism and the dawn of proletarian direct action. He criticized its detractors:

> It is a strange fact. In spite of all the tall talk and all the immense literature ... about Emancipation of Labour, no sooner do the working men anywhere take the subject into their own hands with a will, than up rises at once all the apologetic phraseology of the mouthpieces of present society with its two poles of Capital and Wages Slavery. ... The Commune, they exclaim, intends to abolish property, the basis of all civilisation! Yes, gentlemen, the Commune intended to abolish that class-property which makes the labour of the many the wealth of the few. It aimed at the expropriation of the expropriators. It wanted to make individual property a truth by transforming the means of production, land and capital, now chiefly the means of enslaving and exploiting labour, into mere instruments of free and associated labour.—But this is Communism, "impossible" Communism![90]

Nietzsche's reaction differed profoundly. He said that the communards' battle for survival gave him "the worst day of his life."[91]

Of the Commune as a sign of a growing socialist movement, he remarked,

> In many places in Europe they [socialists] may yet bring off occasional coups and attacks; there will be deep "rumblings" in the stomach of the next century, and the Paris commune...was perhaps no more than a minor indigestion compared to what is coming. But there will always be too many who have possessions for socialism to signify more than an attack of sickness—and those who have possessions are of one mind on one article of faith: "one must possess something in order to *be* something." But this is the oldest and healthiest of all instincts: I should add, "one must want to have more than one has in order to *become* more." For this is the doctrine preached by life itself to all that has life: the morality of development. To have and to want to have more—*growth*, in one word—that is life itself. In the doctrine of socialism there is hidden, rather badly, a "will to negate life."[92]

Nietzsche argues that the socialists' democratic radicalism epitomizes the herd's opposition to higher men. In this, socialists are at one psychologically with their supposed liberal-democratic antagonists: "They [anarchists, democrats, and socialists] are at one with the lot in their thorough and instinctive hostility to every other form of society except that of the *autonomous* herd. . . . They are at one, the lot of them, in their faith in the community as the *savior*, in short, in the herd, in 'themselves.' "[93] Nietzsche refers to socialism as merely an extreme form of the typical nineteenth-century ruse, that is, the egoism of non-egos masquerading as altruism.[94] He says that, as the members of the bourgeoisie are absurd when they deny that the liberal-democratic state originates in exploitation, so socialists are absurd to think that their "good man" will appear.[95] Nietzsche argues that the socialists' promise to abolish exploitation sounds "as if they promised to invent a way of life that would dispense with all organic functions."[96] Consequently, he regards the socialists' society of perfect herd animals as the apotheosis, not the demise, of the state. In a prophetic reference to socialism during *and* after the "dictatorship of the proletariat" he says:

It desires such a wealth of executive power as only despot-
ism has possessed,—indeed, it outdoes everything in the past,
by striving for the downright destruction of the individual, which it sees as an unjustified luxury of nature, and
which it intends to improve into an expedient *organ of the
community.* . . .
    Socialism can serve as a rather brutal and forceful way
to teach, the danger of all accumulations of state power, and
to that extent instill one with distrust of the state itself.[97]

Marx, in turn, argues that aristocratic radicalism expresses
the class interests of bourgeois intellectuals. Aristocratic radicals
find the sources of social revolution not in the finite, coarse,
brutal, dead "mass," but in its opposite, that is, in critical
individuals.[98] In their contempt for the masses, aristocratic
radicals are at one with their supposed bourgeois antagonists:

    All objections urged against the Communistic mode of
    producing and appropriating material products, have . . .
    been urged against the Communistic modes of producing
    and appropriating intellectual products. Just as, to the
    bourgeois, the disappearance of class property is the disap-
    pearance of production itself, so the disappearance of class
    culture is to him identical with the disappearance of all
    culture.
        That culture, the loss of which he laments, is, for the
    enormous majority, a mere training to act as a machine.[99]

While Nietzsche did not want his aristocratic individualism to be
confused with bourgeois individualism, he too can only conceive
of social life as the sacrifice of the individual.[100]
    Marx regards the aristocratic radical's cultural ideal as a
naive nostalgia for the Greek polis in a world which has overcome
its inegalitarian preconditions.[101] Solitary individuals, who attempt to create this ideal with revolutionary pronouncements
alone, are simply staunch conservatives; they merely perpetuate
the status quo.[102] Charismatic individuals, who attempt to create
this ideal by fueling mass movements, do not transcend the state,
but rather perfect its terror. Marx and Nietzsche both regard
Napoleon as such an individual; a comparison of their remarks
about him illustrates Marx's point. Nietzsche glorifies him,

though not without trepidation: "Like a last signpost to the *other* path, Napoleon appeared, the most isolated and late-born man there has ever been, and in him the problem of the *noble ideal as such* made flesh—one might well ponder *what* kind of problem it is: Napoleon, this synthesis of the *inhuman* and *superhuman*."[103] In contrast, Marx says that

> *Napoleon* represented the last battle of *revolutionary terror* against the *bourgeois society* which had been proclaimed . . . Napoleon, of course, already discerned the essence of the *modern state*; he understood that it is based on the unhampered development of bourgeois society, on the free movement of private interest, etc. He decided to recognise and protect this basis. He was no terrorist with his head in the clouds. Yet at the same time he still regarded the *state* as an *end in itself.* . . . He *perfected* the *Terror* by *substituting permanent war* for *permanent revolution*.[104]

It is a tragedy of the twentieth century that Napoleon was not the last battle of revolutionary terror against the bourgeois society. Stalinism and Nazism, regimes founded in Marx's and Nietzsche's names which neither would acclaim as his heir, have legitimated both of their critiques.

Finally, what problems may arise in attempts to synthesize Marx's and Nietzsche's contradictory critiques of the liberal-democratic state? We have seen that Marx would create a free society to overcome the illusory identity of individual and society in liberal democracies, and that Nietzsche would overcome society itself because he thinks it is this illusory identity. This suggests that attempts to synthesize their critiques are caught in a contradiction: is human emancipation to be found in a democratic revolution within society or in an aristocratic escape from it?

Attempts to synthesize the democratic radicalism of socialist revolutionaries and the aristocratic radicalism of bourgeois intellectuals often typify this contradiction, and because of it can fall prey to the worst features of Marx and Nietzsche. As aristocratic radicals, synthesizers may become bourgeois, finding revolutionary consciousness in individuals beyond society, not in the proletariat within it.[105] With this they divorce political activity

from social relations and thereby renounce the structural preconditions for a socialist revolution. As democratic radicals, they
may remain ascetic because they would nonetheless revolutionize, not escape, society.[106] Yet after abandoning the structural
preconditions for a free society they can only create non-conformist theories or inspire charismatic individuals to impose
"freedom."[107] In either case, they reduce scientific socialism to
just another life-denying ideal.

Although syntheses of Marx's and Nietzsche's critiques may
illustrate how politically emancipated individuals remain oppressed, they do not lead beyond the illusory identity of individual and
society in liberal democracies. Such attempts to overcome Marx's
economic and Nietzsche's psychological limitations remain
bound by the economics and psychology of liberal democracy
itself.

CHAPTER SIX

PRODUCTION VERSUS PLAY: CAPITALISM AS SELF-DENIAL

Utility and pleasure are *slave theories* of life: the "blessing of work" is the self-glorification of slaves.—Incapacity for *otium*. (Nietzsche, *The Will to Power*, aphorism #758)

This overcoming of obstacles is itself a liberating activity...the external aims become stripped of the semblance of merely external natural urgencies, and become posited as aims which the individual himself posits—hence as self-realization, objectification of the subject, hence real freedom, whose action is, precisely, labour. (Marx, *Grundrisse*, p. 611)

Few interpreters have seriously considered Nietzsche's views on capitalism. It is often assumed that he had none, or at least none worth considering. This caution was perhaps justified when the association of Nietzsche and Nazism was commonplace. But now, when the tendency is instead to establish the complementarity of Nietzsche's philosophy with Marxism, his economic positions warrant reexamination.[1] They are also in some respects similar to those of Marx. Both argue that man's creative activity involves mastery of nature, and that with capitalist production man's self-assertion becomes his self-denial. However, these similarities conceal deeper differences: Marx argues that men are alienated by the sale of their labor power; Nietzsche argues that labor itself is an ascetic activity. Again, their critiques of modern society are contradictory, not complementary.

This chapter is a comparison of Marx's and Nietzsche's critiques of capitalism. I begin with Marx's historical materialist and Nietzsche's genealogical views of production per se, with their agreement that men produce to master nature and their disagreement about why they do so. Then I compare their specific critiques of capitalist production. Although both criticize capitalism as man's self-denial, they do so from different perspectives which correspond to their different analyses of production. Third, I show how their different perspectives contradict each other. They criticize capitalist production from different perspectives because they see it as a means to incompatible ends. For Marx, it is a means from necessary to free labor. Nietzsche, for whom free labor (like a free society) is a contradiction in terms, sees it as a means from work to play. Here too, each would regard the other's end as the extension of capitalist means. Attempts to synthesize their economic positions are caught in a contradiction between Marx's defense of labor and Nietzsche's attack upon it, and escape neither the economics nor the psychology of capitalism.

What Is Production?

In chapters 2 and 3, I argued that Marx and Nietzsche think that men create themselves historically by expanding their mastery of nature and that they form material and social relations which are functional for doing so. However, their views of why men master nature and hence of the relations they form to do so differ significantly.

According to Marx, men master nature to meet their needs. Their primary needs are material, i.e., they require food, shelter, and clothing to preserve themselves. Marx stresses, "Men must be in a position to live in order to be able to 'make history.' "[2] Men satisfy their needs by appropriating nature and producing commodities which have use value from it.[3] These needs expand historically beyond mere subsistence, but commodity production remains the satisfaction of needs. Marx says, "A commodity is ... an object outside us, a thing that by its properties satisfies human wants of some sort or another. The nature of such wants, *whether, for instance, they spring from the stomach or from fancy, makes no difference.*"[4]

Even socialist society, Marx's realm of freedom, is built upon necessary production.[5] In his early writings, Marx does speak of socialism as overcoming labor and introducing total sensory appropriation of the world.[6] However, in these passages, Marx clearly refers to the overcoming of alienated labor. The total sensory appropriation which he argues is possible beyond necessary production is free production. He describes it:

> This overcoming of obstacles is in itself a liberating activity... the external aims become stripped of the semblance of merely external natural urgencies, and become posited as aims which the individual himself posits—hence as self-realization, objectification of the subject, hence real freedom, whose action is, precisely, labour.[7]

For Marx, labor is man's species-life. Men are purposive producers for whom the overcoming of obstacles is potentially fulfilling. Once men overcome "merely external natural urgencies" or "wants" "from the stomach," labor itself becomes, not merely a means to external needs, but their prime need, their self-realization.[8]

Unlike Marx, for whom production is first and foremost reaction to need, Nietzsche regards man's self-creation as action to incorporate. Nietzsche's biological metaphor for life as will to power is the primitive protoplasm which, he says, "extends its pseudopodia in search of something that resists it—not from hunger but from will to power. Thereupon it attempts to overcome, appropriate, assimilate what it encounters: what one calls 'nourishment' is merely a derivative phenomenon, an application of the original will to become *stronger*."[9] Although Nietzsche does occasionally refer to the non-creative as the non-productive, he consistently abstracts from, even denigrates, material need and material production. He distinguishes between mastering and producing, saying, "We protect artists and poets and those who are masters in anything; but as natures that *are* of a higher kind than these [the industrious], who have only the ability to do something, merely 'productive men,' we do not confound ourselves with them."[10] Mastery involves the transcendence of obstacles by those overflowing with power, whereas production is the overcoming of obstacles to satisfy needs. Mastery is an end in itself, not a means to an end.

Nietzsche does admit that men have metaphysical needs for

horizons. Artists, philosophers, and religious leaders do master nature to meet these needs:

> Man projects his drive to truth, his "goal" in a certain sense, outside himself as a world that has being, as a metaphysical world, as a "thing-in-itself," as a world already in existence. His needs as creator invent the world upon which he works, anticipate it; this anticipation (this "belief" in truth) is his support.[11]

Yet Nietzsche stresses that the metaphysical creations which men need to preserve life are really means for enhancing it. He says, "This is my *basic objection* to all philosophic-moralistic cosmologies and theodicies.... One kind of means has been misunderstood as an end; conversely, life and the enhancement of its power has been debased to a means."[12] That is, even man's seemingly purposive metaphysical creativity is willing to expand. Purposive production as a reaction to need—whether material or metaphysical—remains derivative. Superabundance rather than hunger, prodigality rather than utility, play rather than work, are primary in life as will to power. Nietzsche regards "'play,' the useless—as the ideal of him who is overfull of strength, as 'childlike.' The 'childlikeness' of God, *pais paizon*."[13]

Marx argues that psychologists, who ignore man's material needs and purposive production, are unscientific:

> A *psychology* for which this book [the book of industry] ... is closed, can never become a *real* science with a genuine content. What indeed should we think of a science which *primly* abstracts from this large area of human labour, and fails to sense its own inadequacy, even though such an extended wealth of human activity says nothing more to it perhaps than what can be said in one word—"need," "common need"?[14]

Nietzsche, in turn, argues that materialists, who regard needs and labor as primary, are among the undernourished: "It is not possible to take hunger as the *primum mobile*, any more than self-preservation. To understand hunger as a consequence of undernourishment means: hunger as the consequence of a will to power that no longer achieves mastery."[15] This suggests that, unlike Marx who regards production both for self-preservation and self-expression as man's life activity, Nietzsche will maintain that man's will to power must be freed from it.

This disagreement becomes clearer when production is seen, as Marx and Nietzsche see it, as a social activity. Both argue that men form social relations, specifically a division of labor and property relations, in order to produce. But Marx regards production relations as man's original species-life. Nietzsche instead regards them as derivative and argues that they repress individuals' wills to power.

According to Marx, men form cooperative material relations—divisions of labor—to produce and to procreate. He says, "There exists a materialistic connection of men with one another, which is determined by their needs and their mode of production, and which is as old as men themselves."[16] A particular division of labor corresponds to particular property relations, both of which correspond to a particular level of man's powers. But what is the correspondence between the division of labor and property? Marx speaks of them as "identical expressions: in the one the same thing is affirmed with reference to activity as is affirmed in the other with reference to the product of the activity."[17] However, he also refers to particular property relations as functionally determined by a particular division of labor: "The various stages of development in the division of labour are just so many different forms of ownership, i.e., the existing stage in the division of labour determines also the relations of individuals to one another with reference to the material, instrument, and product of labour."[18] It seems that the division of labor and property relations interact reciprocally, but that the division of labor is functionally determinant. That is, a particular division of labor requires particular property relations, and those property relations establish the control individuals have not only over their products, but also over their productive activity.

This reciprocal interaction apears in Marx's distinction between two general forms of the division of labor, i.e., spontaneous and fixed, which correspond to two general forms of property, i.e., communal and private. The spontaneous division of labor by sex, predisposition, need, and/or accident corresponds to

the production of social use values, i.e., to communal production
of communal property. Marx says of these production relations:
"Wherever the want of clothing forced them to it, the human race
made clothes for thousands of years, without a single man
becoming a tailor."[19] The fixed division of labor corresponds to
the production of exchange values, i.e., to independent production
of private property. Marx says of these production relations: "As
soon as the distribution of labour comes into being, each man has
a particular, exclusive sphere of activity, which is forced upon him
and from which he cannot escape."[20] That is, when some men
become tailors, they must continue to produce and sell coats in
order to buy another man's food. Marx argues that the division of
labor only truly becomes such when a division arises between
material and mental labor. Then the labor of some produces
property for others and is controlled by them. Enjoyment and
labor, consumption and production, devolve on different
classes.[21]

Marx argues that, although the spontaneous division of labor
is a necessary condition for the communal production of use
values, only the private production of exchange values necessitates a fixed division of labor. He expresses this rather paradoxically in the following passage:

> To all the different varieties of values in use there
> correspond as many different kinds of useful labour, clas-
> sified according to the order, genus, species, and variety to
> which they belong in the social division of labour. This
> division of labour is a necessary condition for the production
> of commodities, but it does not follow, conversely, that the
> production of commodities is a necessary condition for the
> division of labour.... Only such products can become
> commodities with regard to each other, as result from
> different kinds of labour, each kind being carried on
> independently and for the account of private individuals.[22]

With this, he suggests that neither fixed roles nor private property
for commodity exchange—coercive divisions of labor and coercive class relations—necessarily characterize man's social production. Marx says of these restrictions on production and
appropriation which developed historically: "The general ex-

change of activities and products, which has become a vital condition for each individual—their mutual interconnection—here appears as something alien to them, autonomous, as a thing."[23]

In contrast to Marx, Nietzsche argues that production and appropriation, as social relations, are necessarily restrictive. He agrees with Marx that the social whole cannot exist without cooperation. However, as we saw in chapter 5, domination creates and preserves that cooperation. Nietzsche says, "All unity is unity only as organization and cooperation—just as a human community is a unity—as opposed to an atomistic anarchy, as a pattern of domination that *signifies* a unity but *is* not a unity."[24]

Nietzsche regards work as one part of the socially imposed division of labor. He speaks of work as a social "virtue" which denies individuals autonomy and reduces them to herd instruments.[25] As he succinctly puts it: work is "the best policeman." He says,

> In the glorification of "work," in the unwearied talk of the "blessing of work," I see the same covert idea as in the praise of useful impersonal actions: that of fear of everything individual. Fundamentally, one now feels at the sight of work—one always means by work that hard industriousness from early till late—that such work is the best policeman, that it keeps everyone in bounds and can mightily hinder the development of reason, covetousness, desire for independence. . . . Thus a society in which there is continual hard work will have more security: and security is now worshipped as the supreme divinity.[26]

This means that Nietzsche is less concerned with the social division among varieties of labor than with the social division between labor and leisure. He says, "A higher culture can come into being only where there are two castes of society: the working caste and the idle caste, capable of true leisure; or, to express it more emphatically, the caste of forced labour and the caste of free labour."[27]

Like Marx, Nietzsche associates particular property relations with particular divisions of labor and even with particular divisions among labor and leisure. Yet as he recognizes no original spontaneous division of labor, so he recognizes no original communal property. Property too is originally private: "Those who have possessions are of one mind on one article of faith: 'one must possess something in order to *be* something.' But this is the oldest and healthiest of all instincts."[28] For Nietzsche, property relations are functionally determined by man's will to power, not by his productive powers.[29] The dominant power which organizes the social division of labor, i.e., the power for which others labor, possesses more because of what it is, not because of what it does. Nietzsche describes the "useless splendor" of these masters:

> This is your thirst: to become sacrifices and gifts yourselves; and that is why you thirst to pile up all the riches in your soul. Insatiably your soul strives for treasures and gems, because your virtue is insatiable in wanting to give. You force all things to and into yourself that they may flow back out of your well as the gifts of your love.[30]

It is an aristocratic leisure class which creates the social whole by enslaving laborers.

Although it is imposed, Nietzsche argues that this aristocratic division between labor and leisure, not some spontaneous social production, is natural. He says,

> Handicraft, trade, agriculture, *science*, the greatest part of art, the whole quintessence of *professional* activity, to sum it up, is compatible only with a mediocre amount of ability and ambition; that sort of thing would be out of place among exceptions; the instinct here required would contradict both aristocratism and anarchism. To be a public utility, a wheel, a function, for that one must be destined by nature: it is *not* society, it is the only kind of *happiness* of which the great majority are capable that makes intelligent machines of them.[31]

Social production belongs among the psychological exchanges which are coterminous with society. In this case, when the exchange occurs between a laboring class and a leisure class, respective debtors and creditors, domination creates a unity which conforms to nature.

Although Marx and Nietzsche both criticize capitalist commodity production as the apotheosis of exchange, they do so from these different perspectives. Nietzsche criticizes it because the psychological exchange of work predominates and the distinction between labor and leisure castes is lost. Nietzsche says, *"Slavery today*: a piece of barbarism! Where are those *for whom* they work?"[32] Marx's contrasting concern is that the economic exchange of capital for labor power predominates and completes the distinction between material and mental labor, proletariat and capitalist classes. He says, "The secret of the self-expansion of capital resolves itself into having the disposal of a definite quantity of other people's unpaid labour."[33] Marx then criticizes capitalist commodity production in the name of social production because production *for* economic exchange alienates man's life activity. Nietzsche, in contrast, criticizes it in the name of play because production *as* psychological exchange denies man's will to power.

Capitalist Commodity Production

What do Marx and Nietzsche mean when they speak of capitalist commodity production as the apotheosis of exchange? How do their critiques of the capitalist division of labor and of capitalist property relations differ?

Production for Exchange

To answer this first question, we must consider what each means by a key term, "exchange," with respect to capitalist economics. This becomes confusing because, although Marx uses exchange to describe an economic relation, Nietzsche regards economic exchange as only one form of psychological exchange. Still, when they refer to capitalist society as the apotheosis of exchange, both are describing an economic relation, specifically capitalist production for commodity exchange. They do approach this economic relation differently, however. Nietzsche explains man's productive activity as the result of the demands placed

upon him by commodity exchange. He criticizes capitalist commodity exchange because it makes labor predominate over leisure
and, in doing so, expresses ascetic herd interests. In contrast,
Marx explains the nature of commodity exchange as the result of
production relations. His target is then capitalist commodity
production. Production, not consumption, elevates exchange
value over use value, reinforcing the interests of the capitalist
class.

Nietzsche, who explains capitalist production in terms of
commodity exchange, refers to commerce as the soul of bourgeois culture.[34] He says that supply and demand (which he also
refers to as consumption), not production or personal need,
determine value:

> The man engaged in commerce understands how to appraise
> everything without having made it, and to appraise it
> *according to the needs of the consumer*, not according to his
> own needs; "Who and how many will consume this?" is his
> question of questions. This type of appraisal he then applies
> instinctively and all the time: he applies it to everything, and
> thus also to the productions of the arts and sciences, of
> thinkers, scholars, artists, statesmen, peoples and parties, of
> the entire age: in regard to everything that is made he
> inquires after supply and demand *in order to determine the
> value of a thing in his own eyes*.[35]

Nietzsche argues that in a society where supply and demand (or
consumption) determines value, power is expressed in trade (or
ability to consume), more precisely, in its prerequisite—money.
He says,

> The means employed by the lust for power have
> changed, but the same volcano continues to glow, the
> impatience and the immoderate love demand their sacrifice:
> and what one formerly did "for the sake of God" one now
> does for the sake of money, that is to say, for the sake of that
> which *now* gives the highest feeling of power and good
> conscience.[36]

Nietzsche argues that, once the value of commodities is
separated from material production for material needs—once

power is expressed in money—then men must produce endlessly to satisfy their now endless needs. Continual chase after gain, which Nietzsche understands as continual work and need, is the capitalist ethic. He describes the "breathless haste" with which men work and their incapacity for leisure:

One is ashamed of resting, and prolonged reflection almost gives people a bad conscience. One thinks with a watch in one's hand, even as one eats one's midday meal while reading the latest news of the stock market; one lives as if one always "might miss out on something." "Rather do anything than nothing."[37]

Nietzsche regards capitalist commodity exchange and its accompanying work ethic as ascetic herd psychology. "Blindly raging industriousness" is a social virtue. It deprives the individual of sensitivity and autonomy, and reduces him to a mere herd instrument.[38] Further, although work creates wealth, it simultaneously precludes enjoyment of that wealth. Nietzsche says, "How frugal our educated—and uneducated—people have become regarding 'joy'! ... More and more, *work* enlists all good conscience on its side; the desire for joy already calls itself a 'need to recuperate' and is beginning to be ashamed of itself."[39] He adds, "(The most industrious of all ages—ours—does not know how to make anything of all its industriousness and money, except always still more money and still more industriousness; for it requires more genius to spend than to acquire.)"[40] Nietzsche is contemptuous of this continual "Doing": squandering, not ambition, leisure, not labor, enjoyment, not effort, characterize the truly rich. He says, "Our time, with its aspiration to remedy and prevent accidental distresses and to wage preventive war against disagreeable possibilities, is a time of the *poor*. Our 'rich'—are poorest of all. The true purpose of all riches is forgotten."[41] Capitalist society is the kingdom of heaven of the poor in spirit. The mediocre middle, i.e., the bourgeois shopkeeper and the toollike laborer, rule it through work and need.[42]

Marx agrees with Nietzsche that men produce for commodity exchange in capitalist society, but he criticizes these exchange relations as expressions of specific class interests, not a general ascetic psychology. Marx argues that, as the division of labor and exchange develop, production and exchange for use value become production and exchange for exchange value. Ultimately, exchange for exchange predominates over exchange for use. Marx describes this historical development:

> The need for exchange and for the transformation of the product into a pure exchange value progresses in step with the division of labour, i.e., with the increasingly social character of production. But as the latter grows, so grows the power of *money*, i.e., the exchange relation establishes itself as a power external to and independent of the producers. What originally appeared as a means to promote production becomes a relation alien to the producers. As the producers become more dependent on exchange, exchange appears to become more independent of them, and the gap between the product as product and the product as exchange value appears to widen.[43]

In capitalist society, the division of labor and exchange are complete. Modern industry requires factory organization and hence the exchange of free labor for accumulated capital. In chapter 5, we glimpsed the free laborer, who is doubly free, i.e., free from ownership of his means of production and free to sell his labor power. I will not examine "primitive accumulation" in detail, but Marx stresses that, as laborers were "freed" from their means of production, those means of production were juxtaposed to them as capital.[44] The free laborer then must sell his labor power (the commodity whose use value exceeds its exchange value) to the capitalist for its exchange value. The capitalist purchases labor power to extract surplus value (the difference between the exchange value and the use value of labor power) in exchange, not to produce use values.[45] Marx says that under capitalism M-C-M' supersedes C-M-C:

> The simple circulation of commodities—selling in order to buy—is a means of carrying out a purpose unconnected with circulation, namely, the appropriation of use-values, the satisfaction of wants. The circulation of money as capital is, on the contrary, an end in itself, for the expansion of value takes place only within this constantly renewed movement. The circulation of capital has therefore no limits.[46]

Marx agrees with Nietzsche that capitalist commodity exchange involves an endless chase after gain: "Use values must therefore never be looked upon as the real aim of the capitalist.... The restless never-ending process of profit-making alone is what he aims at."[47] However, Marx does not agree with Nietzsche that need and work characterize the capitalist's chase. Marx argues that only production creates use values which satisfy human wants. The "rich" may live in "breathless haste," but owning, exchanging, and accumulating capital are not productive activities. The exchange value which capitalists realize in circulation is extracted from the labor of others.

Consequently, although both criticize the division of labor and property relations in capitalist society, they again do so from different perspectives. Nietzsche demystifies capitalist commodity exchange and its accompanying work ethic as expressions of the herd's will to power. The capitalist division of labor and capitalist property relations are ascetic: they make work and want ubiquitous. Marx demystifies capitalist commodity production and its accompanying exchange relations as expressions of capitalist class relations which exploit labor. The capitalist division of labor and capitalist property relations restrict work and want to the proletarian class.

Mental and Manual Labor

According to Nietzsche, the division between labor and leisure not only disappears, but labor also becomes increasingly specialized under capitalist commodity production. As we have seen, Nietzsche praises "a division of labor among the affects within society: so individuals and classes produce an incomplete, but for that reason more useful kind of soul."[48] He even provides an "economic justification" for life-denying virtues, in particular, work: men must become "machines" which perform specialized tasks for the "economy of the species."[49] It is not surprising then that he praises the "machine age" because it "teaches in itself the dove-tailed working of masses of men."[50] However, Nietzsche also criticizes specialized machine production because it "sets in motion hardly any but the lower, unthinking forces of the men who serve it," produces "a despairing ennui of the soul," and "robs the piece of work of its pride, of the individual merits and defects that cling to all work that is not machine-made—in otherwords, of its bit of humanity."[51]

Nietzsche's fear is that the herd, in its endless labor to satisfy endless needs, has "bought the facilitation of labor too dear" and has created an "anonymous and impersonal serfdom."[52] Nietzsche describes industrial culture as a stylized barbarity, not a genuine unity of style. The herd's machine production creates parts without a whole, specialization without synthesis. All men have become mere machines, mere herd functions.

Nietzsche calls for a reverse movement to the herd's specialized utility, one which does not abolish it, but builds upon it. "In opposition to this dwarfing and adaptation of man to a specialized utility, a reverse movement is needed—the production of a synthetic, summarizing, justifying man for whose existence this transformation of mankind into a machine is a precondition, as a base on which he can invent his *higher form of being*."[53] By making all individuals specialized utilities, the herd precludes the development of this individual, who might "create and carry together into One" the "fragments and limbs and dreadful accidents" which now characterize man.[54] That is, the herd's ascetic psychology denies the very utility of its work.

Marx agrees with Nietzsche that specialized machine production robs work of meaning, but he criticizes it as an expression of capitalist class interests, not ascetic herd ones. Marx argues that capitalists try to increase the gap between the use value and the exchange value, i.e., between the surplus and the necessary labor, of the labor power they purchase in order to further their boundless desire for surplus value.[55] A structural antagonism therefore exists between capital and labor: capital extracts more surplus value the more it exploits labor power.[56] This antagonism appears in the capitalist division of labor: the increasingly collective production of use values becomes the increasingly exploitative creation of surplus value.

Marx argues that one way capitalists increase the productivity of labor power is through specialized machine production.[57] With machines they also rob labor of all attraction and independence. Labor loses attraction because capitalist machine production requires laborers repeatedly to perform specialized tasks. Marx says,

> At the same time that factory work exhausts the nervous system to the uttermost, it does away with the many-sided play of the muscles, and confiscates every atom of freedom, both in bodily and intellectual activity. The lightening of the labour, even, becomes a sort of torture since the machine does not free the labourer from work, but deprives the work of all interest.[58]

Labor loses independence as well because work is only possible on the capitalists' machines in the capitalists' factories. Objectified labor as capital dominates living labor: "By means of its conversion into an automaton, the instrument of labour confronts the labourer, during the labour-process, in the shape of capital, of dead labour, that dominates, and pumps dry, living labour-power."[59]

Although Marx's analysis of how the capitalist division of labor stultifies workers' creativity parallels Nietzsche's, a more basic difference remains. Nietzsche criticizes the capitalist division of labor because it undermines the division between labor and leisure, making all men social producers and precluding the possibility of the synthetic "One." For Marx, however, the "One" is the capitalist to whom human production, man's species-activity, is subordinated. Marx says that the creation of such a "One" completes the division between material and mental labor. In the following passage, his language resembles Nietzsche's, but its meaning does not:

> It is a result of the division of labour in manufactures, that the labourer is brought face to face with the intellectual potencies of the material process of production, as the property of another, and as a ruling power. This separation begins in simple cooperation, where the capitalist represents to the single workman, the oneness and the will of the associated labour. It is developed in manufacture which cuts down the labourer into a detail labourer. It is completed in modern industry, which makes science a productive force distinct from labour and presses it into the service of capital.[60]

Unlike Nietzsche, for whom individuals are only truly free beyond production, Marx argues that individuals only cultivate their gifts in all directions through free production. Whereas Nietzsche would transcend labor as the herd's specialized utility, Marx would overcome only its alienated capitalist form.

> The transformation, through the division of labour, of personal powers (relationships) into material powers ... can only be abolished by the individuals again subjecting these material powers to themselves and abolishing the division of labour. This is not possible without the community. Only in community (with others has each) individual the means of cultivating his gifts in all directions; only in the community, therefore, is personal freedom possible.[61]

Marx and Nietzsche agree that particular property relations correspond to the capitalist division of labor. I described these property relations generally as the private appropriation of exchange values, i.e., Nietzsche's "continual chase after gain" and Marx's "restless never-ending quest after profit." But what specific relations exist between capitalists and laborers? Why does Nietzsche criticize those relations as expressions of ascetic herd interests? Why does Marx criticize them as expressions of capitalist class interests?

According to Nietzsche, the ubiquitous work characteristic of the capitalist division of labor corresponds to property relations best described as ubiquitous need. Those relations consist of "bourgeois shop-keepers" dominating "tool-like laborers." We have already seen Nietzsche describe the bourgeoisie's need continually to accumulate money. He thinks that they are possessed by their possessions, and suggests

> only up to a certain point does possession make men feel freer and more independent; one step farther, and possession becomes lord, the possessor a slave. The latter must sacrifice his time, his thoughts to the former, and feels himself compelled to an intercourse, nailed to a spot, incorporated with the State—perhaps quite in conflict with his real and essential needs.[62]

In his continual chase after gain, the bourgeois shopkeeper has forgotten the real purposes of riches—leisure and play.

Nietzsche argues that the bourgeoisie, bent on gain, exploit labor. He describes the laborer's condition: "Here one is at the mercy of brute need; one wants to live and has to sell oneself, but one despises those who exploit this need and *buy* the worker."[63] Nietzsche argues instead that work should express the worker's whole personality; one should not "work in order to be paid."[64] He depicts workers as soldiers who should receive honoraria, not wages.[65]

Nietzsche would not abolish private property in order to abolish need. One must possess something in order to be something. He says of communist society: "Plato's Utopian refrain, which is still sung by Socialists, rests upon a deficient knowledge of men."[66] But he would abolish the extremes of property, the worker's too little and the capitalist's too much, which make need ubiquitous in industrial culture. He argues that transport and trade which favor large accumulations of property should be taken out of private hands.[67] In other words, Nietzsche does not criticize private property because it is exploitative (life as will to power is exploitation), but he does criticize capitalist private property because, when everyone needs, exploitation is *vulgar*. He says,

> Oddly, submission to powerful, frightening, even terrible persons, like tyrants and generals, is not experienced as nearly so painful as this submission [the worker's sale of his labor] to unknown and uninteresting persons, which is what all the luminaries of industry are. What the workers see in the employer is usually only a cunning, bloodsucking dog of a man who speculates on all misery.... The manufacturers and entrepreneurs of business probably have been too deficient so far in all those forms and signs of a *higher race* that alone make a *person* interesting.[68]

He even suggests that the capitalists' vulgarity may be the cause of socialism: "If the nobility of birth showed in their eyes and gestures, there might not be any socialism of the masses. For at bottom the masses are willing to submit to slavery of any kind, if only the higher-ups constantly legitimize themselves as higher, as *born* to command—by having noble manners."[69] It is partially as a response to socialism that Nietzsche calls for "a leisure class whose members make things difficult for themselves and exercise much self-overcoming," squanderers without the "poverty of the rich."[70]

In opposition to Nietzsche, Marx does not argue that need is ubiquitous, under capitalist property relations. On the contrary, it is juxtaposed as labor to capital. According to Marx, when laborers are "freed" from their means of production, those means of production, the conditions for the realization of their labor power, assume an independent existence opposed to them as capital. This separation reproduces itself on an ever-expanding scale as capitalists extract surplus value from labor power. The circle M-C-M is the spiral M-C-M'. This means that labor does not realize itself in production, but rather becomes merely a moment in the realization of capital. Marx says,

> The objective conditions of living labour capacity are pre-supposed as having an existence independent of it, as the objectivity of a subject distinct from living labour capacity and standing independently over against it; the reproduction and *realization*, i.e., the expansion of these *objective conditions*, is therefore at the same time their own reproduction and new production as the wealth of an alien subject.[71]

Marx concludes that the laborer, who produces alien products with alien instruments from alien materials, "becomes poorer by the life forces expended" in production. Under capitalist property relations, whether wages be high or low, "accumulation of wealth at one pole is, therefore, at the same time accumulation of misery, agony of toil, slavery, ignorance, brutality, mental degradation, at the opposite pole, *i.e.*, on the side of the class that produces its own product in the form of capital."[72] The laborer's realization in labor becomes his de-realization; labor becomes not the satisfaction of a need, but a sacrifice for the satisfaction of external needs.

Nietzsche responds to the ubiquitous need which capitalism creates merely by limiting private property, but Marx's different end requires that private property be abolished altogether. For

Nietzsche, the free individual possesses property but without either needing it or laboring for it. Marx argues instead that the free individual realizes labor as his need, as his species-activity, and that he can do so only beyond private property in the social appropriation of his social products. Marx says, "*Communism* is the *positive* supersession of *private property* as *human self-estrangement* and hence the true *appropriation* of the *human* essence through and for man; it is the complete restoration of man to himself as a *social*, i.e., human, being."[73]

Marx and Nietzsche both expose capitalist commodity production as a means for expanding man's powers which he has mistaken for his end. Nietzsche says,

> It is clear, what I combat is economic optimism: as if increasing expenditure of everybody must necessarily involve the increasing welfare of everybody. The opposite seems to me to be the case: *expenditure of everybody amounts to a collective loss*: man is *diminished*—so one no longer knows what *aim* this tremendous process has served. An aim? a new aim?—*that* is what humanity needs.[74]

Marx says,

> The only connection which still links them [laborers] with the productive forces and with their own existence— labour—has lost all semblance of self-activity and only sustains their life by stunting it.... Material life appears as the end, and what produces this material life, labour ... as the means.[75]

They concede that capitalist commodity production is a means, however. Nietzsche argues that the industriousness capitalist property relations foster, and the specialized utility found in the capitalist division of labor, make a "luxury surplus of mankind" possible:

> As the consumption of man and mankind becomes more and more economical and the "machinery" of interests and services is integrated ever more intricately, a counter-movement is inevitable. I designate this as the secretion of a

luxury surplus of mankind . . . My concept, my metaphor for this type is . . . the word "overman."[76]

While all men now work and need, capitalist commodity production will make it possible for some to transcend these conditions.

Marx analogously argues that capitalist commodity production is a means for expanding man's powers. He illustrates how the capitalist division of labor can emancipate labor. The continual revolutionizing and lightening of labor due to modern industry allows, even necessitates, the replacement of specialized, fixed labor by varied, mobile functions.

> Modern industry, indeed, compels society, under penalty of death, to replace the detail-worker of today, crippled by life-long repetition of one and the same trivial operation, and thus reduced to the mere fragment of a man, by the fully developed individual, fit for a variety of labours, ready to face any change of production and to whom the different social functions he performs, are but so many modes of giving free scope to his own natural and acquired powers.[77]

In addition, machine production increases productivity. Marx maintains that "capital here—quite unintentionally—reduces human labour, expenditure of energy, to a minimum. This will redound to the benefit of emancipated labor, and is the condition of its emancipation."[78] Increased productivity also intensifies the contradiction under capitalist property relations between the extraction of surplus value in production and the realization of surplus value in exchange. The enforced cooperation of men under the capitalist division of labor which increases surplus value also increases productivity, often beyond the capacity of consumers (who are, after all, largely the exploited laborers) to purchase products. Organized, social production contradicts anarchic, private consumption. As Marx puts it, capital becomes a barrier to capital. More and more destructive business crises ensue until capitalist property relations are finally overcome and replaced by the social appropriation of man's social products.[79] Some who need do presently produce exchange values for others, but capitalist commodity production makes the social production and social appropriation of use values possible.

Although Marx and Nietzsche agree that capitalist commodity production leads to a future organization of production where man's self-creation becomes his self-realization, they see it as a means to very different ends. For Marx, it is a means from forced to free labor. Once men abolish the coercive division of labor and coercive property relations, they can gain control of their productive activity and their products. With this control, they can produce freely even in the realm of necessity. Marx describes this freedom:

> Freedom [in the realm of necessity] can only consist in socialised man, the associated producers, rationally regulating their interchange with Nature, bringing it under their common control, instead of being ruled by it as by the blind forces of Nature; and achieving this with the least expenditure of energy and under conditions most favorable to, and worthy of, their human nature. But it nonetheless still remains a realm of necessity.[80]

Only beyond necessity, though still based upon it, "begins that development of human energy which is an end in itself, the true realm of freedom."[81] In the realm of freedom, men continue to overcome obstacles and to pursue objects. These are liberating activities in themselves, according to Marx. Yet there for the first time "the external aims become stripped of the semblance of merely external natural urgencies, and become posited as aims which the individual himself posits—hence as self-realization, objectification of the subject, hence real freedom, whose action is, precisely, labour."[82]

Nietzsche, in contrast, understands capitalist commodity production as a means to play. It creates the necessary base of industrious specialized utilities, so that some need not produce. Unlike production, play is effortless and purposeless. It is not a means to ends, be they necessary or free, external or internal, but an end in itself. As such, it transcends human activity and becomes divine: " 'play,' the useless—as the ideal of him who is overfull of strength, as 'childlike.' The 'childlikeness' of God, *pais paizon*."[83]

Production Versus Play

Marx and Nietzsche criticize capitalist production for commodity exchange because it makes man's self-creation his self-denial. However, Marx criticizes production for commodity exchange because labor, man's life activity, becomes an alienating activity. Nietzsche's concern is that labor, the herd's psychological exchange, becomes ubiquitous. Where Marx argues that labor must be freed from capitalist economic interests, Nietzsche maintains that the will to power must be freed from labor, for it is an ascetic herd interest. Here, again, their different critiques of modern society contradict rather than complement one another. In his critique of capitalist commodity production, each once more epitomizes the exchange relation which the other attacks.

Nietzsche adopts his "given" economics to question labor as man's psychological denial. It is the bourgeoisie who cannot conceive of labor except as sacrifice for the species. Engels says that

> the narrow-minded view [of the exploiting classes] that a number of "existences" must under all conditions be condemned to the production of *a single* article [is] the view that desires to perpetuate the "different economic varieties" of men distinguished by their mode of living...people who...have sunk so low that they *rejoice* in their own subjection and one-sidedness.[84]

Marx argues that the notion that material and artistic powers grace different individuals, and that some should labor while others "create," results from the division of labor, instead of justifying it. Nietzsche's notion that squanderers exist on a base of laborers epitomizes the capitalists' squandering of human resources.[85] While not everyone will be a painter in communist society, no "potential Raphael" will be hindered by such a division between material and mental labor. No individual will coerce others to perform his share in productive labor, this natural condition of human existence.[86] Engels says, "It must seem monstrous [to the educated classes] that in time to come there will no longer be any professional porters or architects, and that the man who for half an hour gives instructions as an architect will also push a barrow for a period, until his activity as an architect is once again required."[87] In communist society, "there are no painters but at most people who engage in painting among other activities."[88]

Labor in capitalist society—alienated labor on alien materials with alien instruments to produce alien products—is sacrifice. But labor itself is not. Bourgeois relations are not "inviolable natural laws upon which society in the abstract is founded," but a particular historical mode of production. Once labor is freed from the capitalist division of labor and capitalist class relations, it will no longer be man's self-sacrifice, but rather his self-realization. According to Marx, the "individual, 'in his normal state of health, strength, activity, skill, facility,' also needs a normal portion of work, and of the suspension of tranquillity ... overcoming of obstacles is in itself a liberating activity."[89] In communist society, labor allows the individual to develop all his faculties; it is his species-life, not sacrifice for the species.

Unlike Nietzsche, who adopts his "given" economics and cannot conceive of labor except as sacrifice, Marx adopts his "given" psychology and cannot conceive of activity except as labor. Production as man's self-realization is an ascetic herd ideal. There is an association between Nietzsche's argument against production here and his earlier argument against mechanistic worldviews.[90] Nietzsche links the latter to linear notions of history. He argues that linear histories deny life as will to power not only by binding man to past events he cannot change, but also by positing a future state beyond becoming. Nietzsche would presumably argue that Marx's notion of the dialectical development of man's productive powers posits such an end to history when man realizes his powers. From the perspective of communist society, the past (which man cannot change) is condemned. Further, this ideal is a form of being—an absolute moment—which denies becoming. Nietzsche, like Marx, speaks of modern society as a means to an end, but his end is not a moment. It is the affirmation of all moments by willing their eternal recurrence. Nietzsche argues that eternal recurrence overcomes revenge against life, because in it becoming approximates being. That is, in eternal recurrence men transcend not only progress toward ends but also ends themselves.[91] Life in all its moments is affirmed as an end in itself.

Since Marx argues that evolution continues in communist society, this Nietzschean critique is not entirely fair. Still, Nietzsche has another, stronger argument against Marx. Whether communist society is man's historical end-state or his endless self-realization, it denies life as will to power. In either case, production, a purposive life activity predominates. Nietzsche argues that production requires repression: men must be made to produce for society. In communist societies, where "no individual can throw on the shoulders of others his share of productive labor," all men become mere herd instruments.[92] According to Marx, even activity which is not "directly productive," i.e., free, not necessary, labor, involves overcoming obstacles. That is, productive activity which is an end in itself remains a means to ends. Marx cannot conceive of liberated men except as liberated labor. He says, "Labour becomes attractive work, the individual's self-realization, which in no way means that it becomes mere fun, mere amusement.... Really free working, e.g., composing, is at the same time precisely the most damned seriousness, the most intense exertion."[93] For Nietzsche, labor for needs, even labor as a need, denies life as will to power. Life is the purposeless play of the child. Unlike purposive production to overcome obstacles, play is not a means to an end, but an end in itself. Play expresses life's value in the moment. In contrast, the ascetic "blessing of work" is a reaction against life as it is. It is the revenge against life and the "self-glorification of slaves.—Incapacity for *otium*."[94]

Finally, what problems arise here in attempts to synthesize Marx's and Nietzsche's critiques of capitalist commodity production? Synthesizers often try to explain why capitalist commodity production has not fallen from the contradiction between social production and private appropriation by augmenting Marx's economic analysis of capitalist production with Nietzsche's psychological analysis of herd consumption. In various ways, they argue that commodity exchange—Nietzsche's herd psychology—causes workers to cling to their chains, that is, to cling to work and need.

Again, my concern is that those who try to synthesize Marx's and Nietzsche's critiques will fail to do so. They will fail because Marx explains consumption as determined by production and Nietzsche takes the opposite position, that consumption determines production. From this they arrive at incompatible analyses of modern man's problems: Marx would free man's productive powers from economic exchange and Nietzsche would free man, or at least some men, from production because it is a form of psychological exchange. Attempts to synthesize their critiques consequently confront two related contradictions: Does capitalist economics or herd psychology frustrate men? Does production or play fulfill them? These contradictions expose syntheses to the worst features of each critique; they become as bourgeois as Nietzsche and as ascetic as Marx.

Synthesizers become bourgeois because they criticize production in terms of commodity exchange or herd consumption. Like Nietzsche, synthesizers portray capitalist society as a pervasive psychology—exchange as domination—not a specific mode of production. They consequently cannot identify a basic structure of capitalist production, e.g., the conflict between capital and wage labor. Nor can they find a force within capitalist society capable of transforming it, e.g., the proletariat.[95] They can only suggest that individuals beyond the herd's psychology—a psychology which makes men "mere species-beings" or "mere herd functions"—preserve freedom with their total negativity to commodity culture. Although these individuals negate capitalist production in theory, they perpetuate it in practice. Total negativity to exchange as domination precludes the possibility of a positive position which is not itself an expression of domination. Such a "stance" also precludes the possibility of any coherent class analysis or class strategy. Proletarian and party organizations become repressive collectivities. Production, including the problems of alienation and reification, become man's attempts to appropriate the world, a "species-imperialism." Concrete actions in concrete situations, not total negativity (which Nietzsche argues should be overcome by yea-saying anyway), promote social change. Ironically, by negating the basis for their own critiques, synthesizers affirm life in a manner neither they nor Nietzsche intends.

Synthesizers implicitly acknowledge that they need a positive position, a foundation for their critiques, by incorporating a hidden conception of being. They criticize production as the herd's, not merely the capitalists', psychological repression, but promise liberation in the socialist form of that repression. That is, synthesizers continue to idealize Marx's social producer.[96] However, if production is "sublimated eros" or "ascetic ideology" or "capitalist propaganda," then Marx's vision of man's self-realization is merely another life-denying ideal.[97] There is, then, cause for concern that synthesizers' attempts to overcome the limitations of Marx's and Nietzsche's critiques of capitalist commodity production perpetuate economic and psychological exchange.

CHAPTER SEVEN

THE END OF MODERNITY

Theory is capable of gripping the masses when it demonstrates *ad hominem*, and it demonstrates *ad hominem* as soon as it becomes radical. To be radical is to grasp things by the root. But for man the root is man himself. (Marx, "A Contribution to the Critique of Hegel's *Philosophy of Right*. Introduction," p. 251)

I teach you the overman. Man is something that shall be overcome. (Nietzsche, *Thus Spoke Zarathustra*, p. 124)

We have reached an end, not only of this study of Marx and Nietzsche. In a significant sense the modern project is complete. Man's unprecedented domination of nature is his unprecedented subordination to his own creations. He can now destroy whatever he creates. There is also an increasing awareness that political theory, long part of this modern project, requires reconstruction. This concern spans the disciplines of philosophy and political science. Alisdair MacIntyre contends that in contemporary philosophy "what was once morality has to some large degree disappeared—and that this marks a degeneration, a grave cultural loss."[1] Judith Shklar earlier lamented that "the grand tradition of political theory that began with Plato is ... in abeyance" and declared "a reasoned skepticism" the sanest attitude for a world which knows too much for optimism and too little for despair.[2] More recently, and more optimistically, Scott Warren has stated that "these are exciting times for students of political theory. It is possible that we are riding the crest of a wave of what Richard Bernstein has recently called 'the restructuring of social and political theory.'"[3] Bernstein himself has said, "What is needed is a critique that aims to get at the roots; a rethinking of what it means to live a rational life; and a relating of theory to practice."[4]

Marx and Nietzsche participate in this reconstruction, but controversy continues over what parts they should play. For MacIntyre and Shklar, they extend the problems of modernity; for Warren and Bernstein, they help to solve them.[5] My comparison can further this process of reconstruction by illuminating how Marx and Nietzsche can and cannot contribute to it. As dialecticians, they restructure theory, but their dialectics—whether together or alone—cannot restructure society. With these conclusions in mind, I review where we have been.

I began by examining similarities in Marx's and Nietzsche's dialectical approaches to modern society. In chapter 1, I introduced their dialectics, showing how both question previously unquestioned and presumably unquestionable "given" realities by exposing their historical origins. Marx explores the origins of the "economic laws of motion" of modern society in a specific mode of production, i.e., capitalist production. Nietzsche explains "what the ascetic ideal means" by examining how it expresses and serves herd interests in modern society. Although their dialectical histories lack supra- and/or trans-historical principles of morality and justice, they are not relativistic. By revealing that "given" social structures originate in historical forms of domination, Marx and Nietzsche illuminate their scope and their limits. For both, dialectical history is critical history.

Marx's and Nietzsche's dialectics are not formal methods, however. They are attempts conceptually to convey and to criticize the character of history. This means that they not only have a similar structure, but also share several substantive hypotheses. In chapter 2, I argued that Marx and Nietzsche, as critics of German idealism and their own early alternatives to it, view man as a natural, historical being. Man creates the meaning of history from within history. They agree that men create themselves historically by projecting their powers over nature, that men form social relations as they dominate nature, and that through those social relations they develop their distinctively human capacity to reason. This capacity allows men, unlike animals, to expand their creative powers beyond the mere satisfaction of material needs. Men potentially can create universally and freely.

In chapter 3, I discussed how Marx and Nietzsche think that man's tendency to expand his powers functionally determines the development (rise, functioning, and fall) of societies. Both oppose explanations of history in terms of immanent and/or transcendent teleologies and causal determinants. Both also deny that history is an incoherent collection of events. They regard societies as organic wholes, the order of whose parts is functionally determined and explained by the current level of man's creative powers. A particular social whole will be overcome when its order becomes dysfunctional for, that is, when it contradicts, the continued expansion of man's powers. They agree that such a contradiction exists in modern society. Marx views capitalist economics and Nietzsche views ascetic psychology as social structures which once were functional for man's expanding powers, but which now fetter them. Since each exposes a contradiction in modern society, each maintains that it must and will be overcome.

As dialecticians, Marx and Nietzsche contribute to the restructuring of social and political theory by suggesting that theorists stop regarding the very characteristics of truth, i.e., its conditional nature, as objections to it.[6] Truth is not the non-dialectical correspondence of preordered objects and abstract subjects. We are active, producing, creating subjects, and the objective world which confronts us is partially the product of our historical activity. From this dialectical perspective, truth becomes what we value and what is valuable for us. Such conceptions of truth have been criticized as relativist and historicist. But they are so only to those who seek absolute knowledge.[7] Nietzsche argues that theorists who seek such certainty are truly nihilistic: they continue to pursue what they know is not to be found. In contrast, Marx and Nietzsche suggest how we might redefine truth as conditioned knowledge of a conditional reality. According to this conception of truth, non-dialectical truths are illusions. They mystify their own historical origins and those of the society for which they function. They portray economic, political, and ideological forms which are functional for dominant powers as the fulfillment of eternal, natural laws. By demystifying such truths, indeed such a conception of truth, Marx and Nietzsche reveal that our own creations oppress us and thereby free us to overcome them. Theory and practice can merge, since their interpretations of modern society are meant to change it.

Despite these similarities, Marx's and Nietzsche's critiques of modern society differ radically. Both have dialectical histories, but each has a different historical dialectic. Marx views history as the development of man's productive powers, and Nietzsche sees it as the expansion of his will to power. Since each approaches modern society from his own perspective, they disagree over what oppresses and what can liberate man. Marx argues that the capitalist mode of production alienates men from their products, their productive activity, and their fellow producers. Nietzsche attacks ascetic ideals, especially those of slave moralists, because they sicken man's will to power and prevent him from creating life-affirming values.

My comparison revealed not only how their perspectives differ, but also how each perspective is incomplete. Through a Marxian critique of Nietzsche and a Nietzschean critique of Marx, we saw that neither fully escapes his "given" reality. In fact, neither overcomes what the other identifies as the source of man's oppression. Marx criticizes capitalist economics from an ascetic psychological perspective. He would liberate man as a rational, social producer from the capitalist mode of production. Nietzsche revalues ascetic psychology from the perspective of capitalist economics. He regards rationality, society, and productivity as ascetic ideals. In chapters 4 through 6, I examined their different and incomplete critiques of the ideology, politics, and economics of modern society.

In chapter 4, I compared Marx's and Nietzsche's critiques of modern ideology—Christian and scientific metaphysics—as illusions. Both expose Christian and scientific metaphysics as fetishes of exchange relations, but Marx understands exchange economically and Nietzsche understands it psychologically. For Marx, Christian and scientific fetishes express man's alienation from his species-life in respective illusory communities, social life with God in heaven and social life among commodities on earth. For Nietzsche these fetishes express herd man's denial of individuals in respective illusory subjects, the theistic truth of God and the atheistic truth of matter. Marx demystifies these bourgeois illusions to reveal the truth of man. Nietzsche demystifies truth itself to free man from ascetic ideals. Marx would regard Nietzsche's skepticism as an expression of man's alienation by capitalist economics, and Nietzsche would regard Marx's scientific socialism as the expression of man's denial by ascetic psychology.

These ideologies of modern society correspond to certain political forms. In chapter 5, I compared Marx's and Nietzsche's responses to liberal democracy as human oppression. Marx revealed that liberal democracy expressed economic exchange relations, and Nietzsche portrayed it as the manifestation of psychological exchange. According to Marx, liberal democracy emancipates egoistic man and oppresses species-man. In contrast, Nietzsche argues that it emancipates herd altruism and oppresses aristocratic individualism. Where Marx thinks that social man must be freed from its illusory identity of individual and society, Nietzsche argues that individuals must be freed from society itself because it is this illusory identity. For Marx, Nietzschean individualism expresses man's alienation in capitalist society. For Nietzsche, Marxian socialism expresses man's denial by ascetic psychology.

Marx's and Nietzsche's views on ideology and politics are to some extent based upon their critiques of modern economics. In chapter 6, I examined their critiques of capitalist production—production for commodity exchange—as man's self-denial. Again, they begin from different perspectives: Marx explains economic exchange in terms of production relations; Nietzsche explains production relations in terms of psychological exchange. Where Marx criticizes capitalist production because production for exchange value necessitates the alienation of labor, Nietzsche criticizes capitalist commodity exchange because it makes production, an ascetic herd activity, ubiquitous. Their alternatives differ correspondingly: Marx would overcome forced with free labor; Nietzsche would overcome labor itself with play. To Marx, Nietzsche's critique of labor mistakes alienated labor, the product of capitalist production relations, for labor itself. To Nietzsche, Marx's defense of free labor mistakes an ascetic activity for human fulfillment.

Although Marx and Nietzsche suggest how we might restructure theory dialectically, we cannot adopt either of their dialectics for restructuring society. The limitations of both perspectives can be characterized in their now-familiar terminology of means and ends. Both argue that modern society, a means for expanding man's powers, has been mistaken for man's end. Yet each mistakes the means which the other criticizes for that end. Each projects into the future the problems he neglected in the past. Marx's socialism portrays an ascetic ideal—rational, social, productive individuals—as human nature. Nietzsche's overman portrays a bourgeois ideal—skeptical, individualistic, playful men—as human nature. Their radically different perspectives confront us with a choice: do we want science or skepticism? Socialism or individualism? Production or play? However, we have seen that this is a choice between unacceptable alternatives.

For this reason alone it is not surprising that many twentieth-century social and political theorists have refused to choose between Marx and Nietzsche. Encouraged by the similarities I have discussed, they have tried to overcome the limitations of each perspective by embracing aspects of the other. Their syntheses of Marx and Nietzsche have also been prompted by historical developments. In varying ways, synthesizers argue that the economic forces Marx hoped would liberate man now coincide with the psychological forces Nietzsche fears oppress him: modern science coincides with repressive reason, class conflict coincides with mass politics, capitalist production coincides with herd consumption. This presumed convergence suggests that historical materialism requires redefinition, and that a redefinition which adopts Nietzsche's analysis of man's cultural domination by ascetic psychology might explain why capitalism has not fallen from the weight of its economic contradictions.

Yet combinations of Marx and Nietzsche also cannot direct the restructuring of society. While each perspective is inadequate alone, together they become incoherent. As we have seen, each illuminates but does not obviate the other's limitations. They contradict, not complement, one another, and this is not a dialectical contradiction. Attempts to combine them end in schizophrenia, not synthesis. I have focused less upon the historical circumstances which prompted syntheses of Marx and Nietzsche and more upon the incompatibility of their perspectives. But these concerns are clearly related. If history is structured dialectically, then it will have a discernible logic. History will be the self-creation of the human species, and societies will be wholes whose parts are ordered and reordered by man's expanding powers. Syntheses of Marx and Nietzsche beg a question: how can an incoherent theory explain the coherence of history? Although the logic of history is continually challenged by disparate and irrational events, we cannot afford the synthesizers' response. By adopting Marx and Nietzsche, they abandon logic and history. Their contradictory critiques of modern society resign us to it.

I have not criticized any specific attempt to combine Marx and Nietzsche, but rather have tried to demonstrate the contradictions between their perspectives; the synthesizers should shoulder the burden of proof and show how they avoid or resolve those contradictions. Now, using an "ideal type" synthesizer as a heuristic tool, I can summarize the potential consequences of those contradictions. I must emphasize that this illustration is more and less than a critique of any specific synthesis. As an "ideal-type," this synthesizer is an abstraction. However, his value as a heuristic tool rests upon his character as an abstraction from concrete syntheses. He cannot portray the complex contradictions and attempted resolutions of any specific synthesis, but he can suggest general problems for all such attempts. This picture of him has emerged.

First, as a critic of modern ideology, he simultaneously adopts Nietzschean skepticism and Marxian science. His critique of modern ideology becomes contradictory because, as a Nietzschean skeptic, he rejects rationality as man's psychological repression and, as a Marxian scientist, he liberates man's rationality from economic exploitation. Here, his synthesis shares the worst features of each critique. He becomes bourgeois because as a skeptic he can only reject, not interpret or change, reality. Social criticism directed toward social change requires a rational foundation and collective action. If rationality and collectivity are coterminous forms of psychological repression, then only the speechless, solipsistic individual can be free. Still, as a Marxian scientist, he wants to criticize and to change reality. With socialist ideals, he becomes ascetic, continuing to deny life in the name of man's truth.

Second, as a critic of modern politics, this synthesizer is a Nietzschean individualist and a Marxian socialist. A contradiction is also apparent here. As Nietzschean individualist, he would liberate individuals from herd psychology, but as Marxian socialist, he would liberate species-man from economic individualism. Again, this contradiction means that he shares the worst features of each critique. He becomes bourgeois because he finds revolutionary consciousness only in individuals beyond society, and not in the proletariat within it. With this, he divorces political activity from social relations, renouncing the structural preconditions for a socialist revolution. He is simultaneously ascetic because he insists upon revolutionizing, not escaping, society. Yet, without the structural preconditions for a free society, he can only create non-conformist theories or inspire charismatic individuals to impose "freedom." Scientific socialism remains another life-denying ideal.

Finally, as a critic of modern economics, this synthesizer espouses Nietzschean play and Marxian production. His critique of capitalism is contradictory because Nietzsche wants to free men from production and Marx wants men to produce freely. He also shares the worst features of each economic critique. He becomes bourgeois because he criticizes capitalist production as a part of the herd's psychology—exchange as domination—not as a specific mode of production. Without a scientific analysis of capitalist production, of its structure and of forces within it capable of transforming it, he cannot suggest a coherent class strategy. This synthesizer does suggest that a few individuals beyond herd psychology—beyond production—can criticize it, but he does not suggest how they can change it. He becomes ascetic because, although he criticizes production as the herd's psychological oppression, not merely the capitalist's economic exploitation, of man, he still idealizes production as man's life activity. Synthesizers' attempts to overcome Marx's psychological and Nietzsche's economic limitations perpetuate the economics and the psychology of modern society.

If Marx, Nietzsche, and their mutual heirs cannot solve the problems of modern society, then where does this leave us? In the *Genealogy of Morals* Nietzsche says, " 'What are you really doing, erecting an ideal or knocking one down?' I may perhaps be asked." He answers, "If a temple is to be erected *a temple must be destroyed*: that is the law—let anyone who can show me a case in which it is not fulfilled!"[8] We stand at the end of the tradition of political theory that began with Plato. Our ideals have been knocked down, our temples are destroyed. We have stood here for some time, trying to salvage something of our past. It is time to move on. We are left to create a new practical rationality which renounces domination and retains democracy. This end should be that beginning.

NOTES

I have provided citations to German and English editions. In choosing translations, I have tried to balance accuracy and accessibility.

For Marx, the German edition I have used is the *Marx-Engels Werke*, abbreviated *MEW* and followed by volume and page numbers. Since no definitive English edition of Marx's complete works yet exists, I have cited easily available anthologies.

I cite Nietzsche's works by title and aphorism whenever possible, since these citations correspond for English and German editions. When this is not possible, I cite an English edition and Karl Schlecta's *Werke in drei Bände*, abbreviated *WdB* and followed by volume and page numbers. Although Colli-Montinari is the definitive German edition, I chose Schlecta for acessibility. Given the controversy surrounding the Schlecta edition of the *Nachlass*, I recommend another German edition for references to *Der Wille zur Macht*.

1. The Problem of Modernity

1. Scholars differ regarding the status of alienation in Marx's work. Two extreme interpretations exist: 1) Marx's early humanism has a materialist basis (Avineri, *The Social and Political Thought of Karl Marx*) or Marx's early work on alienation determined his later economic writings (Löwith, *From Hegel to Nietzsche*), that is, it does not make sense to speak of an early versus a late Marx; 2) Marx's work underwent an epistemological break between the *Economic and Philosophical Manuscripts* and *The German Ideology* from a Feuerbachian anthropological problematic to a historical materialist one (Althusser, *For Marx*), that is, the late Marx differs qualitatively from the early Marx.

I do not accept either of these extremes. Instead, I argue that a gradual evolution occurred in Marx's thought from his early, largely philosophical works to his later, more scientific ones. Marx established the need for a materialist view of reality in his *Critique of Hegel's Doctrine of the State* (1843) and in his introduction to "A Contribution to the Critique of Hegel's *Philosophy of Right*" (1843–44); he indicated that this must be an active, i.e., historical, materialism in the *Economic and Philosophical Manuscripts* (1844) and the "Theses on Feuerbach" (1845); he began to develop the premises of historical materialism in *The German Ideology* (1845–46); and he provided his most complete exposition of historical materialism in his analysis of capitalist development in *Capital* (1867–). He retained his concern with alienation throughout his gradual evolution from an anthropological concept of "Man" to historical materialist conceptions of men in capitalist society. He shows his recurring concern with alienated labor by referring to it in *The German Ideology*, *Capital*, and the *Grundrisse*, as well as in his early writings. (For a more detailed discussion of Marx's development, see chapter 2.)

2. *MEW* 23:86; Marx, *Capital*, 1:72.

3. The commodity form of production for exchange is the embryonic form of bourgeois production; money and capital are its later, more developed forms (*MEW* 23:94–95; *Capital* 1:81–82).

4. *WdB* 1:213–214; Nietzsche, *Use and Abuse of History*, pp. 7–8.

5. According to Nietzsche, life itself is will to power: "The world viewed from inside, the world defined and determined according to its 'intelligible character'—it would be 'will to power' and nothing else" (*Beyond*, aphorism #36). As will to power, "life itself is *essentially* appropriation, injury, overpowering of what is alien and weaker; suppression, hardness, imposition of one's own forms, incorporation and at least, at its mildest, exploitation" (*ibid.*, aphorism #259).

6. Nietzsche, *Genealogy*, third essay, section #27.

7. Tracy Strong describes Nietzsche's understanding of this nihilistic condition well: "The present structure of human understanding forces men to continue searching for that which their understanding tells them is not to be found" (*Friedrich Nietzsche and the Politics of Transfiguration*, p. 77).

8. *MEW* 3:21; Marx and Engels, *German Ideology*, p. 42.

9. *WdB* 2:323; Nietzsche, *Zarathustra*, p. 172.

10. Karl Mannheim outlines the pursuit of origins as such a critical enterprise and sparked this understanding of structural similarities in Marx's and Nietzsche's historical methods ("The Sociology of Knowledge").

11. Nietzsche, *Genealogy*, preface, aphorism #6.

12. Nietzsche, *Beyond*, aphorism #6.

13. Nietzsche, *Genealogy*, third essay, section #24.

14. Marx, *Grundrisse*, g8, e87.

15. *MEW* 13:8–9; Marx, "Preface to *A Contribution to the Critique of Political Economy*," p. 425.

16. *MEW* 23:95; Marx, *Capital*, 1:80–81.

17. For an example, see George Sabine, *A History of Political Theory* (Hinsdale, Ill.: Dryden Press, 1973), pp. 810–813.

18. The most recent example of this general orientation is Robert Eden's *Political Leadership and Nihilism*. To his initial question "What becomes of liberal politics if we abandon the plane of theoretical understanding as Weber and Nietzsche do, to reconstitute the liberal cause on the plane of practical historicism?" (p. 35), Eden responds, "One must either rely directly upon political philosophy, and defend liberal democratic institutions by recovering the legislative science of modern liberal politics, or give way before Nietzsche's alternative" (p. 210). (See my review, *American Political Science Review* (March 1985), 79(1):279.) Other examples here include Dannhauser, *Nietzsche's View of Socrates*; MacIntyre, *After Virtue*; Stern, *A Study of Nietzsche*; and Strauss, *Natural Right and History*.

19. In *Nietzsche in German Politics and Society*, Hinton Thomas combats the traditional association of Nietzsche with the Nazis by illustrating his influence upon socialist and anarchist movements.

20. The classic of such interpretations remains Walter Kaufmann's *Nietzsche: Philosopher, Psychologist, Antichrist* (pp. 251–252). More recently, Richard Schacht has followed the same path. In an otherwise superb analysis of Nietzsche's notion of philosophy as interpretation, he acknowledges that life as will to power involves a basic tendency to dominate, but interprets the will to power as "ordering transformation," not exploitation or legislation (*Nietzsche*, p. 228). The latter characterizations he dismisses as rhetorical excesses peripheral to Nietzsche's philosophical project, the revaluation of values. Other such examples include Danto, *Nietzsche as Philosopher*, ch. 4, and Heidegger's *Nietzsche*, especially vol. 1, *The Will to Power as Art*, ch. 10. Heidegger's interpretation has been especially influential among the French new Nietzscheans.

An exception to this tendency in the philosophical literature is Ofelia Schutte's *Beyond Nihilism*. Schutte, in fact, accuses interpreters who ignore Nietzsche's politics of self-deceit or censorship (p. 186). (See my review of Schutte and Schacht, "The Newest Nietzsche.")

21. *MEW, Erganzungsband*, 1:516; Marx, *Economic and Philosophical Manuscripts*, p. 328.

22. *WdB* 2:284; Nietzsche, *Zarathustra*, p. 129.

23. Nietzsche, *Genealogy*, second essay, section #6.

24. Nietzsche, *Will to Power*, aphorism #561.

25. Mark Warren argues that this is precisely how Nietzsche should enter the canon of political philosophy. This typology of Nietzsche interpretations is also adapted from Warren. (See his "Nietzsche and Political Philosophy.")

26. Tillich, "Existential Philosophy," pp. 65–66.

27. Mitzmann, *Iron Cage*, p. 187.

28. Löwith, *From Hegel to Nietzsche*, p. 174.

29. Strong, *Friedrich Nietzsche and the Politics of Transfiguration*, pp. 15, 43, 46.

30. Barth, *Truth and Ideology*, ch. 6.

31. Warren, "Nietzsche and Political Philosophy," pp. 192, 194, 199.

32. Quoted by Mitzmann, *Iron Cage*, p. 182.

33. Franz Mehring, review of Kurt Gisner, *Psychopathia Spiritualis*, *Die neue Zeit*. (1891–92), 10: 668–669. Cited by Warren, "Nietzsche and Political Philosophy," p. 210.

34. Sorel, *Reflections on Violence*.

35. Foucault, *Power/Knowledge*, p. 90.

36. *Ibid.*, pp. 104–105. Also see pp. 52–53.

37. Derrida examines Nietzsche's styles as a method for deconstruction in *Spurs*.

38. Derrida, *Positions*, p. 62. For an attempt to associate the two, see Ryan, *Marxism and Deconstruction*. This attempt is facilitated by Derrida's emphasis upon the method of Nietzsche's philosophy, not its substance. Derrida says, "The question posed by the spurring operation is more powerful than any content, thesis, or meaning" (*Spurs*, p. 107).

39. See Camus' "Nietzsche and Nihilism," *The Rebel*, Merleau-Ponty's *Humanism and Terror*, and Sartre's *Critique of Dialectical Reason*.

40. For occasional remarks about Nietzsche's influence upon critical theory, see Jay, *The Dialectical Imagination*. Jay suggests there that, in the *Dialectic of Enlightenment*, Adorno and Horkheimer "no longer sought answers to cultural questions in the material substructure of society. In fact, their analysis of the exchange principle as a key to understanding western society was as reminiscent of Nietzsche's discussion in the *Genealogy of Morals* as Marx's in *Capital*" (p. 259). For more sustained discussions of that influence, see Pütz, "Nietzsche and Critical Theory," and Rose, *The Melancholy Science*.

41. Controversy continues regarding Marx's concept of justice (or lack thereof) since Allen Wood's "The Marxian Critique of Justice." On this issue, see Cohen et al., eds., *Marx, Justice, and History*; Gilbert, "An Ambiguity in Marx's and Engels' Account of Justice and Equality"; and the review article by Geras, "The Controversy About Marx and Justice."

42. It is interesting to note that Jürgen Habermas remains uneasy with the implications of Nietzsche's philosophy for Marxism. He argues that Nietzsche correctly recognizes the association between knowledge and interest, but incorrectly concludes that it necessitates a profound skepticism about the possibility of truth. Habermas says, "Nietzsche carried to its end the self-abolition of epistemology inaugurated by Hegel and continued by Marx, arriving at the self-denial of reflection" (*Knowledge and Human Interests*, p. 290). Habermas interprets this "position" as "the cynicism of a, as it were, self-denying bourgeois consciousness" (*Legitimation Crisis*, p. 122). He praises Nietzsche's

courage in attacking rationality, however, and portrays the French new Nietzscheans as mere innocents by comparison. They do not feel Nietzsche's pain at the death of God, and even rejoice in the very crisis he feared.

In an effort to prevent the confusion of critical theorists and poststructuralists, Habermas distinguishes between their receptions of Nietzsche. In "The Entwinement of Myth and Enlightenment," he discusses Adorno's and Horkheimer's Nietzschean model in the *Dialectic of Enlightenment*. He argues that in the process of criticizing Enlightenment they destroy the basis of their own critique of ideology: "Critique becomes total: it turns against reason as the foundation of its own analysis" (p. 22). But paradoxically Adorno and Horkheimer want to hold on to the premise of Enlightenment, to continue to use the same critique they have declared false (p. 22). This distinguishes them from the French who, by identifying power and reason, consume critique itself (p. 23). But it also leaves Adorno and Horkheimer caught in an unresolved contradiction, one between Marxian and Nietzschean premises (p. 29).

Others who are uneasy with Nietzsche's influence upon Marxism include Asher, "Deconstruction's Use and Abuse of Nietzsche"; Jay, *Marxism and Totality*, epilogue; Miller, "Some Implications of Nietzsche's Thought for Marxism"; and Veyne, "Ideology According to Marx and According to Nietzsche."

43. *MEW* 3:5–6; Marx, "Theses on Feuerbach," #3.

2. Natural, Historical Man

1. For examples, see Shklar, *After Utopia*, p. 90, and McLellan, *Karl Marx*, pp. 6–29.

2. See, here, Löwith, *From Hegel to Nietzsche*, pp. 179–199, and Miller, "Some Implications of Nietzsche's Thought for Marxism," pp. 27–28.

3. Judith Shklar argues that romanticism is "the unifying element in Nietzsche's thought" (*After Utopia*, p. 52), while Walter Kaufmann says that "the romantic was precisely what he [Nietzsche] opposed" (*Nietzsche: Philosopher, Psychologist, Antichrist*, p. 15).

This opposition arises in part because Shklar and Kaufmann fail to distinguish between early and late German romanticism (cf. Silz, *Early German Romanticism*) and try to compare Nietzsche to an image of the "true" romantic. I think one can (and I will) argue that Nietzsche shares the positive, progressive strains of early romanticism, which he sees in the Feuerbachian Wagner, and rejects the renunciation of late romanticism, which he sees in the Schopenhauerian Wagner. Nietzsche himself distinguishes between early and late romanticism, saying that while romantics may begin as optimists, they end as Christian ascetics. Shklar also makes such a distinction (p. 61, note 150), but she does not sustain it when she analyzes Nietzsche's romanticism.

4. Marx, Letter to Father (November 10, 1837) in *Selected Correspondence*.

5. Dupré, *The Philosophical Foundations of Marxism*, p. xiii.

6. McLellan, *Karl Marx*, p. 121.

7. *WdB* 2:1114; Nietzsche, *Ecce Homo*, p. 736; Nietzsche, *Gay Science*, aphorism #357.

8. McLellan, *The Young Hegelians*, p. 125.

9. Löwith, *From Hegel to Nietzsche*, p. 185.

10. Nietzsche, Letters to Taine (July 4, 1887) and Brandes (December 2, 1887) in *Selected Letters*; *WdB* 2:1114; Nietzsche, *Ecce Homo*, p. 734.

11. Löwith, *From Hegel to Nietzsche*, pp. 174–175.

12. McLellan, *The Young Hegelians*, p. 80.

13. Hayman discusses Nietzsche's indirect connection to Marx through the Feuerbachian Wagner (*Nietzsche*, p. 134). For a discussion of the tensions between Nietzsche's Wagnerian and Schopenhauerian roots, see Love, *Young Nietzsche*, pp. 56–58.

14. Wagner, *My Life*, p. 522.

15. *Ibid.*, p. 615.

16. *Ibid.*, p. 731.

17. Nietzsche, *Genealogy*, third essay, section #3.

18. Nietzsche, *Case of Wagner*, section #5.

19. *MEW, Erganzungsband*, 1:8; Marx, Letter to Father (November 10, 1837) in *Selected Correspondence*.

20. Nietzsche, *Birth of Tragedy*, "Self-Criticism," aphorism #6; Love, *Young Nietzsche*, p. 39.

21. Marx, Letter to Father (November 10, 1837) in *Selected Correspondence*.

22. *Ibid.*

23. *Ibid.*

24. *WdB* 2:961; Nietzsche, *Twilight*, p. 484.

25. Nietzsche, *Birth of Tragedy*, section #18, and *Daybreak*, aphorism #198.

26. Nietzsche, *Will to Power*, aphorism #414.

27. For a critique of interpretations of Nietzsche as a radical Kantian, see Strong, "Text and Pretexts," p. 167.

28. Nietzsche, *Will to Power*, aphorism #253.

29. *Ibid.*

30. *WdB* 2:958–959; Nietzsche, *Twilight*, p. 481.

31. *MEW, Erg.*, 1:584; Marx, *Economic and Philosophical Manuscripts*, p. 396.

32. *MEW* 4:127; Marx, *Poverty of Philosophy*, p. 106.

33. *MEW* 1:241; Marx, *Critique of Hegel's Doctrine of the State*, p. 98.

34. *WdB* 1:263–264; Nietzsche, *Use and Abuse of History*, pp. 52–53.

35. Nietzsche, *Gay Science*, aphorism #357.

36. *MEW, Erg.*, 1:574; Marx, *Economic and Philosophical Manuscripts*, pp. 385–386.
37. *MEW, Erg.*, 1:575; *Economic and Philosophical Manuscripts*, p. 386.
38. *MEW, Erg.*, 1:575–576; *Economic and Philosophical Manuscripts*, p. 387.
39. *MEW, Erg.*, 1:577; *Economic and Philosophical Manuscripts*, p. 389.
40. *WdB* 2:300–301; Nietzsche, *Zarathustra*, p. 146.
41. *MEW* 3:7; Marx, "Theses on Feuerbach," #11.
42. Nietzsche, *Will to Power*, aphorism #423.
43. I refer here especially to the first generation of critical theorists, members of the Institute for Social Research under the direction of Max Horkheimer. For Horkheimer himself and his frequent collaborator, Theodor Adorno, the declaration that theorizing is practice springs as much from conviction as necessity. Their conviction, one manifest in Adorno's critique of identity and Horkheimer's attack upon instrumental reason, is that marxists' (if not Marx's) insistence that practice proves the truth merely extends the anthropomorphic objectification of life characteristic of the dialectic of enlightenment. In response to those who would characterize their position as Left Hegelian, Adorno argues that "the call for unity of theory and practice has irresistibly degraded theory to a servant's role, removing the very traits it should have brought to that unity. . . . Whereas theory succumbed in the vaunted mixture, practice became nonconceptual, a piece of the politics it was supposed to lead out of; it became the prey of power" (*Negative Dialectics*, p. 143). There is also an element of necessity here, however. Horkheimer laments that in the administered nightmare of the twentieth century, theory is the only form of praxis still open to honest men. (Jay, *Dialectical Imagination*, p. 280).
   Herbert Marcuse's analysis of one-dimensionality contributes to this pervasive pessimism. Although he identifies forces on the margins of society—the outsiders and the outcast—which might revolutionize it, the forces containing qualitative change predominate: "The chance is that the historical extremes may meet again: the most advanced consciousness of humanity, and its most exploited force. It is nothing but a chance. The critical theory of society possesses no concepts which could bridge the gap between the present and its future: holding no promise and showing no success, it remains negative" (*One-Dimensional Man*, p. 201).
44. Nietzsche, *Beyond*, aphorism #252.
45. *MEW* 3:21; Marx and Engels, *German Ideology*, p. 42.
46. Bertell Ollman advances this argument in its most extreme form. He maintains that Marx's writings are "expressions of a single theoretical scheme . . . [that], despite the fact that anthropology and psychology cease to be major subjects, man continues, of necessity, to occupy a central position in Marx's theories. And the men who act and interact in

Marx's later writings are no different from those who appear in his early works. The conception of human nature with which he began has hardly altered" (*Alienation*, p. xiv). Proponents of less extreme forms of this argument admit that Marx's focus changed from primarily philosophical critiques of German idealism and political economy to primarily historical materialist critiques of capitalism, but argue that Marx maintains a particular theory of man's essence throughout. Consequently, they find the seeds of Marx's later materialism in his early humanism—"The humanistic vision of the young Marx was based on a materialist epistemology" (Avineri, *The Social and Political Thought of Karl Marx*, p. 12)—or the fulfillment of Marx's early humanism in his later materialism—"Labor and capital are not at all for Marx only economic categories; they were anthropological categories, imbued with a value judgment which is rooted in his humanistic position" (Fromm, *Marx's Concept of Man*, p. 40)—or both: "What must be seen and understood is that economics and politics have become the economic-political basis of the theory of revolution through a quite particular philosophical interpretation of human existence and its historical realization.... The revolutionary critique of political economy itself has a philosophical foundation, just as conversely, the philosophy underlying it already contains revolutionary praxis." (Marcuse, "Foundation of Historical Materialism," pp. 4–5).

47. Althusser, *For Marx.*

48. *Ibid.*, p. 67.

49. *Ibid.*, p. 68.

50. *Ibid.*

51. *Ibid.*, p. 46.

52. *Ibid.*, pp. 89–93.

53. *Ibid.*, p. 83.

54. *Ibid.*, pp. 110, 158.

55. *Ibid.*, p. 227.

56. *Ibid.*, p. 214.

57. *Ibid.*, p. 229.

58. *Ibid.*, p. 227.

59. *MEW, Erg.*, 1:512, 515; Marx, *Economic and Philosophical Manuscripts*, pp. 324, 327; *MEW* 23:86–87, 93, 649; Marx, *Capital*, 1:72, 79, 621.

60. Marx, Letter to Ruge (March 13, 1843) in *Selected Correspondence.*

61. *MEW* 1:378, 385; Marx, "A Contribution to the Critique of Hegel's *Philosophy of Right*. Introduction," pp. 244, 251.

62. *MEW* 3:6, 7; Marx, "Theses on Feuerbach," #6, #7; *MEW* 3:41–45; Marx and Engels, *German Ideology*, pp. 60–64.

63. *MEW, Erg.*, 1:543; Marx, *Economic and Philosophical Manuscripts*, p. 355.

64. Althusser, *For Marx*, p. 83.

65. In *Reading Capital,* Althusser refers to his interpretation of Marx, an interpretation that denies Marx's self-proclaimed debt to Hegel's dialectic, as a "symptomatic reading." By this he means that his interpretation reveals the qualitatively new questions which Marx answers but cannot formulate because he must operate with "borrowed" idealist and/or empiricist concepts. Althusser says, "We have simply tried to apply to Marx's reading the '*symptomatic*' reading . . . by measuring the problematic initially visible in his writings against the invisible problematic contained in the paradox of *an answer which does not correspond to any question posed*" (p. 28). And he argues that, given the intellectual uncertainty surrounding changes of problematics, "there is nothing incomprehensible in the paradoxical fact that Marx treated his original method of analysis as a method that already existed even in the instant when he invented it, and in the fact that he thought he was borrowing from Hegel even in the instant when he broke his Hegelian moorings" (p. 51).

This symptomatic reading is suspect to me for several reasons. First, once one abandons Marx's own remarks about his dialectic, one cannot distinguish—as Althusser does—between scientific and ideological formulations of "unasked questions." Necessary standards of evidence are lacking. Second, since Marx's own remarks about his dialectic are coherent, I see no justification for explaining away those remarks by probing for some "inner darkness of exclusion" (p. 26). Perhaps such an approach is justifiable if it reveals hidden coherence in an ostensibly incoherent philosophy; this is not the case with Althusser's interpretation of Marx. Third, Althusser's method of reading Marx presumes a notion of science—development through "epistemological breaks"—which contradicts Marx's own notion of dialectical development. A reading which presents Marx's historical materialism as an *Aufhebung* of Feuerbachian materialism and Hegelian dialectics seems more consistent with Marx's explicit remarks and with his general philosophical orientation.

66. *MEW* 3:5; Marx, "Theses on Feuerbach," #1.

67. *MEW* 23:27; Marx, *Capital*, 1:19–20.

68. *MEW* 21; Engels, *Ludwig Feuerbach*, ch. 2.

69. Although Marx criticizes Hegel and Feuerbach for viewing man's objectification as *naturally* a process of alienation as well as externalization (*MEW, Erg.*, 1:575, 579, 601, 603, 604; *Economic and Philosophical Manuscripts*, pp. 387, 391, 393, 395, 396), he too occasionally uses such ahistorical language *MEW, Erg.*, 1:597, 603; *Economic and Philosophical Manuscripts*, pp. 389, 395).

70. *MEW, Erg.*, 1:597, 603; *Economic and Philosophical Manuscripts*, pp. 389, 395.

71. *MEW, Erg.*, 1:477; *Economic and Philosophical Manuscripts*, p. 289.

72. *MEW* 3:217–218; Marx and Engels, *German Ideology*, p. 103.

73. *MEW* 3:21; *German Ideology*, p. 42; *MEW* 23:193; *Capital* 1:178.

74. Marx, *Grundrisse*, g15, e94.

75. *MEW* 23:528-529; Marx, *Capital*, 1:506; Marx, *Grundrisse*, g374, e470. Note the similarities in the following references, for example:

"In the sphere of political economy this realization of labour appears as a *loss of reality* for the worker" (*MEW, Erg.*, 1:512; *Economic and Philosophical Manuscripts*, p. 324).

"This realization process is at the same time the de-realization process of labour" (*Grundrisse*, g358, e454).

"The only connection which still links them with the productive forces and with their own existence—labour—has lost all semblance of self-activity and only sustains their life by stunting it" (*MEW* 3:67; *German Ideology*, p. 92).

76. Nietzsche, Letter to Overbeck (received February 11, 1883) in *Selected Letters*.

77. Nietzsche, *Case of Wagner*, #4.

78. Nietzsche, *Genealogy*, third essay, section #5.

79. *WdB* 2:1109-1110; Nietzsche, *Ecce Homo*, p. 728.

80. *WdB* 2:1111; *Ecce Homo*, p. 729.

81. *WdB*, 2:1118-1119; *Ecce Homo*, p. 740.

82. *WdB* 2:1108-1109; *Ecce Homo*, pp. 726-727. It is a mistake, I think, to interpret Nietzsche in this passage (as Deleuze does) as rejecting dialectics per se.

83. *MEW* 3:45; Marx and Engels, *German Ideology*, p. 64.

84. Nietzsche, *Birth of Tragedy*, "Self-Criticism," section #7.

85. See Marx's remarks in *The Holy Family* on French materialism, including the following assessment of the direct connection between materialism and socialism: "If man draws all his knowledge, sensation, etc., from the world of the senses and the experience gained in it, then what has to be done is to arrange the empirical world in such a way that man experiences and becomes accustomed to what is truly human in it and that he becomes aware of himself as man" (p. 154; *MEW* 2:138).

86. *MEW* 3:27; Marx and Engels, *German Ideology*, pp. 47-48.

87. Nietzsche, *Beyond*, aphorism #36.

88. *MEW, Erg.*, 1:578; Marx, *Economic and Philosophical Manuscripts*, p. 389.

89. *MEW, Erg.*, 1:578; *Economic and Philosophical Manuscripts*, p. 390.

90. *MEW* 3:21; Marx and Engels, *German Ideology*, p. 42.

91. *MEW* 23:192; Marx, *Capital*, 1:177.

92. *MEW, Erg.*, 1:542; Marx, *Economic and Philosophical Manuscripts*, p. 354. Also see *MEW* 3:30; Marx and Engels, *German Ideology*, p. 50.

93. *WdB* 2:977-978; Nietzsche, *Twilight*, p. 500.

94. Nietzsche, *Will to Power*, aphorism #552.

95. *WdB* 2:371; Nietzsche, *Zarathustra*, p. 227.

96. Nietzsche, *Will to Power*, aphorism #704.

97. Marx, *Grundrisse*, g7, e85.

98. Nietzsche, *Will to Power*, aphorism #692.

99. *Ibid.*, aphorism #577; *MEW*, *Erg.*, 1:578; Marx, *Economic and Philosophical Manuscripts*, p. 390.

100. *MEW* 23:193; Marx, *Capital*, 1:179.

101. *MEW* 23: 196; *Capital* 1:181.

102. Nietzsche, *Beyond*, aphorism #12.

103. Nietzsche, *Will to Power*, aphorism #635.

104. *Ibid.*

105. *Ibid.*, aphorism #569.

106. *Ibid.*, aphorism #617.

107. Nietzsche, *Beyond*, aphorism #36.

108. Nietzsche, *Will to Power*, aphorism #634.

109. *Ibid.*, aphorism #552.

110. In *Gay Science* (aphorism #344), Nietzsche suggests: It is still a *metaphysical faith* upon which our faith in science rests—that even we seekers after knowledge today, we godless anti-metaphysicians still take our fire, too, from the flame lit by a faith that is thousands of years old, that Christian faith which was also the faith of Plato, that God is the truth, that truth is divine."

111. *MEW* 23:195; Marx, *Capital*, 1:180.

112. Marx, *Grundrisse*, g9, e87.

113. See Locke, *Second Treatise of Government*, ch. V, section 27, for this theory of property based on possessive individualism.

114. *MEW*, *Erg.*, 1:537–538; Marx, *Economic and Philosophical Manuscripts*, p. 349.

115. *MEW* 3:21; Marx and Engels, *German Ideology*, p. 42.

116. *MEW*, *Erg.*, 1:517; Marx, *Economic and Philosophical Manuscripts*, p. 329.

117. *MEW* 3:28; Marx and Engels, *German Ideology*, p. 49.

118. *MEW* 25:828; Marx, *Capital*, 3:820.

119. *MEW* 25:828; *Capital* 3:820.

120. *MEW* 25:828; *Capital* 3:820.

121. *MEW*, *Erg.*, 1:539; Marx, *Economic and Philosophical Manuscripts*, p. 351.

122. *MEW*, *Erg.*, 1:516; *Economic and Philosophical Manuscripts*, p. 328.

123. *MEW* 3:21; Marx and Engels, *German Ideology*, p. 42.

124. For example, see *MEW*, *Erg.*, 1:530, 539; *Economic and Philosophical Manuscripts*, pp. 342, 351; *MEW* 3:49, 69–70; *German Ideology*, pp. 61, 94.

125. *MEW*, *Erg.*, 1:516; Marx, *Economic and Philosophical Manuscripts*, p. 328.

126. *MEW* 3:30; Marx and Engels, *German Ideology*, p. 51.

127. Nietzsche, *Will to Power*, aphorism #552.

128. *WdB* 1:213; Nietzsche, *Use and Abuse of History*, pp. 7–8.

129. Nietzsche, *Will to Power*, aphorism #617.

130. Nietzsche, *Beyond*, aphorism #6.

131. *Ibid.*, aphorism #259.

132. *WdB* 2:370; Nietzsche, *Zarathustra*, p. 226.

133. Nietzsche, *Beyond*, preface.

134. Nietzsche, *Will to Power*, aphorism #704.

135. Nietzsche, *Genealogy*, second essay, section #2.

136. *WdB* 1:209–210; Nietzsche, *Use and Abuse of History*, pp. 3–4.

137. Nietzsche, *Genealogy*, second essay, section #1.

138. Nietzsche, *Gay Science*, aphorism #354.

139. Nietzsche, *Will to Power*, aphorism #707.

140. *MEW*, *Erg.*, 1:516; Marx, *Economic and Philosophical Manuscripts*, pp. 328–329.

141. *MEW* 3:30; Marx and Engels, *German Ideology*, p. 50.

142. *MEW* 3:29–30; *German Ideology*, p. 50.

143. *MEW* 3:31; *German Ideology*, p. 51.

144. *MEW* 3:31; *German Ideology*, p. 51.

145. *MEW* 3:31; *German Ideology*, p. 51.

146. *MEW* 3:32; *German Ideology*, pp. 51–52.

147. *MEW*, *Erg.*, 1:542; Marx, *Economic and Philosophical Manuscripts*, p. 354.

148. *MEW* 1:538–539; *Economic and Philosophical Manuscripts*, p. 350.

149. *MEW* 1:538; *Economic and Philosophical Manuscripts*, p. 349.

150. Nietzsche, *Gay Science*, aphorism #354.

151. *Ibid.*

152. *Ibid.* Freud in fact said that Nietzsche's "premonitions and insights often agree in the most amazing way with the laborious findings of psycho-analysis" (Hayman, *Nietzsche*, p. 200).

153. Nietzsche, *Will to Power*, aphorism #387.

154. Nietzsche, *Gay Science*, aphorism #354.

155. Nietzsche, *Genealogy*, second essay, section #17.

156. *Ibid.*, second essay, section #3.

157. *Ibid.*, second essay, section #16.

158. *WdB* 2:322; Nietzsche, *Zarathustra*, p. 170.

159. Nietzsche, *Beyond*, aphorism #260.

160. *Ibid.*

161. *Ibid.*

162. Strong, *Friedrich Nietzsche and the Politics of Transfiguration*, p. 240.

163. Nietzsche, *Genealogy*, second essay, section #3.

164. *Ibid.*, second essay, section #4.

165. *Ibid.*, second essay, section #16.

166. *Ibid.*, third essay, section #20.

167. *Ibid.*, second essay, section #16.
168. Nietzsche, *Gay Science*, aphorism #360.
169. Nietzsche, *Will to Power*, aphorism #766.
170. Nietzsche, *Beyond*, aphorism #258.
171. Nietzsche, *Will to Power*, aphorism #124.

3. Dialectical History

1. When I refer to Nietzsche's genealogy as a view of human history, I do not mean that it is a worldview. It must be distinguished from the latter in several ways. First, Nietzsche differentiates between the character of organic life and that of the world. It is in contrast to the organic that Nietzsche describes the world as chaotic and unamenable to our aesthetic anthropomorphisms. Because all events in organic life involve mastery, because the will to power is operative in them, they have characteristic tendencies and patterns of organization which the world lacks and which we should not attribute to it. Genealogy concerns the evolution of man from pre-man and of the overman from man as events in organic life.

Second, even our understanding of organic life is problematic. Nietzsche clearly thinks that a reality exists beyond the knower to be known. As we have seen, his critique of the Kantian thing-in-itself is less an argument about whether other beings and things exist than about how they exist: they exist objectively, but not structured as objects. His critique of Kant has implications for how we are to know reality, however. As Kantian knowers, i.e., as unified subjects who have an interpretation of reality, our perspectives are merely perspectives grounded in our species. That is, we project our identity—man as subject—upon life and the world in attempts to make them equivalent to reason. Nietzsche's perspectivism is not a defense of having multiple such subjects, each projecting from a different human angle. Instead, he defends reconstitution of the subject as a multiplicity. That is, his knower no longer abstracts himself as knowing subject from the world of which he has knowledge. His "subject" knows as a multiplicity "constituted" by his manifold relations to other beings and things. This allows his "subject" to begin to know things as they are. Although there is only a perspective knowing, some perspectives are more complete and objective than others: "There is *only* a perspective seeing, *only* a perspective 'knowing'; and the *more* affects we allow to speak about one thing, the *more* eyes, different eyes, we can use to observe one thing, the more complete will our 'concept' of this thing, our 'objectivity,' be" (*Genealogy*, third essay, section #12). It is as the most complete and objective perspective upon organic life that I speak of Nietzsche's theory of history. (For detailed discussions of Nietzsche's perspectivism, see Nehamas, "Immanent and Transcendent Perspectivism in Nietzsche," and Strong, "Text and Pretexts.")

2. Wood, *Karl Marx*. Although Allen Wood explicitly denies that Marx is an anthropological teleologist (pp. 108–110), his characterization of man's expanding productive powers in Aristotelian language as the actualization of potential implies otherwise. This language does emphasize, however, that Marx identifies historical tendencies, and that they are human tendencies. G. A. Cohen, who describes Marx's theory of history as functional, not teleological, avoids implying that Marx is an anthropological teleologist, but also de-emphasizes the fact that human capacities create the functionally determinant tendencies. If Wood's language implies too close an association between human and historical development, Cohen's implies too great a separation. What seems to be needed is an exposition which stresses the human character of the tendencies without implying the existence of an anthropological *telos*.

3. Ernest Nagel, in *The Structure of Science* (Indianapolis: Hackett, 1979), argues that many teleological explanations do not postulate purposes or ends in view, but only specify functions which things or processes possess (p. 402). However, his functional conception of teleological explanation still involves "goal-directed" (p. 411) organization, i.e., parts are functionally determined and hence explained as they *maintain* the whole. Marx and Nietzsche not only deny the existence of theological or anthropological ends in view, but also of end states per se (pp. 401–408).

4. *WdB* 2:977–978; Nietzsche, *Twilight*, p. 500.

5. *MEW* 3:28; Marx and Engels, *German Ideology*, p. 58.

6. *WdB* 2:977–978; Nietzsche, *Twilight*, p. 500.

7. Nietzsche, *Will to Power*, aphorism #332. By using this example, Nietzsche reveals his opposition to the Aristotelian notion that as there is in an acorn a tendency to become an oak, so there is in the human race a tendency to become happy, moral, etc. By using a biological example, he also reveals an unacknowledged affinity between his philosophy and aspects of teleological explanation in the biological sciences. (See below.)

8. *WdB* 2:972; Nietzsche, *Twilight*, p. 493.

9. *WdB* 2:971; *Twilight*, p. 491.

10. *MEW* 3:69; Marx and Engels, *German Ideology*, pp. 93–94.

11. *MEW* 3:45; *German Ideology*, pp. 57–58

12. *MEW* 3:45; *German Ideology*, p. 57.

13. Marx, Letter to Annenkov (December 28, 1846) in *Selected Correspondence*.

14. Nietzsche, *Will to Power*, aphorism #552.

15. *Ibid.*, aphorism #1001.

16. *Ibid*, aphorism #995.

17. *Ibid*, aphorism #1067.

18. Nietzsche explicitly says, "We deny end goals: if existence had one it would have to have been reached" (*Will to Power*, aphorism #55). He also denies that the overman is an ideal type of man, an evolutionary apotheosis:

"The word 'overman', as the designation of a type of supreme achievement, as opposed to 'modern' men, to 'good' men, to Christians and other nihilists—a word that in the mouth of a Zarathustra, the annihilator of morality, becomes a very pensive word—has been understood almost everywhere with the utmost innocence in the sense of those very values whose opposite Zarathustra was meant to represent—that is, as an 'idealistic' type of a higher kind of man, half 'saint,' half 'genius.'

Other scholarly oxen have suspected me of Darwinism on that account" (*WdB* 2:1101; *Ecce Homo*, p. 717).

19. *MEW, Erganzungsband*, 1:536; Marx, *Economic and Philosophical Manuscripts*, p. 348.

20. *MEW* 23:790–791; Marx, *Capital*, 1:763.

21. Nietzsche, *Will to Power*, aphorism #20.

22. *Ibid*, aphorism #30.

23. *MEW* 4:182; Marx, *Poverty of Philosophy*, p. 175. "It is only in an order of things in which there are no more classes and class antagonisms that *social evolutions* will cease to be *political revolutions*." Also see *MEW* 25:828; Marx, *Capital*, 3:820, on human activity in the realm of freedom.

24. *MEW* 3:35; Marx and Engels, *German Ideology*, p. 56.

25. *MEW* 20:121–122; Engels, *Anti-Dühring*, p. 147.

26. *MEW* 3:69; Marx and Engels, *German Ideology*, p. 94.

27. Nietzsche, *Will to Power*, aphorism #526.

28. *WdB* 2:972; Nietzsche, *Twilight*, p. 493.

29. *MEW* 13:9; Marx, "Preface to *A Contribution to the Critique of Political Economy*," p. 425.

30. Nietzsche, *Will to Power*, aphorism #552.

31. *Ibid*.

32. Engels, Letter to Mehring (July 14, 1893) in *Selected Correspondence*.

33. Engels, Letter to Bloch (September 21–22, 1890) in *Selected Correspondence*.

34. *MEW* 3:37–38; Marx and Engels, *German Ideology*, p. 58, emphasis mine.

35. Engels, Letter to Bloch (September 21–22, 1890) in *Selected Correspondence*.

36. Kaufmann, *Nietzsche: Philosopher, Psychologist, Antichrist*, p. 265. His apology also mistakenly presumes the causal relations Nietzsche would reject.

37. Althusser, *For Marx*, pp. 108–110.

38. Foucault, "Nietzsche, Genealogy, History," p. 148.

39. Nietzsche, *Genealogy*, second essay, section #12.

40. *MEW* 13:8; Marx, "Preface to *A Contribution to the Critique of Political Economy*," p. 425.

41. Marx's and Nietzsche's reactions to Darwin indicate their affinity for some aspects of teleological explanations. Marx praises Darwin's explanation of historically progressive tendencies in rational, scientific

teleological terms, not speculative theological or anthropological ones. "Darwin's book is very important and serves me as a natural-scientific basis for the class struggle in history. One has to put up with the crude English method of development, of course. Despite all the deficiencies, not only is the death-blow dealt here for the first time to 'teleology' in the natural sciences but its rational meaning is empirically explained" (Letter to Lasalle (January 16, 1861) *Selected Correspondence*). Nietzsche, while he too sees deficiencies in Darwinism, agrees that life evolves—"The organic is rising to yet higher levels" (*Will to Power*, aphorism #676)— and that apparent theological or anthropological purposes merely reflect naturalistic tendencies: "All 'purposes,' 'aims,' 'meaning' are only modes of expression and metamorphoses of one will that is inherent in all events: the will to power. To have purposes, aims, intentions, *willing* in general, is the same thing as willing to be stronger, willing to grow—and, in addition, willing the means to this" (*Will to Power*, aphorism #675).

Both view as Darwin's primary deficiency his elevation of the Malthusian "struggle for existence," a principle of modern society, to the historical tendency of nature. Nietzsche says that Darwin mistakes a fatalistic Christian-democratic principle, survival through adaptation, for nature (*Twilight*, p. 471). Marx says that Darwin mistakes an exploitative bourgeois principle, competition, for nature (*Capital* 1:372–373). Nietzsche disputes Darwin's Malthusian principle because, while life is struggle, it is overwhelmingly a struggle for power and only incidentally a struggle for existence; Marx disputes it because life is essentially cooperative and free, not competitive and impoverished. Both agree that the struggle for existence typifies modern society, and both agree that the mediocre or the bourgeois who "survive" are not the "fittest."

These remarks not only reveal structural similarities in their theories of history, but also foreshadow substantive differences in their critiques of modern society.

42. *MEW* 3:21; Marx and Engels, *German Ideology*, p. 42.
43. Marx, *Grundrisse*, g14, e93.
44. *Ibid.*, g20, e99.
45. Nietzsche, *Beyond*, aphorism #36.
46. Nietzsche, *Genealogy*, second essay, section #8.
47. *WdB* 2:972; Nietzsche, *Twilight*, p. 493.
48. Nietzsche, *Beyond*, aphorism #13.
49. *MEW* 3:46; Marx and Engels, *German Ideology*, p. 64.
50. Nietzsche, *Will to Power*, aphorism #676.
51. *MEW* 3:72; Marx and Engels, *German Ideology*, p. 87.
52. *MEW* 4:467; Marx and Engels, *Communist Manifesto*, pp. 477–478.
53. Nietzsche, *Genealogy*, third essay, section #20.
54. *MEW* 4:467; Marx and Engels, *Communist Manifesto*, p. 477.
55. Nietzsche, *Genealogy*, third essay, section #13.
56. *MEW* 3:72; Marx and Engels, *German Ideology*, p. 87–88.

57. *MEW* 3:54; *German Ideology*, p. 72.

58. Nietzsche, *Will to Power*, aphorism #881.

59. *Ibid.*

60. *Ibid.*, aphorism #1063.

61. *Ibid.*, aphorism #1062.

62. *Ibid.*, aphorism #1066.

63. *Ibid.*, aphorisms #1053, #1056, #1058.

64. *Ibid.*, aphorism #1057.

65. *Ibid.*, aphorism #1067. Also see Schacht's *Nietzsche*, pp. 253–266, upon which I draw.

66. *MEW* 23:16; Marx, *Capital*, 1:10.

67. *MEW* 3:31; Marx and Engels, *German Ideology*, p. 51.

68. Nietzsche, *Genealogy*, second essay, section #17.

69. *MEW* 4:474; Marx and Engels, *Communist Manifesto*, p. 483.

70. Nietzsche, *Genealogy*, third essay, section #27.

71. *MEW* 23:16; Marx, *Capital*, 1:10.

72. *MEW* 23:94–96; *Capital* 1:80.

73. Nietzsche, *Genealogy*, third essay, section #23.

74. Nietzsche, *Gay Science*, aphorism #370.

75. *MEW* 4:131; Marx, *Poverty of Philosophy*, p. 110.

76. *WdB* 1:232; Nietzsche, *Use and Abuse of History*, p. 23.

77. *MEW* 4:126; Marx, *Poverty of Philosophy*, p. 104.

78. Nietzsche, *Beyond*, aphorism #13, and *Genealogy*, third essay, section #26.

79. Marx, *Grundrisse*, g11, e90.

80. *Ibid.*, g20, e99.

81. Nietzsche, *Gay Science*, aphorism #109.

82. *Ibid.*

83. Nietzsche, *Genealogy*, second essay, section #12.

84. *Ibid.*

85. *WdB*, 2:371; Nietzsche, *Zarathustra*, p. 227. In his *Nietzsche*, Richard Schacht argues that Nietzsche's world as will to power is only chaotic by our ordinary standards of order (as it is only valueless by our ordinary standards of value). The world has its necessities, but they do not correspond to our aesthetic anthropomorphisms (p. 196). Ofelia Schutte takes this argument a step further, maintaining that Nietzsche should also have recognized that life as will to power had sufficient order without a moral imperative of nature (*Beyond Nihilism*, conclusion).

86. Nietzsche, *Beyond*, aphorism #188.

87. Nietzsche, *Beyond*, aphorism #19.

88. Nietzsche, *Will to Power*, aphorism #561.

89. *WdB*, 2:393; Nietzsche, *Zarathustra*, p. 250.

90. *Ibid.*, 2:317–318, 322–324. *Ibid.*, pp. 160–161, 170–172.

91. Nietzsche, *Genealogy*, second essay, section #12.

92. Nietzsche, *Will to Power*, aphorism #20.

93. *Ibid.*, aphorism #585. Martin Jay also discusses how Nietzsche,

unlike many of his professed heirs, retains the concept of totality (*Marxism and Totality*, epilogue).

94. *MEW*, 13:9; Marx, "Preface to *A Contribution to the Critique of Political Economy*," p. 425. I only provide a brief outline of the relationships which Marx analyzes. For more detailed discussions of historical materialism, see Cohen, *Karl Marx's Theory of History*; Shaw, *Marx's Theory of History*; and Wood, *Karl Marx*. I draw extensively from their work.

95. *MEW* 3:72; Marx and Engels, *German Ideology*, p. 87.

96. *MEW* 3:29-30; *German Ideology*, p. 50.

97. Marx, Letter to Annenkov (December 28, 1846) in *Selected Correspondence*.

98. *MEW* 4:130; Marx, *Poverty of Philosophy*, p. 109.

99. *MEW* 3:22; Marx and Engels, *German Ideology*, p. 43.

100. *MEW* 4:149; Marx, *Poverty of Philosophy*, p. 133.

101. *MEW* 4:464; Marx and Engels, *Communist Manifesto*, p. 475.

102. *MEW* 3:46; Marx and Engels, *German Ideology*, p. 64.

103. *MEW* 3:31-32; *German Ideology*, pp. 51-52.

104. Engels, Letter to Bloch (September 21-22, 1890) in *Selected Correspondence*.

105. Nietzsche, *Will to Power*, aphorism #552.

106. Deleuze, *Nietzsche and Philosophy*, ch. 4. Deleuze schematizes this development. It begins with the topology of *ressentiment*, that is, the invasion of consciousness by memory, a displacement of reactive forces which manifests itself in the inability to forget and to act. The man of *ressentiment* blames others affecting him for his own impotence. His topology allows a new type, the Judaic priest (and the first slave moralist) to arise and to reverse values: the masters' good, as we saw in chapter 2, becomes the slaves' evil. Nietzsche illustrates this reversal with the parable of the lamb and the hawk. In that story, a lamb suggests that a hawk might not eat lambs, declares the hawk who continues to do so evil, and asks "its opposite, a lamb—would he not be good?" (*Genealogy*, first essay, section #13). The presumption that hawks might behave as lambs already separates active force from what it can do, but in book two of the *Genealogy* Nietzsche describes how this separation is internalized in the bad conscience. The Christian priest is the relevant type here. Priests now teach the hawk—to continue Nietzsche's example—to find the source of its suffering its own strength. They teach masters to internalize the slaves' morality. Finally, in book three, Nietzsche discusses ascetic ideals, the instruments ascetic priests use to make   *ressentiment* and the bad conscience bearable.

107. Schutte discusses this limitation of Deleuze's argument (*Beyond Nihilism*, pp. 87-90).

108. Nietzsche, *Genealogy*, first essay, section #2.

109. *Ibid.*, second essay, section #16.

110. *Ibid.*

111. *Ibid.*, second essay, section #8. For an analysis of Nietzsche's critique of society as an exchange relation, see Deleuze, "Nomad Thought." I compare Nietzsche's and Marx's critiques of the exchange principle in chapter 6.

112. Nietzsche, *Genealogy*, second essay, section #3.

113. *Ibid.*, first essay, sections #6, #7.

114. *WdB* 2:322; Nietzsche, *Zarathustra*, p. 170.

115. Nietzsche, *Daybreak*, aphorism #109. Walter Kaufmann, who discusses Nietzsche's concept of reason sublimating the passions (*Nietzsche: Philosopher, Psychologist, Antichrist*, ch. 8), mistakenly concludes, because reason has this role, that Nietzsche had greater faith in individual and scientific reason than he himself or others generally acknowledged. What Kaufmann ignores is that reason, which "causes" a particular ordering of the passions, is itself functionally determined by the will to power. In fact, Nietzsche thinks that reliance on autonomous reason for individual and social order merely reflects the inability of the will to power to command.

116. Still, Nietzsche's masters and slaves differ from Marx's bourgeoisie and proletariat because, unlike the latter, the former are not necessarily defined by sociological status. That is, masters are known more by the nature of their will to power than by their place within society.

117. Nietzsche, *Will to Power*, aphorism #707.

118. *Ibid.*

119. Deleuze, *Nietzsche and Philosophy*, p. 195, and Kaufmann, *Nietzsche: Philosopher, Psychologist, Antichrist*, p. 235.

120. Nietzsche, *Will to Power*, aphorism #529.

121. *Ibid.*, aphorism #430.

122. *Ibid.*, aphorism #507.

123. *WdB* 2:953; Nietzsche, *Twilight*, p. 476.

124. Marx, however, does speak of his inversion of Hegel's dialectic as the discovery of the "rational kernel within the mystical shell" (*MEW* 23:27; *Capital* 1:20). As I discussed in chapter 2, Nietzsche would argue that Marx does not question "given" realities radically enough. By accepting the notion of a dialectic of subject and object (even if that subject is producing man, not spirit, and that object is matter, not spirit's self-actualization), Marx retains Hegel's metaphysical language and retains his faith in the existence of a world accessible to reason. Marx may "invert" Hegel, but he only substitutes scientific for theological metaphysics. Nietzsche would regard both as untenable in a universe without truth.

Yet, in spite of his attempts to avoid "metaphysical language," Nietzsche's notion of life as will to power seems vulnerable to similar criticisms. As I have shown, Nietzsche does think that there is some "intelligibility" at least to organic life. But if truth is dead, what is the status of the will to power itself? Is the will to power the truth about life?

If it is the truth about life, would it not consequently be false? Nietzsche seems to argue simultaneously that there are no truths and that the will to power is true. He may ultimately be an ethical naturalist, i.e., he may argue that life has built-in values—that power, exploitation, overcoming, are good and that weakness, pity, decline (all of which appear in ascetic ideals), are bad. But if Nietzsche is an ethical naturalist, then something— however tentatively it is expressed—is true and his philosophy is incoherent. In addition, although they disagree on what the values are, his argument that life has built-in values is strikingly similar to Marx's.

125. *MEW* 20:348; Engels, *Dialectics of Nature*, p. 26. Although the applicability of these "laws" to Marx has been questioned (in part because they have been misunderstood as formal scientific laws, not structural hypotheses), the evidence points to Marx's agreement with them. First, Engels derives the laws from Hegel, to whose dialectic Marx acknowledges his debt. Second, the laws describe, among other things, developmental tendencies of organisms, and the concept of organic development is fundamental to Marx's theory of history. Third, Marx explicitly argues that historical and natural development are interrelated, and criticizes the empiricists who regard matter as dead (*German Ideology*, pp. 48, 62–63).

126. Nietzsche, *Will to Power*, aphorism #564.

127. Nietzsche, *Beyond*, aphorism #2.

128. *MEW* 13:9; Marx, "Preface to *A Contribution to the Critique of Political Economy*," pp. 425–426.

129. *WdB* 2:371; Nietzsche, *Zarathustra*, p. 227.

130. *MEW* 4:474; Marx and Engels, *Communist Manifesto*, p. 483.

131. Nietzsche, *Genealogy*, third essay, section #27.

132. Kaufmann, *Nietzsche: Philosopher, Psychologist, Antichrist*, pp. 235–236.

133. Deleuze, *Nietzsche and Philosophy*, pp. 85, 121.

134. *Ibid.*, p. 180.

135. *Ibid.*, pp. 170, 179.

136. *MEW* 19:19; Marx, "Critique of the Gotha Program," p. 529.

137. *MEW* 19:21; "Critique of the Gotha Program," p. 531.

138. Nietzsche, *Genealogy*, third essay, section #11.

139. *WdB* 2:371; Nietzsche, *Zarathustra*, p. 227.

140. See my "Reason, Repression, and Reality in Marxism."

141. Nietzsche, *Genealogy*, third essay, section #25.

142. *MEW* 3:212–213; Marx and Engels, *German Ideology*, p. 102.

143. *MEW* 3:35; *German Ideology*, p. 57.

144. Nietzsche, *Will to Power*, aphorism #674. Much has been written on Nietzsche's notion of ascending and descending life. The major question posed has been: How can Nietzsche, after denying the existence of truth, evaluate particular societies as ascendant or decadent? What are his standards of judgment? If my analysis is correct, Nietzsche evaluates individual and social organisms in terms of certain values or

tendencies built in to life as will to power. This understanding of life as will to power is neither subjective nor objective; it is a peculiar combination of both as the most complete perspective on life so far. (See note 1.) However, to repeat, if Nietzsche is an ethical naturalist, then something—no matter how tentatively it is expressed—is true, and his philosophy is incoherent.

145. Nietzsche, *Genealogy*, third essay, section #28.

146. *MEW* 4:482; Marx and Engels, *Communist Manifesto*, p. 491.

147. Nietzsche, *Genealogy*, third essay, section #27.

4. Science Versus Skepticism: Ideology as Illusion

1. Paul Ricoeur argues that Marx, Freud, and Nietzsche constitute the modern "School of Suspicion" over illusions of consciousness (*Freud and Philosophy*, Dennis Savage, tr. [New Haven: Yale University Press, 1970], pp. 32–36). Louis Althusser concurs, citing the three of them as progenitors of symptomatic readings (*Reading Capital*, preface). The following works combine aspects of Marx's and Nietzsche's critiques of ideology: Adorno, *Minima Moralia* and *Negative Dialectics*; Adorno and Horkheimer, *Dialectic of Enlightenment*, especially excursus II; Derrida, *Spurs*; Foucault, "Nietzsche, Genealogy, History"; Mannheim, "Sociology of Knowledge"; Weber, "The Meaning of Ethical Neutrality in Sociology and Economics," "Objectivity in Social Science and Social Policy," "Politics as a Vocation," "Science as a Vocation," and *The Protestant Ethic and the Spirit of Capitalism*.

2. *MEW* 3:31; Marx and Engels, *German Ideology*, p. 51.

3. Nietzsche, *Gay Science*, aphorism #354.

4. *MEW* 3:46; Marx and Engels, *German Ideology*, p. 64.

5. *WdB* 2:322; Nietzsche, *Zarathustra*, p. 170.

6. Nietzsche, *Genealogy*, second essay, section #4.

7. *MEW* 13:8; Marx, "Preface to *A Contribution to the Critique of Political Economy*," p. 425.

8. *MEW* 3:26–27; Marx and Engels, *German Ideology*, p. 47.

9. *MEW* 4:469–471; Marx and Engels, *Communist Manifesto*, pp. 479–481.

10. *MEW* 8:198; Marx, *Eighteenth Brumaire*, p. 608.

11. Though he makes the point too strongly, arguing that "there is no sense in which the will to power could be said to 'underlie' interpretation," I am indebted to Mark Warren for this insight into ideology as morphology ("Nietzsche's Concept of Ideology," p. 550).

12. Nietzsche, *Beyond*, aphorism #6.

13. *Ibid.*

14. Nietzsche, *Genealogy*, third essay, section #11.

15. *WdB* 3:314; Nietzsche, "Truth and Falsity," p. 180.

16. Nietzsche, *Will to Power*, aphorism #707.

17. *MEW* 3:47–48; Marx and Engels, *German Ideology*, pp. 65–66.

18. *WdB* 1:214; Nietzsche, *Use and Abuse of History*, p. 7.

19. Nietzsche, *Beyond*, aphorism #3.

20. Nietzsche, *Genealogy*, third essay, section #28.

21. *MEW* 3:47; Marx and Engels, *German Ideology*, p. 66.

22. Nietzsche, *Genealogy*, third essay, section #11.

23. Marx, *Grundrisse*, g8, e87.

24. Nietzsche, *Beyond*, aphorism #202.

25. Nietzsche, *Beyond*, aphorism #211.

26. *MEW* 1:385; Marx, "A Contribution to the Critique of Hegel's *Philosophy of Right*. Introduction," p. 251.

27. Nietzsche, *Beyond*, aphorism #210.

28. *MEW* 1:385; Marx, "A Contribution to the Critique of Hegel's *Philosophy of Right*. Introduction," p. 251.

29. Feuerbach, *Essence of Christianity*, pp. xii, xli.

30. *MEW* 1:378; Marx, "A Contribution to the Critique of Hegel's *Philosophy of Right*. Introduction," p. 244.

31. *WdB* 2:943; Nietzsche, *Twilight*, p. 467.

32. *MEW* 1:378; Marx, "A Contribution to the Critique of Hegel's *Philosophy of Right*. Introduction," p. 244.

33. *MEW* 4:464-465; Marx and Engels, *Communist Manifesto*, p. 475.

34. *MEW* 1:355; Marx, "On the Jewish Question,"p. 220.

35. *MEW* 1:355; "On the Jewish Question," p. 220.

36. *MEW* 1:360; "On the Jewish Question," p. 225.

37. *MEW* 1:376; "On the Jewish Question," p. 240.

38. Nietzsche, *Genealogy*, third essay, section #28.

39. *Ibid.*

40. *Ibid.*, third essay, section #20.

41. *Ibid.*, second essay, section #22.

42. *WdB* 2:971-978; Nietzsche, *Twilight*, pp. 492-501.

43. *WdB* 2:973; *Twilight*, p. 495.

44. *WdB* 2:973; *Twilight*, p. 495.

45. Nietzsche, *Genealogy*, first essay section #13. The herd's morality declares the virtues of strong, healthy men (power, subtlety) to be evil and the virtues of sick, weak men (pity, patience, humility, industry) to be good.

46. Nietzsche, *Will to Power*, aphorism #252.

47. Nietzsche, *Genealogy*, first essay, section #9.

48. *MEW* 21:275; Engels, *Ludwig Feuerbach*, p. 22.

49. *MEW* 3:26; Marx and Engels, *German Ideology*, p. 47; *MEW* 23:27; Marx, *Capital*, 1:19.

50. *MEW* 21:276; Engels, *Ludwig Feuerbach*, p. 22. For a detailed discussion of practical knowledge, see Doyal and Harris, "The Practical Foundations of Human Understanding."

51. *MEW* 19:205; Engels, "Socialism: Utopian and Scientific," p. 696.

52. *MEW* 3:20; Marx and Engels, *German Ideology*, p. 52. Marx argues that Hegel (and presumably Kant) were the philosophers of political economy: "It is self-evident . . . that 'spectres,' 'bonds,' 'the higher being,' 'concept,' 'scruple,' are merely the idealistic, spiritual expression, the conception apparently of the isolated individual, the image of the very empirical fetters and limitations, within which the mode of production of life and the form of intercourse coupled with it move."

53. *MEW* 3:7; Marx, "Theses on Feuerbach," #9.

54. *MEW* 23:825; Marx, *Capital*, 3:817.

55. *MEW* 3:7; Marx, "Theses on Feuerbach," #10.

56. *MEW* 23:86; Marx, *Capital*, 1:72.

57. *MEW* 23:90; *Capital* 1:76.

58. Nietzsche, *Genealogy*, third essay, section #25.

59. *WdB* 2:973; Nietzsche, *Twilight*, p. 495.

60. Nietzsche, *Beyond*, aphorism #36. Nietzsche equated materialism and atomism in the following passage: "As for materialistic atomism, it is one of the best refuted theories there are . . . thanks chiefly to the Dalmation Boscovich. . . . Boscovich has taught us to abjure the belief in the last part of the earth that 'stood fast'—the belief in 'substance,' in 'matter,' in the earth-residuum and particle-atom: it is the greatest triumph over the senses that has been gained on earth so far" (*Beyond*, aphorism #12).

61. Nietzsche, *Will to Power*, aphorism #569.

62. *Ibid.*, aphorism #635.

63. Nietzsche, *Genealogy*, third essay, section #27.

64. Nietzsche, *Beyond*, aphorism #229.

65. Nietzsche, *Gay Science*, aphorism #344.

66. Nietzsche, *Will to Power*, aphorism #12.

67. *Ibid.*, aphorism #584.

68. *MEW* 4:467; Marx and Engels, *Communist Manifesto*, p. 477.

69. Nietzsche, *Genealogy*, third essay, section #28.

70. Marx, *Grundrisse*, g8, e87.

71. Nietzsche, *Beyond*, aphorism #202.

72. *MEW* 1:390; Marx, "A Contribution to the Critique of Hegel's *Philosophy of Right*. Introduction," p. 256.

73. *MEW* 1:390; "A Contribution to the Critique of Hegel's *Philosophy of Right*. Introduction," p. 256.

74. I am not suggesting that this is a truth of anthropological "Man," but of "natural, historical men." For details see chapters 2 and 3.

75. Cohen, *Karl Marx's Theory of History*, p. 331.

76. *MEW* 3:5–6; Marx, "Theses on Feuerbach," #2.

77. *MEW* 25:825; Marx, *Capital*, 3:817.

78. Nietzsche, *Genealogy*, third essay, section #27.

79. *WdB* 2:441; Nietzsche, *Zarathustra*, p. 306.

80. Nietzsche, *Beyond*, #22. Nietzsche also thinks that the will to power is an "interpretation with a difference." (The phrase is from

Richard Schacht's *Nietzsche*.) It is the most complete and objective perspective on life so far. This suggests that the will to power may be a truth of life akin to socialist society as a truth of man. If so, Nietzsche's philosophy, particularly his critique of Marx, becomes incoherent. That is, if the will to power is true, it is also false.

81. *MEW* 19:210; Engels, "Socialism: Utopian and Scientific," p. 701.

82. Nietzsche, *Will to Power*, aphorism #512.

83. *Ibid.*, aphorism #339.

84. Karl Mannheim recognizes, but does not resolve, this contradiction. He suggests that Marxian, as well as bourgeois, science reifies reason: "There is a tendency to abide by the particular view that is immediately obtainable, and to prevent the question from being raised as to whether the fact that knowledge is bound up with existence is not inherent in the human thought structure itself. . . . For instance, one is not even allowed to raise the question whether 'impersonalization' (*Verdinglichung*), as elaborated by Marx and Lukács, is a more or less general phenomenon of consciousness, or whether capitalistic impersonalization is merely one particular form of it" ("The Sociology of Knowledge," pp. 177–178).

Max Weber is aware of a similar problem. He says that "an empirical science cannot tell anyone what he *should* do—but rather what he *can* do—and under certain circumstances—what he wishes to do" ("Objectivity in Social Science," p. 54). Herbert Marcuse attacks Weber's notion of formal rationality as itself bourgeois reason. In doing so, Marcuse reveals Weber's dilemma: "For Max Weber this possibility [reason as liberation] was utopian. Today it looks as if he was right. But if contemporary industrial society triumphs over its own potentialities, then this triumph is no longer that of Max Weber's bourgeois reason. It is difficult to see reason at all in the ever more solid 'shell of bondage' which is being constructed. Or is there perhaps already in Max Weber's concept of reason the irony that understands but disavows? Does he by any chance mean to say: And this you call 'reason'?" ("Industrialization and Capitalism in the Work of Max Weber," pp. 225–226).

For Marcuse, who asks, "And this you call reason?" and for other twentieth-century marxists, the contradiction between science and skepticism persists. Adorno and Horkheimer illustrate this contradiction most clearly. In the *Dialectic of Enlightenment*, they say, "Bourgeois society is ruled by equivalence. It makes the dissimilar comparable by reducing it to abstract quantities" (p. 7). This principle of equivalence originates with the Enlightenment, which they describe as "totalitarian": "Number became the canon of the Enlightenment. The same equations dominate bourgeois justice and commodity exchange" (p. 7). They maintain, however, that "this logical necessity is not conclusive. It remains tied to domination" (p. 37). In fact, Nietzsche's critique of the bourgeois "ratio" "implicitly liberates from its hiding-place the utopia contained in the Kantian notion of reason as in every great philosophy: the utopia of a humanity which, itself no longer distorted, has no further need to distort" (p. 119). What they do not explain is why, if reason establishes equivalents and dominates reality, Marxist reason liberates us. They beg the question: Is the domination of logic, not merely the logic of domination, repressive?

5. Socialism Versus Individualism: Liberal Democracy as Oppression

1. Among such aristocratic critiques are Edmund Burke's attack upon "levellers" who "change and pervert the natural order of things" (*Reflections on the Revolution in France* [Great Britain: Penguin Books, 1982], p. 138) and Alexis de Tocqueville's warning that democrats will "endure poverty, servitude, barbarism, but ... not ... aristocracy (*Democracy in America* [New York: Vintage Books, 1945] 2:102). Although he described himself as a long-term socialist, John Stuart Mill's short-term conservatism, especially his plans for proportional representation and plural voting, also places him here. Jean-Jacques Rousseau's characterization of the social contract as a ploy by the rich to dupe the poor provides the clearest example of the democratic position (*Discourse on the Origins of Inequality* in *The Social Contract and Discourses*, G. D. H. Cole, tr. [London: Everyman, 1982] p. 89).

2. A number of analyses of the state and its ideological apparatuses draw upon Marx and Nietzsche. For a start, see Adorno and Horkheimer, *Dialectic of Enlightenment*, ch. 4; Horkheimer, "The Authoritarian State"; Marcuse, "Some Social Implications of Modern Technology" and *One-Dimensional Man*; Althusser, "Ideology and Ideological State Apparatuses" (Althusser only acknowledges Freud's influence here, but there is also a Nietzschean influence which he acknowledges in the introduction to *Reading Capital*); Foucault, *Discipline and Punish*; Sorel, *Reflections on Violence*; Weber, *The Theory of Social and Economic Organization*, part three, "The Types of Authority and Imperative Co-Ordination."

3. George Brandes used this phrase to describe Nietzsche's politics in a letter to him (November 26, 1887). Nietzsche was delighted and responded, calling it "the shrewdest comment on me I have so far read" (December 2, 1887) (*Selected Letters*).

4. By referring to Marx's and Nietzsche's political target as the liberal-democratic state, I am painting with very broad strokes. This is justified, however, because neither Marx nor Nietzsche was particularly concerned with distinctions within liberalism, i.e., between natural right and utilitarian theorists, or with distinctions between liberal theorists' emphasis on individual freedom and democratic theorists' emphasis on egalitarian community. For both, these schools merge because all portray political life as an exchange relation among egoistic individuals. Marx speaks of Hobbes', Locke's, Bentham's, Mill's, and Rousseau's political theories as bourgeois democracy; each subordinates all relations to

"economic exploitation" (*German Ideology*, p. 110). Nietzsche speaks of English liberals, English utilitarians, and French democrats (not to mention anarchists and socialists) as ascetic herd moralists; they are "at one . . . in their thorough and instinctive hostility to every other form of society except that of the autonomous herd." (*Beyond*, aphorism #202).

5. *MEW*, 21:164; Engels, *Origin of the Family, Private Property and the State*, p. 228.

6. *MEW*, 21:165; Engels, *Origin of the Family, Private Property, and the State*, p. 229.

7. For references to the gens, see Nietzsche, *Human All Too Human*, aphorism #472, and *Genealogy*, second essay, sections #19, #20. A more detailed description of the "morality of mores" may be found in *Human All Too Human*, aphorisms #96, #99; *Daybreak*, aphorisms #9, #16, #18; *Genealogy*, second essay, sections #2, #16, #17.

While Marx and Engels distinguish between the barbarian and the civilized gens, Nietzsche's analogous distinction is between the "morality of mores" and "peoples." It is interesting to note that they identify many of the same societies, e.g., pre-Socratic Greece, pre-Christian Rome, and the German Mark (Nietzsche adds the Jews and the Persians) as civilized gens or peoples. A more detailed comparison of their analyses of the characteristics and degeneration of these societies would shed additional light on the ideological nature of the pursuit of origins. (See part III below for a brief discussion of this.)

8. Nietzsche, *Human All Too Human*, aphorism #99.

9. Nietzsche, *Genealogy*, second essay, section #8.

10. *MEW* 4:482; Marx and Engels, *Communist Manifesto*, p. 490.

11. *MEW* 21:167; Engels, *Origin of the Family, Private Property, and the State*, p. 231.

12. Nietzsche, *Genealogy*, first essay, section #6.

13. Nietzsche, *Will to Power*, aphorism #752.

14. *MEW* 25:352; Marx, *Capital*, 3:339–340.

15. Nietzsche, *Genealogy*, second essay, section #12.

16. On the existence of language, see *MEW* 3:30–31; Marx and Engels, *German Ideology*, pp. 50–52.

On the economic determination of the primacy of political and theological explanations of the state, Marx says: "In the whole conception of history up to the present this real [economic] basis of history has either been totally neglected or else considered as a minor matter quite irrelevant to the course of history. . . . The exponents of this conception of history have consequently only been able to see in history the political actions of princes and States, religious and all sorts of theoretical struggles, and in particular in each historical epoch have had to *share the illusion of that epoch*" (*MEW* 3:39; *German Ideology*, pp. 59–60). He concludes, "This is explained perfectly easily from their practical position in life, their job, and the division of labour" (*MEW* 3:49–50; *German Ideology*, p. 68).

17. On the existence of property, see Nietzsche, *Genealogy*, second essay, section #8, and *Will to Power*, aphorism #125. On the psychological determination of the primacy of economic explanations of the state, Nietzsche says: "Formerly one had the theory of the state as a calculating utility: now one has the practice as well!—The age of kings is past because the peoples are no longer worthy of them: they do not *want* to see the symbol of their ideal in kings, but a means for their profit.—That is the whole truth!" (*Will to Power*, aphorism #725).

18. *MEW* 1:204; Marx, *Critique of Hegel's Doctrine of the State*, p. 60.

19. *MEW* 3:33; Marx and Engels, *German Ideology*, p. 53.

20. Nietzsche, *Human All Too Human*, aphorism #99.

21. *MEW* 21:152; Engels, *Origin of the Family, Private Property, and the State*, p. 217.

22. *WdB* 2:323–324; Nietzsche, *Zarathustra*, pp. 171–172.

23. The decay of the gens or peoples and the rise of individualism is both a local and a world-historical process. For Marx and Engels, once individualism (fostered by the development of the division of labor and exchange) arises within a gens, the decay of that society is inevitable. The gens cannot reconcile the contradiction between particular and general interests socially; it can only regulate it politically. For Nietzsche, individualism (fostered by the decline of the "unfavorable conditions" which made communal discipline necessary) is a segment of a people's life cycle of birth, death, and rebirth. Commanders form individuals into "peoples," communal discipline declines, individualism arises, and a new commander, who developed strength in the struggle against the old morality, forms a new people. As examples of this, Nietzsche discusses the "rebirth" of classical values in Renaissance Italy and Napoleonic France. (See *Beyond*, aphorism #262, for a discussion of "peoples' cycle"; see *Genealogy*, first essay, section #16, for a discussion of these periodic rebirths.)

Marx and Nietzsche both argue that these local developments are increasingly becoming part of a world-historical process. According to Marx, the development of the world market is destroying the isolation of previously separate nationalities. According to Nietzsche, the development of cultural relativism is destroying the isolation of particular peoples. Hence, the gens or peoples are gradually being overcome throughout the world by increasingly illusory states. (See Nietzsche, *Human All Too Human*, aphorism #475; Marx and Engels, *German Ideology*, p. 58; *MEW* 3:37.)

24. *MEW* 1:234; Marx, *Critique of Hegel's Doctrine of the State*, p. 91.

25. *MEW* 1:354–355; Marx, "On the Jewish Question," p. 220.

26. *WdB* 1:233; Nietzsche, *Use and Abuse of History*, p. 25.

27. *WdB* 1:284–285; *Use and Abuse of History*, p. 73. On the state as the "death of peoples," see *WdB* 2:323–324 and *Zarathustra*, pp. 160–161; on the state as the decay of the state, see *Human All Too Human*,

aphorism #472; on the "oldest States," see note 7 above; on feudal states as "mixed cultures," see *Human All Too Human*, aphorism #222, and *Beyond*, aphorism #260. The final aphorism is also relevant for an understanding of the difference between Nietzsche's radical aristocrats and previous ones.

28. *WdB* 2:323–324; Nietzsche, *Zarathustra*, pp. 160–161.

29. *MEW* 2:123; Marx and Engels, *Holy Family*, p. 137.

30. *MEW* 22:197–198; Marx, *Civil War in France*, p. 627.

31. Nietzsche, *Will to Power*, aphorism #886.

32. Nietzsche, *Beyond*, aphorism #199.

33. *WdB* 2:284; Nietzsche, *Zarathustra*, p. 130.

34. Tönnies, *Community and Society*, p. 33.

35. *MEW* 4:464–465; Marx and Engels, *Communist Manifesto*, p. 475.

36. Nietzsche, *Human All Too Human*, aphorism #476.

37. *MEW* 21:80–81; Engels, *Origin of the Family, Private Property, and the State*, pp. 142–143.

38. Nietzsche, *Gay Science*, aphorism #358.

39. *MEW* 1:360–361; Marx, "On the Jewish Question," p. 226.

40. Nietzsche, *Will to Power*, aphorism #215.

41. Nietzsche says, "Step by step, private companies incorporate state business; even the most stubborn vestige of the old work of governing (For example, that activity, which is supposed to secure private parties against other private parties) will ultimately be managed by private contractors" (*Human All Too Human*, aphorism #472).

Marx says, "To this modern private property corresponds the modern State, which, purchased gradually by the owners of property by means of taxation, has fallen entirely into their hands through the national debt" (*MEW* 3:62; *German Ideology*, p. 79).

42. *MEW* 3:311; Marx and Engels, *German Ideology*, p. 106.

43. Nietzsche, *Daybreak*, aphorism #112.

44. Nietzsche, *Beyond*, aphorism #199.

45. *Ibid.*, aphorism #202.

46. *MEW* 4:476; Marx and Engels, *Communist Manifesto*, p. 486.

47. *MEW* 23:24; Marx, *Capital* 1:26.

48. Marx, *Pre-Capitalist Economic Formations*, p. 111.

49. *MEW* 25:827; Marx, *Capital*, 3:819.

50. *MEW* 1:365; Marx, "On the Jewish Question," p. 230.

51. Nietzsche, *Will to Power*, aphorism #783.

52. Nietzsche, *Genealogy*, second essay, section #8.

53. *Ibid.*

54. Nietzsche, *Beyond*, aphorism #259.

55. *Ibid.*, aphorism #212.

56. *MEW* 23:100; Marx, *Capital* 1:85.

57. *MEW* 23:182; *Capital* 1:168.

58. Marx, *Pre-Capitalist Economic Formations*, p. 114.

59. *MEW* 1:365, 366; Marx, "On the Jewish Question," p. 230.
60. Nietzsche, *Beyond*, aphorism #201.
61. *Ibid.*, aphorism #262.
62. Nietzsche, *Genealogy*, second essay, section #11.
63. Nietzsche, *Daybreak*, aphorism #9.
64. Nietzsche, *Will to Power*, aphorism #285.
65. *Ibid.*, aphorism #873.
66. *MEW* 1:366; Marx, "On the Jewish Question," p. 230.
67. Nietzsche, *Will to Power*, aphorism #770.
68. *WdB* 2:371; Nietzsche, *Zarathustra*, p. 226-227.
69. *WdB* 2:326; *Zarathustra*, p. 175.
70. *MEW* 3:76; Marx and Engels, *German Ideology*, p. 84.
71. Marx, *Grundrisse*, g81, e164.
72. *MEW* 1:368; Marx, "On the Jewish Question," p. 231.
73. Nietzsche, *Will to Power*, aphorism #766.
74. Marx, *Pre-Capitalist Economic Formations*, p. 84.
75. *MEW* 20:99; Engels, *Anti-Dühring*, p. 117.
76. *MEW* 4:482; Marx and Engels, *Communist Manifesto*, pp. 490-491.
77. Nietzsche, *Will to Power*, aphorism #14.
78. Nietzsche, *Beyond*, aphorism #242.
79. Nietzsche, *Genealogy*, second essay, section #10.
80. Nietzsche, *Will to Power*, aphorism #124.
81. Nietzsche, *Beyond*, aphorism #258.
82. *MEW*, *Erganzungoband*, 1:538; Marx, *Economic and Philosophical Manuscripts*, p. 352.
83. Marx and Engels, *German Ideology*, pp. 102-103.
84. Nietzsche, *Will to Power*, aphorism #373.
85. Nietzsche, *Genealogy*, second essay, section #6.
86. Nietzsche, *Beyond*, aphorism #199.
87. *MEW* 23:90; Marx, *Capital*, 1:76.
88. Marx, *Pre-Capitalist Economic Formations*, p. 96.
89. Compare *MEW* 23:102; Marx, *Capital*, 1:87; Nietzsche, *Genealogy*, second essay, section #8.
90. Marx, *Civil War in France*, p. 635.
91. Letter to Wilhelm Vischer-Bilfinger (May 27, 1871). Nietzsche's comment upon the fighting in which the communards shot hostages, burned the Tuileries and the Hotel de Ville, and, according to German reports, burned the Louvre was: "What use is an intellectual faced with such a cultural earthquake? One feels like an atom; One uses one's whole life and the greatest part of one's strength to come to a better understanding of one cultural period and to expound it. How is this profession to be regarded when in a single wretched day the most precious documents of such periods are burned to ashes?" (quoted by Hayman, *Nietzsche*, p. 141).
92. Nietzsche, *Will to Power*, aphorism #125.

93. Nietzsche, *Beyond*, aphorism #202.

94. Nietzsche, *Will to Power*, aphorism #784.

95. *Ibid.*, aphorism #755.

96. Nietzsche, *Beyond*, aphorism #259.

97. Nietzsche, *Human All Too Human*, aphorism #473.

98. *MEW* 2:99; Marx and Engels, *Holy Family*, p. 111.

99. *MEW* 4:477–478. Marx and Engels, *Communist Manifesto*, pp. 486–487.

100. Marx and Engels, *German Ideology*, pp. 104, 118.

101. Marx, *Grundrisse*, g30, e110–111.

102. *MEW* 3:19; Marx and Engels, *German Ideology*, p. 41.

103. Nietzsche, *Genealogy*, first essay, section #16.

104. *MEW* 2:130; Marx and Engels, *Holy Family*, p. 145.

105. Although they all locate revolutionary consciousness in individuals, they differ on which individuals: Althusser finds revolutionary consciousness in the "theoretical practice" of the "scientist" ("To pose these problems [the problems of ideology] correctly and to resolve them in reality, they must be called by their names, *their scientific names*," For *Marx*, p. 247). Foucault says that he would like to slip unnoticed into the discourse about discourse, presumably to avoid having to explain his own privileged position beyond it (*Archaeology*, p. 215). Adorno finds revolutionary consciousness in the philosophical individual ("In face of the totalitarian unison with which the eradication of difference is proclaimed as a purpose in itself, even part of the social force of liberation may have temporarily withdrawn to the individual sphere. If critical theory lingers there, it is not only with a bad conscience," *Minima Moralia*, p. 18).

Marcuse finds it in those outside the "democratic process" ("the substratum of the outcasts and outsiders, the exploited and persecuted of other races and other colours, the unemployed and the unemployable," *One-Dimensional Man*, p. 201). Sorel finds it in the "passionate individualism" of the oppressed eager for the general strike ("These groups ... picture the Revolution as an immense uprising which yet may be called individualistic; each working with the greatest possible zeal, each acting on his own account, and not troubling himself much to subordinate his conduct to a great and scientifically combined plan," *Reflections on Violence*, p. 241). Weber finds it in the charismatic leader ("The term 'charisma' will be applied to a certain quality of an individual personality by virtue of which he is set apart from ordinary men and treated as endowed with supernatural, superhuman, or at least specifically exceptional powers or qualities. These are such as are not accessible to the ordinary person, but are regarded of divine origin or as exemplary, and on the basis of them the individual concerned is treated as a leader. ... In traditionally stereotyped periods, charisma is the greatest revolutionary force," *Theory of Social and Economic Organization*, pp. 359–363).

106. Even Weber becomes an apologist for rationalization as civilization. Sorel attempts to preserve both individuality and solidarity through permanent revolution. Marcuse insists that society releases, not represses, individuality; only the direction of that release—toward guilt, not innocence—has been repressive (*Eros and Civilization*, p. 108). Adorno and Horkheimer claim that Nietzsche's "ratio" "implicitly liberates from its hiding-place the utopia contained in the Kantian notion of reason ... the utopia of a humanity which, itself no longer distorted, has no further need to distort" (*Dialectic of Enlightenment*, p. 119). Althusser argues that present historical tasks call for new forms of organization, and Foucault responds to the disappearance of the subject by declaring subjectivity to be artificial (*For Marx*, p. 239, and *Archaeology*, p. 211).

107. Examples of the former appear in Adorno's insistence that "avant-garde theory" serves a "true collective" but his inability to explain how (Buck-Morss, *Origin of Negative Dialectics*, p. 41) and Marcuse's relegation of revolution to accident ("The chance is that the historical extremes may meet again: the most advanced consciousness of humanity, and its most exploited force. It is nothing but a chance. The critical theory of society possesses no concepts which could bridge the gap between the present and its future: holding no promise and showing no success, it remains negative," *One-Dimensional Man*, p. 201).

Examples of the latter appear in Althusser's ambivalent attitude toward Stalinism: he declares it to be merely a superstructural error (*For Marx*, p. 240). They may also be found in Sorel's ambivalence toward fascist regimes and Weber's reliance upon a charismatic leader to counteract the rationalization of life.

6. Production Versus Play: Capitalism as Self-Denial

1. See again Adorno and Horkheimer, *Dialectic of Enlightenment*, especially chs. 1 and 4; Adorno, *Minima Moralia*, aphorism #144; Heinrich Regius (a pseudonym for Horkheimer), *Dämmerung*, p. 181. Also see Marcuse, "On Hedonism" and "Industrialization and Capitalism in the Work of Max Weber"; *One-Dimensional Man*, chs. 3 and 6; and *Eros and Civilization*, p. 105–112.

2. *MEW* 3:28; Marx and Engels, *German Ideology*, p. 48.

3. *MEW* 23:198; Marx, *Capital*, 1:183.

4. *MEW* 23:49; *Capital*, 1:35, emphasis mine.

5. *MEW* 25:828; *Capital* 3:820.

6. For example, Marx refers to "labor itself" as unable to exist except in opposition to capital, i.e., except as a consequence of private property and the division of labor (*MEW* 3:66; *German Ideology*, p. 92). He then says that "the communist revolution is directed against the preceding *mode* of activity, does away with *labour*, and abolishes the rule of all

classes with the classes themselves" (*MEW* 3:69–70; *German Ideology*, p. 94).

In the *Economic and Philosophical Manuscripts*, he contrasts how "man appropriates his integral essence in an integral way" with appropriation restricted to "crude practical need," i.e., with "estranged labor" under "private property" (pp. 351–353; *MEW, Erganzungsband*, 1:39–41).

Numerous similar references clearly refer to alienated labor when read in context.

7. Marx, *Grundrisse*, g505, e611.
8. *MEW* 3:20; Marx and Engels, *German Ideology*, p. 42.
9. Nietzsche, *Will to Power*, aphorism #702.
10. *Ibid.*, aphorism #943.
11. *Ibid.*, aphorism #552.
12. *Ibid.*, aphorism #707.
13. *Ibid.*, aphorism #797.
14. *MEW, Erg.*, 1:543; Marx, *Economic and Philosophical Manuscripts*, p. 354.
15. Nietzsche, *Will to Power*, aphorism #652.
16. *MEW* 3:30; Marx and Engels, *German Ideology*, p. 50.
17. *MEW* 3:32; *German Ideology*, p. 53.
18. *MEW* 3:21; *German Ideology*, p. 43.
19. *MEW* 23:57; Marx, *Capital*, 1:42.
20. *MEW* 3:33; Marx and Engels, *German Ideology*, p. 53.
21. *MEW* 3:32; *German Ideology*, p. 52.
22. *MEW* 23:56–57; Marx, *Capital*, 1:42.
23. Marx, *Grundrisse*, g75, e157.
24. Nietzsche, *Will to Power*, aphorism #561.
25. Nietzsche, *Gay Science*, aphorism #21.
26. Nietzsche, *Daybreak*, aphorism #173.
27. Nietzsche, *Human All Too Human*, aphorism #439.
28. Nietzsche, *Will to Power*, aphorism #125.
29. Nietzsche, *Genealogy*, first essay, section #5.
30. *WdB*, 2:337; Nietzsche, *Zarathustra*, pp. 186–187.
31. Nietzsche, *Anti-Christ*, aphorism #57.
32. Nietzsche, *Will to Power*, aphorism #758.
33. *MEW* 23:556; Marx, *Capital*, 1:534.
34. Nietzsche, *Daybreak*, aphorism #174.
35. *Ibid.*, aphorism #175.
36. *Ibid.*, aphorism #204.
37. Nietzsche, *Gay Science*, aphorism #329.
38. Nietzsche, *Will to Power*, aphorism #792.
39. Nietzsche, *Gay Science*, aphorism #329.
40. *Ibid.*, aphorism #21.
41. Nietzsche, *Will to Power*, aphorism #61.
42. *Ibid.*, aphorism #94.
43. Marx, *Grundrisse*, g64–65, e146.

44. For a discussion of the "so-called primitive accumulation," see *MEW* 23:742ff; Marx, *Capital*, 1:714ff; and Marx, *Pre-Capitalist Economic Formations*, pp. 106–108. Hobsbawm's introduction also provides an excellent analysis of Marx's and Engel's treatment of the breakdown of feudalism and the rise of capitalism.

45. *MEW* 23:249–251; Marx, *Capital*, 1:235–236.

46. *MEW* 23:167; *Capital* 1:151–152.

47. *MEW* 23:167; *Capital* 1:151–152.

48. Nietzsche, *Will to Power*, aphorism #719.

49. *Ibid.*, aphorism #888.

50. Nietzsche, *Wanderer and His Shadow*, aphorism #218.

51. *Ibid.*, aphorisms #220, #288.

52. *Ibid.*, aphorism #288.

53. Nietzsche, *Will to Power*, aphorism #866.

54. *WdB* 2:394; Nietzsche, *Zarathustra*, pp. 250–251.

55. *MEW* 23:249; Marx, *Capital*, 1:235.

56. *MEW* 23:200–202; *Capital* 1:186–187.

57. Machines enable capitalists to increase surplus value not only by increasing the productivity of labor, but also by allowing (even requiring, since machines lose use value and exchange value when they sit idle) longer working days and multiple shifts, by intensifying labor, and by facilitating cheaper female and child labor. Marx stresses, as I will presently discuss, that machine production itself does not alienate men; capitalists who put machines to the wrong use—who use them to exploit labor—do. It is the bourgeoisie who cannot conceive of "any employment of machinery except by capital." Marx is not an enemy of technological advances, but rather of their capitalist employment.

58. *MEW* 23:445–446; Marx, *Capital*, 1:422–423.

59. *MEW* 23:446; *Capital* 1:423.

60. *MEW* 23:382; *Capital* 1:361.

61. *MEW* 3:74; Marx and Engels, *German Ideology*, p. 83.

62. Nietzsche, *Miscellaneous Maxims and Opinions*, aphorism #317.

63. Nietzsche, *Gay Science*, aphorism #40.

64. *Ibid.*, aphorism #42.

65. Nietzsche, *Will to Power*, aphorism #763.

66. Nietzsche, *Wanderer and His Shadow*, aphorism #285.

67. *Ibid.*

68. Nietzsche, *Gay Science*, aphorism #40.

69. *Ibid.*

70. Nietzsche, *Will to Power*, aphorism #94.

71. Marx, *Grundrisse*, g365–366, e462.

72. *MEW* 23:675; Marx, *Capital*, 1:645. I have chosen this passage, although it is a reference to Marx's controversial thesis that as capital accumulates, so does an industrial reserve army (that is, a mass of workers made obsolete by machines, who compete with other workers for limited jobs, depressing wages), because it is clear even in this passage that Marx is not merely, perhaps not even primarily, attacking

the quantitative decrease of wages under capitalist production. Even if the quantitative decrease of wages were his main target, he could be defended against those who would refute him by claiming that, contrary to his presumed predictions, workers' wages have increased. Marx argues that there is a historical/moral component, i.e., the customary degree of comfort in a society, which enters into the determination of the value of labor power (*MEW* 23:185; *Capital* 1:171). Consequently, wage laborers may be impoverished relative to social conditions, even if their absolute wages increase.

In any case, Marx says, "But all methods for the production of surplus-value are at the same time methods of accumulation; and every extension of accumulation becomes again a means for the development of those methods. It follows therefore that in proportion as capital accumulates, the lot of the laborer, *be his payment high or low*, must grow worse" (emphasis mine). Marx is arguing that the laborer is "poorer" because his domination of nature produces his subordination to his own creations as capital. Capital makes his life activity and his products his self-alienation, not his self-realization. This argument about the quality of labor in capitalist society survives, even if the quantity of wages increases relatively as well as absolutely.

73. *MEW*, *Erg.*, 1:536; Marx, *Economic and Philosophical Manuscripts*, p. 348.

74. Nietzsche, *Will to Power*, aphorism #866.

75. *MEW* 3:67; Marx and Engels, *German Ideology*, p. 92.

76. Nietzsche, *Will to Power*, aphorism #866.

77. *MEW* 23:511–512; Marx, *Capital*, 1:487–489.

78. Marx, *Grundrisse*, g608, e701.

79. *MEW* 4:467–468; Marx and Engels, *Communist Manifesto*, p. 478.

80. *MEW* 25:828; Marx, *Capital*, 3:820.

81. *MEW* 25:828; *Capital* 3:820.

82. Marx, *Grundrisse*, g505, e611.

83. Nietzsche, *Will to Power*, aphorism #797. It should be remembered that play, for Nietzsche, is neither *laisser aller* nor hedonism; Nietzsche's leisure caste exercises the greatest self-overcoming. Play is the activity of the individual who is free of revenge, who no longer *reacts against* life. This individual transcends all "earthly seriousness," the renunciation of the reverent and the rebellion of the nihilist (*WdB* 2:294; *Zarathustra*, p. 139). But it is only with this that the "great seriousness" begins. For the child consciously affirms himself and life as it is by willing their eternal recurrence. Beyond life-denying illusions, he consciously creates non-ascetic meaning for life. Nietzsche describes his "play" in greater detail: "Another ideal runs ahead of us, a strange, tempting, dangerous ideal . . . the ideal of a spirit who plays naively—that is, not deliberately but from overflowing power and abundance—with all that was hitherto called holy, good, untouchable, divine; for whom those

supreme things that people naturally accept as their value standards, signify danger, decay, debasement, or at least recreation, blindness, and temporary self-oblivion; the ideal of a human, superhuman well-being and benevolence that will often appear *inhuman*—for example, when it confronts all earthly seriousness so far, all solemnity in gesture, word, tone, eye, morality, and task so far, as if it were their most incarnate and involuntary parody—and in spite of all of this, it is perhaps only with him that *great seriousness* really begins, that the real question mark is posed for the first time, that the destiny of the soul changes, the hand moves forward, the tragedy *begins"* (*Gay Science*, aphorism #382).

84. *MEW* 20:273; Engels, *Anti-Dühring*, p. 320.

85. *MEW* 25:96; Marx, *Capital*, 3:86. Marx says: "However, it is not only the alienation and indifference that arise between the labourer, the bearer of living labor and the economical, i.e., rational and thrifty, use of the material conditions of his labour. In line with its contradictory and antagonistic nature, the capitalist mode of production proceeds to count the prodigious dissipation of the labourer's life and health...as an economy...as a means of raising the profit."

86. *MEW* 20:273; Engels, *Anti-Dühring*, p. 320.

87. *MEW* 20:277; *Anti-Dühring*, p. 221.

88. *MEW* 3:379; Marx and Engels, *German Ideology*, p. 109.

89. Marx, *Grundrisse*, g505, e611.

90. Nietzsche, *Will to Power*, aphorism #758.

91. Nietzsche, *Will to Power*, aphorism #1066.

92. *Ibid.*, aphorism #757.

93. Marx, *Grundrisse*, g505, e611.

94. Nietzsche, *Will to Power*, aphorism #758.

95. For example: In the *Dialectic of Enlightenment*, Adorno and Horkheimer say, "Bourgeois society is ruled by equivalence. It makes the dissimilar comparable by reducing it to abstract quantities." They trace this principle of equivalence to the Enlightenment, which is "totalitarian," saying, "Number became the canon of the Enlightenment. The same equations dominate bourgeois justice and commodity exchange" (p. 7). From the principle of Enlightenment/exchange as domination, they conclude, "The impotence of the worker is not merely a stratagem of the rulers, but the logical consequence of the industrial society into which the ancient Fate—in the very course of the effort to escape it—has finally changed" (p. 37). They nonetheless maintain that "this logical necessity is not conclusive. It remains tied to domination, as both its reflection and its tool" (p. 37).

But it is hard to see how one escapes, let alone revolutionizes, this logic of domination. At the very least, it seems that Marx's emphasis upon man's nature as a social producer shares this logic. It is not surprising then that Adorno and Horkheimer try to distance themselves from it. "To make labor into a transcendent category," says Horkheimer, "is an ascetic ideology. ... In that socialists adhere to this general concept, they make themselves carriers of capitalist propaganda" (*Dämmerung*, p. 181). Following Weber, Horkheimer argues that it is bourgeois to emphasize self-preservation and self-fulfillment. Instead of production— a realm of necessity, Adorno notes critically, even in socialist society— they stress "purposive purposelessness."

Marcuse also argues that commodity culture is totalitarian; it participates in the logic of domination, not gratification. In *One-Dimensional Man*, he describes this totalitarian "economic—technical coordination": "The distinguishing feature of advanced industrial society is its effective suffocation of those needs which demand liberation— liberation also from that which is tolerable and rewarding and comfortable—while it sustains and absolves the destructive power and repressive function of the affluent society. Here, the social controls exact the overwhelming need for the production and consumption of waste; the need for stupefying work where it is no longer a real necessity; the need for modes of relaxation which soothe and prolong this stupefication; the need for maintaining such deceptive liberties as free competition at administered prices, a free press which censors itself, free choice between brands and gadgets" (p. 7). Marcuse asks, "How can the people who have been the object of effective and productive domination by themselves create the conditions of freedom?" (p. 6). He too uses Nietzsche to illustrate the contrast between the logic of domination and that of gratification, suggesting as well that production partakes of the former.

96. Although Adorno and Horkheimer describe and criticize a logical, not merely a capitalist, connection between labor as the domination of nature and the domination of men, they nonetheless suggest that the unity of the collectivity and domination can be overcome: "To the individual, domination appears to be the universal: reason in actuality. Through the division of labor imposed on them, the power of all the members of society—for whom as such there is no other course [!]— amounts over and over again to the realization of the whole, whose rationality is reproduced in this way. What is done to all by the few, always occurs as the subjection of individuals by the many: social repression always exhibits the masks of repression by a collective. It is this unity of the collectivity and domination, and not direct social universality, solidarity, which is expressed in thought forms" (*Dialectic of Enlightenment*, p. 22).

In the following passage, Marcuse emphasizes the separation of labor and pleasure in capitalist society. However, he also implies that pleasure has value separate from, even superior to, value-creating labor. "Where the prevailing social relationship is the relation of men to one another as owners of commodities and where the value of every commodity is determined by the abstract labor time applied to it, enjoyment has no value in itself. For all that it is in this society, it is in separation from labor. In enjoyment the individual expends no labor power, nor does he reproduce labor power. He behaves as and acknowledges himself to be a private person. When value, the standard of the equity of exchange is created only by abstract labor, then pleasure may not be a value" ("On Hedonism," p. 185).

For an extended critique of labor as imposition of being versus eros as acceptance of becoming, see Marcuse's *Eros and Civilization*, ch. 4. Especially see pp. 108–110 for a discussion of the association between play and the eternal recurrence in Nietzsche.

97. For psychological critiques of Marxian rational producers informed by Nietzsche, see Sigmund Freud, *Civilization and Its Discontents*, especially chs. 3 and 5, specifically on Marx, pp. 59–63; Jean Baudrillard, *The Mirror of Production*.

7. The End of Modernity

1. MacIntyre, *After Virtue*, p. 21.
2. Shklar, *After Utopia*, p. 272.
3. Warren, *Emergence of Dialectical Theory*, p. 1.
4. Bernstein, *Restructuring of Social and Political Theory*, p. xxiv.
5. In *After Virtue*, MacIntyre says, "The Nietzschean stance turns out not to be a mode of escape from or an alternative to the conceptual scheme of liberal individualist modernity, but rather one more representative moment in its internal unfolding" (p. 241). He argues that Marxism also perpetuates modernity: "As Marxists move towards power they always tend to become Weberians.... When Marxism does not become Weberian social democracy or crude tyranny, it tends to become Nietzschean fantasy" (pp. 243–244).

In *After Utopia*, Shklar is also skeptical about Nietzsche's and Marx's contributions to the restructuring of society. She argues that romantics, Nietzsche among them, typify "the unhappy consciousness": "They can offer us no coherent account of nature, man, history or society. They do not even try, for the defeat of the spirit lies in just this: that everything has become incomprehensible.... The romanticism of defeat is simple submission to this otherness of nature and society" (p. 163). In her more recent "Subversive Genealogies," Shklar does recognize Nietzsche's contribution as a genealogist to the debunking of Western values. She also argues, however, that Nietzsche recognized "the paradox of his own efforts. For his genealogy is also a pursuit of truth" (p. 146). Shklar argues that socialists (and liberals) have become equally, though differently, pessimistic: "Certainly, neither liberals nor socialists today believe in inevitable progress or in the ability of free, rational men to live without coercion in a perfectly harmonious society" (*After Utopia*, p. 220).

In *The Emergence of Dialectical Theory*, Scott Warren is more optimistic about Marx's and Nietzsche's capacity to contribute to the restructuring of political inquiry. Although "Marx's development too readily allowed for the emergence of an instrumentalist positivism,"

Warren defends a "dialectical Marxism" which "avoids the two extremes of abolishing all reflective inquiry as such and of transforming philosophy into positivist science" (pp. 60–65). Because he does not regard Nietzsche as a dialectician, Warren says little about his philosophy (p. 218, n. 33). But he defends a dialectical theory informed by the *Lebensphilosophen* who recovered spiritual, vital dimensions of humanity from abstract rationalism and social conformity.

In *The Restructuring of Social and Political Theory*, Bernstein also praises Marx's (and Hegel's) use of critique, though he argues that Marx's original critique of political economy needs to be radically revised, partially because so many of Marx's predictions have been realized in contemporary society (pp. 170, 180–184). In "Nietzsche or Aristotle?" he defends Nietzsche by arguing polemically that "MacIntyre decoded is the champion of Nietzsche." This is because MacIntyre "not only shows that there are incompatible and incommensurable lists and theories of virtue, but has failed *thus far* to show how we can 'rationally' adjudicate among rival claimants" (p. 9). Bernstein concludes that "the problem today is how we can live with the conflict and tension between the 'truth' implicit in the tradition of the virtues and the 'truth' of the Enlightenment" (p. 28).

6. Warren argues that dialectical theory addresses some of the problems shared by traditional political theory and behavioral political science. (See *The Emergence of Dialectical Theory*, ch. 1.)

7. In *The Emergence of Dialectical Theory*, Warren notes that all thinkers who stand outside positivism and revived classical theory are often relegated to the "monolithic ideological prison of historicism." He cites one such classification which includes Kant, Hegel, Marx, Nietzsche, Husserl, Spengler, Dewey, G. H. Mead, Bergson, Sartre, Dilthey, Mannheim, Heidegger, Merleau-Ponty, Wittgenstein, Cassierer, Kuhn, Hwa Yol Jung, John Gunnell, and Henry Kariel. He concludes, "This is quite a collection, and one that is not altogether helpful" (p. 189). In chapter 7, "Prologue to the Future," he differentiates between dialectical theory and historicism.

8. Nietzsche, *Genealogy*, second essay, section #24.

SELECTED BIBLIOGRAPHY

PRIMARY SOURCES

Karl Marx and Frederick Engels

Engels, Frederick. *Dialectics of Nature* (1873–83). Clemens Dutt ed. and tr. New York: International Publishers, 1940.

___ *Herr Eugen Dühring's Revolution in Science* (1876–77). New York: International Publishers, 1935.

___ *Ludwig Feuerbach and the Age of Classical German Philosophy* (1886). New York: International Publishers, 1941.

___ *On Authority* (1874). In *The Marx-Engels Reader*, pp. 730–734.

___ *The Origin of the Family, Private Property, and the State: In the Light of the Researches of Lewis H. Morgan* (1884). New York: International Publishers, 1973.

___ "Socialism: Utopian and Scientific" (1880). In *The Marx-Engels Reader*, pp. 683–713.

Marx, Karl. *Capital*. Vol. 1 (1867). New York: International Publishers, 1967.

___ *Capital*. Vol. 2 (1885). Frederick Engels, ed. New York: International Publishers, 1967.

___ *Capital*. Vol. 3 (1894). Frederick Engels, ed. New York: International Publishers, 1967.

___ *The Civil War in France* (1871). In *The Marx-Engels Reader*, pp. 618–653.

___ "A Contribution to the Critique of Hegel's *Philosophy of Right*. Introduction" (1843–44). In *Early Writings*, pp. 243–258.

____ "Critique of the Gotha Program" (1875). In *The Marx-Engels Reader*, pp. 525–541.

____ *Critique of Hegel's Doctrine of the State* (1843). In *Early Writings*, pp. 57–198.

____ *Early Writings*. Quinton Hoare, ed.; Gregor Benton and Rodney Livingstone, trs. New York: Random House, 1975.

____ *Economic and Philosophical Manuscripts* (1844). In *Early Writings*, pp. 279–400.

____ *The Eighteenth Brumaire of Louis Bonaparte* (1852). In *The Marx-Engels Reader*, pp. 594–617.

____ *Grundrisse* (1857–58). Berlin: Dietz, 1974. (Fotomechanischer Nachdruck der Ausgabe Moskau 1939 and 1941.)

____ *Grundrisse* (1857–58). Martin Nicolaus, tr. New York: Random House, 1973.

____ "On the Jewish Question" (1843). In *Early Writings*, pp. 211–242.

____ *The Poverty of Philosophy* (1946–47). New York: International Publishers, 1975.

____ *Pre-Capitalist Economic Formations* (1857–58). Jack Cohen, tr., introduction by E. J. Hobsbawm. New York: International Publishers, 1964.

____ "Preface to *A Contribution to the Critique of Political Economy*" (1859). In *Early Writings*, pp. 424-428.

____ "Reflections of a Youth on Choosing an Occupation" (1835). Loyd D. Easton and Kurt Guddat, trs., pp. 35–39. In *Writings of the Young Marx on Philosophy and Society*, Garden City, N.Y.: Double day, 1977.

____ "Theses on Feuerbach" (1845). In *Early Writings*, pp. 422–423.

Marx, Karl and Frederick Engels. *The Communist Manifesto*. In *The Marx-Engels Reader*, pp. 469–500.

____ *The German Ideology* (1945–46). C. J. Arthur, ed. New York: International Publishers, 1977.

____ *The Holy Family, or a Critique of Critical Criticism* (1844). 2d ed. Moscow: Progress Publishers, 1975.

____ *The Marx-Engels Reader*. Robert C. Tucker, ed. 2d ed. New York: Norton, 1978.

____ *Marx-Engels Werke*. Berlin: Dietz, 1961–66.

____ *Selected Correspondence.* Moscow: Foreign Languages Publishing, 1956.

Friedrich Nietzsche

Nietzsche, Friedrich. *The AntiChrist* (1888). In *The Portable Nietzsche, pp. 569–660.*
____ *Basic Writings of Nietzsche.* Walter Kaufmann, tr. New York: Random House, 1966.
____ *Beyond Good and Evil* (1886). In *Basic Writings of Nietzsche,* pp. 181–435.
____ *The Birth of Tragedy* (1872). In *Basic Writings of Nietzsche,* pp. 3–144.
____ *The Case of Wagner* (1888). In *Basic Writings of Nietzsche,* pp. 609–648.
____ *The Complete Works of Friedrich Nietzsche.* Oscar Levy, ed. New York: Gordon Press, 1974.
____ *David Strauss, Confessor and Writer* (1873). In *The Complete Works of Friedrich Nietzsche,* 4:1–98.
____ *Daybreak* (1881). R. J. Hollingdale, tr. Cambridge: Cambridge University Press, 1982.
____ *Ecce Homo* (1888). In *Basic Writings of Nietzsche,* pp. 671–791.
____ *The Gay Science* (1882). Walter Kaufmann, tr. New York: Random House, 1974.
____ *The Genealogy of Morals* (1887). In *Basic Writings of Nietzsche,* pp. 459–599.
____ *Human All Too Human* (1878). Marion Faber and Stephen Lehmann, trs. Lincoln: University of Nebraska Press, 1984.
____ *Miscellaneous Maxims and Opinions* (1879). In *The Complete Works of Friedrich Nietzsche,* 7:11–178.
____ *Nietzsche Contra Wagner.* In *The Portable Nietzsche,* pp. 661–683.
____ *Nietzsche Werke. Kritische Gesamtausgabe.* Giorgio Colli and Mazzini Montinari, eds. Berlin: Walter de Gruyter, 1967.
____ *The Portable Nietzsche.* Walter Kaufmann, tr. and ed. New York: Viking Press, 1968.

___ *Richard Wagner in Bayreuth* (1876). In *The Complete Works of Friedrich Nietzsche*, 4:99–204.

___ *Schopenhauer as Educator* (1874). James W. Hellesheim and Malcolm R. Simpson, trs. South Bend, Ind.: Regnery-Gateway, 1965.

___ *Selected Letters of Friedrich Nietzsche*. Christopher Middleton, ed. and tr. Chicago: University of Chicago Press, 1969.

___ *Thus Spoke Zarathustra* (1883–84). In *The Portable Nietzsche*, pp. 112–439.

___ "Truth and Falsity in Their Ultra-Moral Sense." In *The Complete Works of Friedrich Nietzsche*, 1:171–192.

___ *Twilight of the Idols* (1888). In *The Portable Nietzsche*, pp. 464–563.

___ *The Use and Abuse of History* (1874). Adrian Collins, tr. New York: Bobbs-Merrill, 1957.

___ *The Wanderer and His Shadow* (1880). In *The Complete Works of Friedrich Nietzsche*, 7:179–366.

___ *Werke in drei Bänden*. Karl Schlecta, ed. Munich: Carl Hanser, 1966.

___ *The Will to Power* (1886–88). Walter Kaufmann and R. J. Hollingdale, trs. and eds. New York: Random House, 1968.

SECONDARY SOURCES

Adorno, Theodor. *Minima Moralia: Reflections from Damaged Life.* E. F. N. Jephcott, tr. London: New Left Books, 1978.

___ *Negative Dialectics*. E. B. Ashton, tr. New York: Continuum Books, 1983.

Adorno, Theodor and Max Horkheimer. *Dialectic of Enlightenment.* John Cumming, tr. New York: Seabury Press, 1972.

†Allison, David, ed. *The New Nietzsche*: *Contemporary Styles of Interpretation*. New York: Dell, 1977.

Althusser, Louis. *For Marx*. Ben Brewster, tr. London: New Left Books, 1977.

---

*Works on Marx and Engels
†Works on Nietzsche

____ "Ideology and Ideological State Apparatuses." Ben Brewster, tr. In *Lenin and Philosophy and Other Essays*, pp. 127–188. New York: Monthly Review Press, 1971.

Althusser, Louis and Etienne Balibar. *Reading Capital.* London: New Left Books, 1977.

Andrew, Edward. "A Note on the Unity of Theory and Practice in Marx and Nietzsche." *Political Theory* (August 1975), 3(3):305– 316.

Arato, Andrew and Eike Gebhardt, eds. *The Essential Frankfurt School Reader.* New York: Continuum Books, 1982.

Asher, Kenneth. "Deconstruction's Use and Abuse of Nietzsche." *Telos* (Winter 1984–85), 62:169–179.

*Avineri, Shlomo. "The Hegelian Origins of Marx's Political Thought." *Review of Metaphysics* (September 1967), 21:33– 56.

*____ *The Social and Political Thought of Karl Marx.* Cambridge: Cambridge University Press, 1968.

*Ball, Terrence and James Farr, eds. *After Marx.* Cambridge: Cambridge University Press, 1984.

Barth, Hans. *Truth and Ideology.* Frederic Lilge, tr. Berkeley and Los Angeles: University of California Press, 1976.

Bathrick, David and Paul Breines. "Marx und/oder Nietzsche." In Reinhold Grimm and Jost Hermann eds., *Karl Marx und Friedrich Nietzsche*, pp. 119–135. Konigsten/Ts.: Athenaum-Taschenbucher, 1978.

Baudrillard, Jean. *The Mirror of Production.* Mark Poster, tr. Saint Louis: Telos Press, 1975.

*Berki, R. N. *Insight & Vision: The Problem of Communism in Marx's Thought.* London: J. M. Dent, 1984.

Bernstein, Richard. "Nietzsche or Aristotle?: Reflections on MacIntyre's *After Virtue.*" *Soundings* (Spring 1984), 67 (1):6–30.

____ *The Restructuring of Social and Political Theory.* New York: Harcourt Brace Jovanovich, 1976.

Buck-Morss, Susan. *The Origin of Negative Dialectics: Theodor*

Adorno, Walter Benjamin, and the Frankfurt Institute. New York: Free Press, 1977.

†Camus, Albert. "Nietzsche and Nihilism." In *The Rebel*, A. Bower, tr. New York: Vintage Books, 1956.

*Cohen, G. A. "Karl Marx and the Withering Away of Social Science." *Philosophy and Public Affairs* (1972), 1:182–203. Reprinted as an appendix to *Karl Marx's Theory of History: A Defence.*

*____ *Karl Marx's Theory of History: A Defence.* Princeton, N.J.: Princeton University Press, 1978.

*____ "Marx's Dialectic of Labor." *Philosophy and Public Affairs* (Spring 1974), 3(3):235–261.

*____ Review of Wood, *Karl Marx. Mind* (1983), 92:440–445.

*Cohen, Marshall, Thomas Nagel, and Thomas Scanlon, eds., *Marx, Justice, and History.* Princeton, N.J.: Princeton University Press, 1980.

†Dannhauser, Werner. *Nietzsche's View of Socrates.* Ithaca, N.Y.: Cornell University Press, 1974.

†Danto, Arthur. *Nietzsche as Philosopher.* New York: Columbia University Press, 1970.

†Deleuze, Giles. *Nietzsche and Philosophy.* Hugh Tomlinson, tr. New York: Columbia University Press, 1983.

†____ "Nomad Thought." In David Allison, ed., *The New Nietzsche*, pp. 142–147. New York: Dell Publishing Co., 1977.

Derrida, Jacques. *Positions.* Alan Bass, tr. Chicago: University of Chicago Press, 1981.

†____ *Spurs: Nietzsche's Styles.* Barbara Harlow, tr. Chicago: University of Chicago Press, 1979.

Doyal, Len and Roger Harris. "The Practical Foundations of Human Understanding." *New Left Review* (May–June 1983), 139:59–78.

*Draper, Hal. *Karl Marx's Theory of Revolution.* Part 1, *State and Revolution.* New York and London: Monthly Review Press, 1977.

*Dupré, Louis. *The Philosophical Foundations of Marxism.* New York: Harcourt, Brace, and World, 1966.

*Works on Marx and Engels
†Works on Nietzsche

Eagleton, Terry. *Literary Theory: An Introduction*. Minneapolis: University of Minnesota Press, 1983.

† Eden, Robert. *Political Leadership and Nihilism: A Study of Weber and Nietzsche*. Gainesville: University of Florida Presses, 1984.

Feuerbach, Ludwig. *The Essence of Christianity*. George Eliot, tr. New York: Harper and Row, 1957.

Foucault, Michel. *The Archaeology of Knowledge*. A. M. Sheridan Smith, tr. New York: Pantheon Books, 1972.

___ *Discipline and Punish: The Birth of the Prison*. Alan Sheridan, tr. New York: Random House, 1979.

†___ "Nietzsche, Genealogy, History." In Donald F. Bouchard, ed., *Language, Countermemory, Practice*, pp. 139–164. New York: Cornell University Press, 1977.

___ *Power/Knowledge: Selected Interviews and Other Writings, 1972–1977*. Colin Gordon, ed. New York: Pantheon Books, 1980.

Freud, Sigmund. *Civilization and Its Discontents*. James Strachey, ed. New York: Norton, 1961.

*Fromm, Eric. *Marx's Concept of Man*. New York: Unger, 1977.

*Geras, Norman. "The Controversy About Marx and Justice." *New Left Review* (March-April 1985), 150:47–88.

Gerth, H. H. and C. Wright Mills, eds. *From Max Weber*. New York: Oxford University Press, 1946.

*Gilbert, Allen. "An Ambiguity in Marx's and Engels' Account of Justice and Equality." *American Political Science Review* (June 1982), 76(2):328–346.

Habermas, Jürgen. "The Entwinement of Myth and Enlightenment: Re-Reading *Dialectic of Enlightenment*." *New German Critique* (Spring-Summer 1982), 26:13–32.

___ *Knowledge and Human Interests*. J. J. Shapiro, tr. Boston: Beacon Press, 1971.

___ *Legitimation Crisis*. Thomas McCarthy, tr. Boston: Beacon Press, 1973.

___ "Modernity Versus Post Modernity." *New German Critique* (Winter 1981), 22:3–14.

*Works on Marx and Engels
†Works on Nietzsche

_____ "Toward a Reconstruction of Historical Materialism." Thomas McCarthy, tr. In *Communication and the Evolution of Society*, pp. 130–177. Boston: Beacon Press, 1979.

†Hayman, Ronald. *Nietzsche: A Critical Life.* New York: Penguin Books, 1982.

†Heidegger, Martin. *Nietzsche.* 2 vols. Pfullingen: Gunther Neske, 1961.

†_____ *Nietzsche.* Vol. 1. *The Will to Power as Art.* David Farrell Krell, tr. San Francisco: Harper and Row, 1979.

†_____ *Nietzsche.* Vol. 4. *Nihilism.* Frank Capuzzi, tr. San Francisco: Harper and Row, 1982.

*Hobsbawm, Eric J. Introduction to *Pre-Capitalist Economic Formations.* New York: International Publishers, 1980.

†Hollingdale, R. J. *Nietzsche: The Man and His Philosophy.* London: Routledge and Kegan Paul, 1973.

Horkheimer, Max. "The Authoritarian State." In Andrew Arato and Eike Gebhardt, eds., *The Essential Frankfurt School Reader*, pp. 95–117.

_____ *Dämmerung.* (Zurich, 1934) under pseudonym Heinrich Regius.

†Jaspers, Karl. *Nietzsche: An Introduction to the Understanding of His Philosophical Activity.* Charles F. Wallraff and Frederick J. Schmiltz, trs. Chicago: Regnery, 1965.

Jay Martin. *The Dialectical Imagination: A History of the Frankfurt School and the Institute for Social Research, 1923–1950.* Boston: Little, Brown, 1973.

_____ *Marxism and Totality: The Adventures of a Concept from Lukács to Habermas.* Berkeley and Los Angeles: University of California Press, 1984.

†Kaufmann, Walter. *Nietzsche: Philosopher, Psychologist, Antichrist.* Princeton, N.J.: Princeton University Press, 1974.

*Kolakowski, Leszek. *Toward a Marxist Humanism: Essays on the Left Today.* Jane Zielonko Peel, tr. New York: Grove Press, 1968.

†Love, Frederick R. *Young Nietzsche and the Wagnerian Experi-*

*Works on Marx and Engels
†Works on Nietzsche

ence. Chapel Hill: University of North Carolina Press, 1963.

† Love, Nancy. "The Newest Nietzsche." *Review of Politics.* (October 1985), 47(4):631–637.

____ "Reason, Repression, and Reality in Marxism." Paper presented at the American Political Science Association Meeting, Washington, D.C., September 1984.

† Löwith, Karl. *From Hegel to Nietzsche: The Revolution in 19th Century Thought.* Garden City, N.Y.: Anchor Books, 1967.

† ____ *Nietzsches Philosophie der ewigen Wiederkehr des Gleichen.* Stuttgart: W. Kohlhammer, 1956.

Lukács, Georg. *The Destruction of Reason.* Peter Palmer, tr. New Jersey: Humanities Press, 1981.

____ *History and Class Consciousness.* Rodney Livingstone, tr. Cambridge, Mass.: MIT Press, 1971.

MacIntyre, Alisdair. *After Virtue: A Study in Moral Theory.* Notre Dame, Ind.: University of Notre Dame Press, 1981.

____ "Bernstein's Distorting Mirrors: A Rejoinder." *Soundings* (Spring 1984), 67(1):30–41.

*McLellan, David. *Karl Marx: His Life and Thought.* New York: Harper and Row, 1971.

____ *The Young Hegelians and Karl Marx.* New York: Praeger, 1969.

† Magnus, Bernd. *Nietzsche's Existential Imperative.* Bloomington: Indiana University Press, 1978.

*Mandel, Ernest. *The Formation of the Economic Thought of Karl Marx.* Brian Pearce, tr. New York: Monthly Review Press, 1971.

* ____ *Marxist Economic Theory.* 2 vols. Brian Pearce, tr. New York and London: Monthly Review Press, 1968.

Mannheim, Karl. "The Sociology of Knowledge." Louis Wirth and Edward Shils, trs. In *Ideology and Utopia,* pp. 264–311. New York: Harcourt, Brace, & World, 1936.

Marcuse, Herbert. *Eros and Civilization: A Philosophical Inquiry Into Freud.* New York: Vintage Books, 1955.

____ "The Foundation of Historical Materialism." Joris de Brés, tr.

---

*Works on Marx and Engels
† Works on Nietzsche

In *Studies in Critical Philosophy*, pp. 1–48. Boston: Beacon Press, 1973.

———. "Industrialization and Capitalism in the Work of Max Weber." In *Negations*, pp. 201–226.

———. *Negations*. Jeremy Shapiro, tr. Boston: Beacon Press, 1969.

———. *One-Dimensional Man: Studies in the Ideology of Advanced Industrial Society*. Boston: Beacon Press, 1964.

———. "On Hedonism." In *Negations*, pp. 159–200.

———. *Reason and Revolution: Hegel and the Rise of Social Theory*. Boston: Beacon Press, 1960.

———. "Some Social Implications of Modern Technology," pp. 138–162. In *The Essential Frankfurt School Reader*.

*Mehring, Franz. *Karl Marx: The Story of His Life*. New Jersey: Humanities Press, 1956.

Merleau-Ponty, Maurice. *Humanism and Terror: An Essay on the Communist Problem*. John O'Neill, tr. Boston: Beacon Press, 1969.

Miller, James. "Some Implications of Nietzsche's Thought for Marxism." *Telos* (Fall 1978), 37:22–41.

Miller, Richard. "Methodological Individualism and Social Explanation." *Philosophy of Science* (1978), p. 45.

Mitzmann, Arthur. *The Iron Cage*. New York: Grosset and Dunlap, 1969.

†Nehamas, Alexander. "Immanent and Transcendent Perspectivism in Nietzsche." *Nietzsche-Studien* 12:473–490. Berlin: Walter de Gruyter, 1983.

*Nicolaus, Martin. "The Unknown Marx." *New Left Review* (1968), 48:41–62.

*Ollman, Bertell. *Alienation: Marx's Conception of Man in Capitalist Society*. London: Cambridge University Press, 1976.

*Plamenatz, John. *Karl Marx's Philosophy of Man*. Oxford: Clarendon Press, 1975.

†Pütz, Peter. "Nietzsche and Critical Theory." *Telos* (Winter 1981–82) 50:103–114.

*Robinson, Joan. *An Essay in Marxian Economics*. London: Macmillan, 1947.

*Works on Marx and Engels
†Works on Nietzsche

Rose, Gillian. *The Melancholy Science: An Introduction to the Thought of Theodor Adorno.* New York: Columbia University Press, 1978.

*Rotenstreich, Nathan. *Basic Problems of Marx's Philosophy.* New York: Bobbs-Merrill, 1965.

*Ryan, Michael. *Marxism and Deconstruction.* Baltimore: Johns Hopkins University Press, 1982.

Sartre, Jean-Paul. *Critique of Dialectical Reason.* Alan Sheridan Smith, tr., Jonathan Ree, ed. Atlantic Highlands, N.J.: Humanities Press, 1976.

†Schacht, Richard. *Nietzsche.* London: Routledge and Kegan Paul, 1984.

Scheler, Max. *Ressentiment.* William W. Holdheim, tr. New York: Schocken Books, 1972.

†Schutte, Ofelia. *Beyond Nihilism: Nietzsche Without Masks.* Chicago: University of Chicago Press, 1984.

*Shaw, William H. *Marx's Theory of History.* Stanford: Stanford University Press, 1978.

Shils, Edward A. and Henry A. Finch, eds. *The Methodology of the Social Sciences.* New York: Free Press, 1949.

Shklar, Judith. *After Utopia.* Princeton, N.J.: Princeton University Press, 1957.

_____ "Subversive Genealogies." *Daedalus* (Winter 1972), 101(1): 129–154.

Silz, Walter. *Early German Romanticism.* Cambridge, Mass.: Harvard University Press, 1929.

Sorel, Georges. *Reflections on Violence.* T. E. Hulme and J. Roth, trs. New York: Collier Macmillan, 1972.

†Stambaugh, Joan. *Nietzsche's Thought of Eternal Return.* Baltimore: Johns Hopkins University Press, 1972.

†Stern, J. P. *A Study of Nietzsche.* Cambridge: Cambridge University Press, 1979.

_____ On Andrew: "Theory and Practice in Marx and Nietzsche." *Political Theory* (1976), 4(4):506–508.

Strauss, Leo. *Natural Right and History.* Chicago: University of Chicago Press, 1953.

*Works on Marx and Engels
†Works on Nietzsche

†Strong, Tracy. "Comment on A. Nehemas: 'Immanent and Transcendent Perspectivism in Nietzsche.'" *Nietzsche-Studien* 12:491–494. Berlin: Walter de Gruyter, 1983.

†___ *Friedrich Nietzsche and the Politics of Transfiguration.* Berkeley and Los Angeles: University of California Press, 1975.

†___ "Text and Pretexts: Reflections on Perspectivism in Nietzsche." *Political Theory* (May 1985), 13:164–182.

*Sweezy, Paul. *The Theory of Capitalist Development: Principles of Marxian Political Economy.* New York and London: Monthly Review Press, 1970.

†Thomas, R. Hinton. *Nietzsche in German Politics and Society, 1890–1918.* Manchester: Manchester University Press, 1983.

Thompson, E. P. "The Poverty of Theory." In *The Poverty of Theory and Other Essays,* pp. 1–120. New York: Monthly Review Press, 1978.

Tillich, Paul. "Existential Philosophy." *Journal of the History of Ideas* (1944), pp. 44–70.

†___ "Nietzsche and the Bourgeois Spirit." *Journal of the History of Ideas* (1945), 6:307–309.

Tönnies, Ferdinand. *Community and Society.* Charles P. Loomis, tr. New York: Harper and Row, 1963.

Veyne, Paul. "Ideology According to Marx and According to Nietzsche." Jeanne Ferguson, tr. *Diogenes* (Fall 1977), 99:80–102.

Wagner, Richard. *My Life.* New York: Dodd, Mead, 1911.

†Warren, Mark. "Nietzsche and Political Philosophy." *Political Theory* (May 1985), 13(2):183–212.

†___ "Nietzsche's Concept of Ideology." *Theory and Society* (July 1984), 13(4):541–565.

Warren, Scott. *The Emergence of Dialectical Theory: Philosophy and Political Inquiry.* Chicago: University of Chicago Press, 1984.

Weber, Max. "The Meaning of Ethical Neutrality in Sociology and

*Works on Marx and Engels
†Works on Nietzsche

Economics." In Shils and Finch, eds., *The Methodology of the Social Sciences*, pp. 1-47.

___ "Objectivity in Social Science and Social Policy." In Shils and Finch, eds., *The Methodology of the Social Sciences*, pp. 50-112.

___ "Politics as a Vocation." In Gerth and Mills, eds., *From Max Weber*, pp. 77-129.

___ *The Protestant Ethic and the Spirit of Capitalism*. Talcott Parsons, tr. New York: Scribner, 1958.

___ "Science as a Vocation." In Gerth and Mills, eds., *From Max Weber*, pp. 129-156.

___ *The Theory of Social and Economic Organization*. A. M. Henderson and Talcott Parsons, trs. New York: Collier Macmillan, 1964.

†Wilcox, John T. *Truth and Value in Nietzsche: A Study of His Metaethics and Epistemology*. Ann Arbor: University of Michigan Press, 1974.

*Wood, Allen W. *Karl Marx*. Boston: Routledge and Kegan Paul, 1981.

*___ "The Marxian Critique of Justice." *Philosophy and Public Affairs* (Spring 1972), 1(3):244-282.

*Works on Marx and Engels
†Works on Nietzsche

Index

Active/reactive types, 61-64, 99-101, 106-7
Adorno, Theodor, 13-14, 30, 211*n*43, 228*n*84, 235*n*106, 235*n*107, 239-40 *n*95, 240*n*96
Affirmation, 26, 39-40, 91, 105-7, 138, 193; *see also* Negation
Alienation: alienated labor as basis of, 36, 191; capitalist production as cause of, 2-3, 237-38*n*72, 239*n*85; and commodity fetishism, 2-3, 129-30, 135; development of Marx's concept of, 36-38, 205-6*n*1, 214*n*75; distinct from objectification, 43-44, 49-52, 170-71, 213*n*69; and division of labor, 182-83, 186-87; as frustrated life activity, 65, 109-10; left Hegelian view of, 28-30; as necessary stage of history, 110-11; and private property, 177, 179-81; and religion, 122-24; and state, 143-44, 146-50, 151-61
Althusser, Louis, 32-38, 78-79, 213*n*65, 234*n*105, 235*n*106, 235*n*107
Altruism, 157, 165
America, 72
Anarchism, 11, 165, 176, 230*n*4
Anthropology, 32-35, 70-74, 122, 205-6*n*1, 217*n*1, 218*n*2, 221*n*85
Antiquity, 85, 147, 150, 159
Anti-Semitism, 9
Appearance/reality, 25-26, 48-49, 89, 129-30, 135-36
Appropriation, 49-54, 170-72; *see also* Property
Aristocracy, 11, 141-42, 145, 150, 160, 176, 232*n*27
Aristotle, 25, 92, 218*n*7

Art/artists, 20-22, 38-40, 115-16, 148, 171-72, 190-91, 194
Ascending/declining life, 224-25*n* 144; *see also* Morality, master/slave
Ascetic ideals, 3-4, 7, 16, 34, 63, 87, 89, 99, 101, 105, 107, 109-10, 118, 124, 126, 130, 134, 191; *see also* Asceticism
Ascetic interests, 88, 118-20, 151-52, 182, 184, 190; *see also* Asceticism
Asceticism: and consumption, 178-79, 184-85; and culture, 16, 61-64, 83, 99, 106-8, 118, 222*n*106; as necessary historical stage, 110; and religion, 124-27; and science, 132-33; and truth, 130-32, 134, 138-39; and work, 175, 179, 239-40*n*95; *see also* Ascetic ideals; Ascetic interests; Ascetic priests; Sickness
Ascetic priests, 63, 83-84, 88, 107-8, 118, 120, 124, 133; *see also* Asceticism
Atomism, 41-42, 47-48, 130-31, 227*n* 52; *see also* Matter; Materialism; Object; Subject; Thing

Bachelard, Gaston, 33
Bacon, Francis, 41
Barth, Hans, 12
Bauer, Bruno, 21-22
Being/becoming, 28, 40-41, 47-48, 53, 126, 191, 241*n*96
Bentham, Jeremy, 229*n*4
Bernstein, Richard, 195-96, 242*n*5
Biologism, 75-78, 104; *see also* Determinism, causal
Body, 29, 48, 82, 93, 125; *see also* Will to power